D1566350

# The Inner Dream

# The Inner Dream.

## CÉLINE AS NOVELIST

## J. H. Matthews

SYRACUSE UNIVERSITY PRESS    1978

Matthews, J. H.
   The inner dream.

   Includes index.
   1.   Destouches, Louis Ferdinand, 1894–1961—Criticism
and interpretation.   I.   Title.
PQ2607.E834Z774            843'.9'12            78-11324
ISBN 0-8156-2197-3

*Manufactured in the United States of America*

*for Garnet Rees,*
*from one he taught.*

J. H. Matthews, Docteur de l'Université de Montpellier, D.Litt., University of Wales, is Professor of French at Syracuse University and editor of *Symposium: A Quarterly Journal in Modern Foreign Literatures*. He has served as guest editor for special numbers of *La Revue des Lettres modernes* on Albert Camus (1961) and the French New Novel (1964). His publications include *Les deux Zola* (1957), a selection of short stories by Guy de Maupassant (1959), *Surrealism and the Novel* (1966), *The Custom-House of Desire: A Half-Century of Surrealist Short Stories* (1975), and ten other books on surrealism.

# CONTENTS

# CONTENTS

# The Inner Dream

"In truth, Sartre, Camus, Miller, etc. ... . . . are really furious to know I'm still alive; they aren't gifted those snots—They lack an Inner Dream."

# INTRODUCTION

SOME CREATIVE WRITERS live lives on the surface so sedentary and featureless that they appear to have had no existence outside their published works. An extreme case is that of Gustave Flaubert, who was quite content to refer to himself as *l'homme-plume*, a kind of human pen. Others, like Samuel Beckett, while not concealing their identity still take care to keep their private lives to themselves, shrouded in a mystery sometimes more interesting than what it conceals. With others again, it seems that their way of life is quite important to the public, authenticating their literary creations. This is true of André Malraux, Antoine de Saint-Exupéry, and even the Marquis de Sade—each a man of action who, in his own way, gives weight to his novels by his conduct. Others still actually live dual lives. Paul Claudel was at once diplomat, poet, and dramatist. The man who saw military and consular service as Henri Beyle wrote novels as Stendhal.

Usually it does not make much difference to the literary critic how and under what circumstances a writer produces, for it is normally no harder for him to approach authors in the second and third categories than those in the first. How, though, to deal with a writer who has been an habitual criminal and who confesses openly to being homosexual at a time when it is not yet socially acceptable—let alone quite fashionable—to do so and, moreover, draws upon his prison life and sexual experiences for the material of his novels? If the writer's name is Jean Genet and he has had the good fortune to attract the notice of so influential a sponsor as Jean-Paul Sartre, then he may well find himself treated as a saint. Society and the conditions it imposes on every one of us often are held responsible, these days, for behavior patterns that deviate from the accepted norm. And so it is not difficult for some people to persuade themselves, and others too, that the crimes com-

1

mitted by Chester Himes in his youth are the sole responsibility of the
world into which he was born black.

What, now, if the writer's politics are exceedingly unpopular and
all too easily can be taken as signifying a brutalized sensibility or perhaps as inexcusable proof of indifference to common decency, striking
us for this reason as alarmingly contradictory, next to his literary
productions? Should his name be Ezra Pound, most people would find
it possible, in the long run anyway, to separate the man from his work
and to look upon his art as sufficient compensation for either character
weakness or aberrant belief. What happens, though, when he goes by
the name of Louis-Ferdinand Céline and his political stance is no less
repugnant? How do we approach the work of a man who, during the
thirties, publishes in France statements to the effect that Fascism offers
the best way—the only way—of handling Jews, while at the same time
repeatedly declaring in private that he will prove Adolph Hitler to be
Jewish? What if, having won the *Médaille militaire* in 1914 at the age
of twenty, he lives to experience the unenviable distinction among
twentieth-century French writers of being arrested in 1945, at the request of the French government, in Denmark (where he has sought
asylum), and is held on Death Row for seventeen months in a Copenhagen prison before being condemned in 1950, at the age of fifty-six, to
national disgrace and confiscation of half his property?

Supposing, now, that he leaves us little or no chance of gen-
erously dissociating the author from the works he puts out, because his
life history is apparently the very substance of his novels and, incidentally, he assures everyone who asks him why he writes that he does
so only to make money? What if, in addition, outside his novelistic universe, just as much as in it (for example, he falsely claims to have
sustained head injuries requiring trepanation, during the incident that
earned him his military decoration), he lies incessantly and apparently
compulsively? And what if, misleading readers and listeners alike, he is
supposedly in full agreement with the narrator of one of his novels,
who declares, "You must choose, to die or to lie. Me I've never been
able to kill myself"?[1] Well, if he answers to the name of Louis-
Ferdinand Céline, then dealing with him and his work presents special
problems.

1. Louis-Ferdinand Céline, *Voyage au bout de la nuit*, I, 148. Unless otherwise indicated, all page references are to Jean A. Ducourneau, ed., *Œuvres de
Louis-Ferdinand Céline*, five volumes, published by André Balland (Paris,
1966–69).

Céline was born Louis-Ferdinand-Auguste Destouches in Courbevoie, in the Seine département of France, May 27, 1894. His father was employed in a position of some responsibility by an insurance company named Le Phénix. His mother, who dealt in quality lace, set up shop in the Passage Choiseul once the family moved to Paris, where Louis Destouches spent his childhood.

Louis (throughout his life he identified himself by the first of his given names) did not pursue formal studies very far. While he was still a boy, his parents sent him abroad to learn languages they believed might be useful to him in a business career. He spent a year (1908) in Diepholz, Lower Saxony, before being recalled and placed for the following year in an English boarding school. After his return from England he held a variety of jobs with commercial companies, while working on his own for his high school diploma, the *baccalauréat*, obtained in 1912. Only a few months later, not yet eighteen, he enlisted for three years in the 12th Regiment of the Cuirassiers, a cavalry unit based in Rambouillet.

Destouches's first known writings date from this time. In 1914 he entrusted to another soldier a black notebook where the first of his penciled jotting reads, "I couldn't say what impels me to set down in writing what I think." Another notation is less vague: "These notes that are as one can judge of a translucent paleness are only purely personal and it's with the sole aim of marking a period . . . the first really painful one I've gone through, but maybe not the last."[2]

The peacetime army offered him no haven. His notebook confides that he even began to think of desertion as "the only way out of this calvary." By the time war broke out in 1914, however, he had been promoted sergeant. On October 25, near Ypres, having volunteered for a dangerous mission, he was seriously wounded. Cited for bravery, he was awarded the Military Medal from the hands of Joffre himself. After treatment in one hospital after another, he was released from active duty. Extended convalescent leave was followed by a term of residence in London. Here, while his discharge was being processed, he was attached to the French Passport Office.

Granted a medical discharge at the end of 1915, Destouches went to the Cameroons to work as an agent for a French lumber company. While in the Tropics he contracted dysentery and malaria, poor health finally necessitating his repatriation. Back in France, in July

2. "Carnet du cuirassier Destouches," in *L'Herne*, No 5 (1965), 9–11.

1919 he presented himself successfully for the second part of the *baccalauréat*. He was already twenty-five years old and had been hired by the Rockefeller Foundation to travel through Brittany (he would never cease to regard himself as Breton), lecturing on the diagnosis and cure of tuberculosis. He was now in a position to hope for the realization of an ambition he later would claim to have cherished for a long time. He entered the medical school in Rennes, qualifying in 1923.

The year 1928 found Louis Destouches in private practice in Clichy, a working-class district of Paris. From the beginning of 1931 he worked too at the Dispensaire de Clichy. Supposedly totally occupied with his professional duties, he was engaged nevertheless, throughout this period and into 1932, in writing his first novel, *Voyage au bout de la nuit*. This controversial book was as fervently admired by some as it was passionately condemned by others. Its appearance brought to wide attention a personality no less controversial, though by no means as likely to draw admiration as to provoke detestation. Throughout his career Céline would take care to project a repellent public image that was to stand between many of his readers and balanced judgment of his achievement as a fiction writer of stature.

While the "Papa" Hemingway myth has helped the sales and reputation of Hemingway novels, Céline's mythomania did more to alienate the critics and large sections of the public. He knew this well enough. "To place confidence in men means already letting oneself be killed a little," says the storyteller of *Voyage au bout de la nuit* (I, 162). "The more you are hated, I find," remarks Céline in *Bagatelles pour un massacre*, "the more you rest easy."[3] Profoundly mistrustful of

3. Louis-Ferdinand Céline, *Bagatelles pour un massacre* (Paris: Denoël, 1937), p. 216. Subsequent parenthetical page references are to this edition. Cf. Céline's letter to Lucien Combelles, written some time in 1940:

> I do and will do everything I can to be and remain if not the richest man in France at least the most unpopular. At this cost I retain all my calm and my independence.
> This total contempt for humanity is extremely pleasant to me. (*L'Herne*, No 5, pp. 64–65)

See also a letter to Albert Paraz dated June 1, 1947: "An enormous hatred keeps me alive. I'd live a million years if I could be sure I'd see the world croak." Cited in Albert Paraz, *Le Gala des vaches* (Paris: Editions de l'Elan, 1948), p. 86.

people in general, he developed a hearty contempt for journalists, specifically those among them who report on literature. In a letter to Albert Paraz he once asserted that the duty of journalists is to "cover us with shit."[4] Hence hostility to such people prompted him to put up a front very often, to deliberately confuse them. Reporting on an interview they had had, André Parinaud quoted Céline as saying, "Gentle as a lamb, the Céline foaming at the mouth or spitting. What do you want today? There was *L'Express* that came to Meudon [the small surburban community where he spent his last years]. I'd decked out the station with all my puke to greet them!... They're going to edify their readers with good conscience."[5] After reading the report subsequently published in *L'Express* on June 14, 1957 under the title "Voyage au bout de la haine" ("Journey to the end of hate"), Céline commented to a friend, "I gave in to my habitual sacrificial mania. . . . I don't give a damn for my image. I'm a Mohamedan: I detest seeing my own face."[6] In *L'Ecole des cadavres*, written in 1938, he had observed, "The unfortunate thing is that people always judge you according to their own tendencies, and they are almost all for sale, any day, in any weather."[7]

A variety of journalists have confessed to feelings of uneasiness at the prospect of interviewing Céline. After the event, though, few of them indeed seem to have had any misgivings about putting down on paper whatever they have heard him say. In Céline's presence each of them presumably was well satisfied that to *him*, at least, Louis-Ferdinand Céline had been both frank and truthful. The novelist's every word, therefore, could be taken at face value and considered pertinent, whether one was concerned with reaching a better understanding of the man or of his outlook on life, or his fiction. At no time did Céline seem to have spoken more openly than when saying the very things his interviewer particularly wished to hear. Thus Robert Poulet does not appear to have doubted for an instant that his own assessment of Céline's second novel, *Mort à crédit* (1936) as "the drama of guilty conscience" found unimpeachable support in a remark made by Céline

---

4. See the letter reproduced in Paraz, *Le Gala des vaches*, p. 229.
5. See *Arts*, No 625, June 25, 1957. Robert Kirsch has remarked, "Céline presents a Hamlet-like problem to the critics. Is he a madman or an artist assuming the symptoms of a madman?" "Céline's 'Castle,' a fascinating Freak Out," *Los Angeles Times*, April 2, 1969.
6. See André Brissaud, "Voyage au bout de la tendresse," in *L'Herne*, No 3 (1963), pp. 226–27.
7. Louis-Ferdinand Céline, *L'Ecole des cadavres* (Paris: Denoël, 1938), p. 229. Subsequent parenthetical page references are to this edition.

during one of their conversations: "Even as a child, I had a very clear feeling of culpability."[8] Poulet gives no hint of having wondered whether Céline might not have made this statement precisely because it was consistent with the interpretation of *Mort à crédit* as an auto-biographical novel, almost universally held by the critics. And yet he should have known as well as anyone that Céline was quite capable of doing such a thing: the novelist always found amusement in de-liberately making inaccurate statements that, having the ring of truth, would find glad and unquestioned acceptance among the public. Such was his pleasure in disinformation that the more earnestly he asserted something, the more skeptical one needed to be about what he said. Aggravated beyond endurance, Milton Hindus exclaimed, "Céline is as tightly packed with lies as a boil is with pus."[9]

It would simplify the problem of dealing with Céline and his work if, with clear conscience, we could ignore everything he said in newspaper and magazine interviews and if, too, we could be assured that he hid the truth behind falsehood even in his private letters. Un-fortunately, like the boy who cried wolf, Céline did not always lie, even though he contrived to cast the shadow of doubt upon everything he had to say. For this reason, one cannot afford to dismiss every single comment he made on life or on his own work. We have no right to classify his public and private pronouncements as invariably untrust-worthy or as consistently designed to misinform. Even when putting on the kind of performance expected of him by the representative of *L'Express*, Céline still had something important to say about the tech-nique employed in *Voyage au bout de la nuit* that sets his later novels in a perspective from which scarcely any critic has bothered to con-sider them.

8. Robert Poulet, *Entretiens familiers avec L.-F. Céline* (Paris: Plon, 1958), p. 75.
9. Milton Hindus, *The Crippled Giant* (New York: Boar's Head Books, 1950), p. 69. Commenting on the things Céline told journalists about himself in later years, Patrick McCarthy remarks, "Not everything was false, but the total impression was quite wrong" (*Céline: a biography* [1975], Penguin Books, 1977, p. 28). The information supplied by Céline was certainly inaccurate, but it was not wrong, from his point of view. The novelist intended to give an impression of irascible, lawless insensitivity, paradoxically seeming to resent being disliked or again revelling in his unpopularity, as when he boasted on one occasion of having been thrown out of a Paris café just a few days before.

Mythomania in Louis-Ferdinand Céline tended to find expression in ways that impress many an observer as perverse, not to say indicative of mental or emotional imbalance. To those who can see *Mort à crédit* as no more than an essay in autobiography, this novel seems to offer a madly distorted image of his childhood and boyhood in the Passage Choiseul, grossly falsifying facts and maligning his parents out of rampant detestation of his immediate family. How then are we to explain Céline's use of one of his mother's first names as his *nom de plume*? And how do we explain his motives in asking her never to read *Mort à crédit*?

In his *Voyage au bout de la nuit* this man who had risked his life, been seriously wounded, and decorated for valor never ceased to extol the commonsense virtues of cowardice and self-preservation. During his interview for *L'Express* he declared, "One must be the opposite of what one writes. That's the surprise." Was this statement intended to confuse the public, or was it to be taken seriously, as an essential clue to be used in accounting for the puzzling conduct of a writer who urged people to detest him so that they would like him more? Whichever way we turn, we face enigmatic paradoxes in Céline's character and behavior, veiled in baffling ambiguity. In 1939, seven years after publishing *Voyage au bout de la nuit,* he volunteered for war service. Was this an act of courage and selfless patriotism, or was it simply a gesture, an attempt to disarm some of his opponents? Volunteering is not a serious step, when you know your medical disability rating will make sure you never have to serve. How fair is it, though, to be cynical about Céline's display of patriotism? He did serve as ship's doctor aboard the *Shella,* an armed passenger ship plying between Marseilles and Casablanca, damaged in an encounter with a British patrol boat in 1940.

Something of a professional brute on the literary scene, Céline is said to have evidenced exemplary concern for and devotion to his patients. He continued to practice in Clichy after the success of *Voyage*—bringing him suddenly out of obscurity—could have guaranteed him a lucrative living in far less depressing surroundings. Later, when the Allied invasion of Normandy brought him to the conclusion that it would be wiser to leave Occupied France than to face charges of pro-German sympathies, he and his second wife, Lucette, resided briefly among collaborationist French refugees in Sigmaringen, Germany. There, this man reputed to be loyal only to money, offered his services as a physician. He claimed later that he used to pay for patients' medical supplies out of his own pocket. Was

it perhaps, rather, out of the lining of his top coat, in which he is said
to have sewn a substantial number of bank notes before leaving France
in 1944? Or was he lying, in reporting on his altruism, for the same
reason as he occasionally would share the food on which his companions
subsisted: to cover up the fact that his means permitted him to enjoy
certain comforts, including a far more appetizing diet, in the privacy
of his room at the Löwen Hotel?

Was Céline someone consistently and redeemingly dedicated to
the medical profession? It is hard to argue the contrary. How, though,
did Louis Destouches, in his mid-twenties before he completed his
high school education, manage to become qualified in medicine so that,
at last, aged twenty-nine, he could serve humanity as a physician, a
general practitioner specializing in children's illnesses?

> No matter what the price. Compromise, hypocrisy, calculated
> smiles—any path would be worth taking.
> Even courting the daughter of the director of the medical
> school.

We have only to read these words by one of Céline's biographers[10] to
notice how easily Céline attracts suspicion, even calumny. It seemed
natural to him that he should do so, for calumny confirmed his estimate
of the people around him. All we know for certain is that in 1919 marriage followed courtship. Yet, within six years, Destouches had abandoned the practice his father-in-law's reputation as professor of
medicine had enabled him to take over in Rennes. Abandoned too were
his first wife, Edith, née Follet, and his five-year-old daughter.
Destouches had left France to spend two years as a doctor for the
League of Nations, first in Switzerland, then traveling to the United
Kingdom and the Cameroons, the United States, Cuba, and Canada.

10. Erika Ostrovsky, *Voyeur Voyant: A Portrait of Louis-Ferdinand Céline*
(New York: Random House, 1971), p. 35. Cf. Michel Brochard's statement in
"Céline à Rennes": "After finishing his *bachot* late, Louis Destouches was able to
do medicine at Rennes only through his marriage to Edith" (*L'Herne*, No 3, p.
16). McCarthy is more tactful, but still offers the same interpretation, when he
writes, "Yet by work and a certain ruthlessness he had achieved his great ambition"
(p. 28).

Numerous contradictions come to light as soon as we scrutinize Céline's life history. Far from resolving or making sense of them, his writings emphasize and even exaggerate them, leaving readers perplexed, provoked, or outraged perhaps. Visiting him in exile after his imprisonment in Copenhagen, Milton Hindus saw him as no more than a crippled giant, for whom he appears to have felt mingled pity and horror. Dominique de Roux, writing a few years after Céline's death, cast him in the unfamiliar role of saint, but was to remain virtually alone in doing so. Discussing his work in the light of Jung's theories, Bettina L. Knapp views him exclusively as a man of hate. And if Erika Ostrovsky is willing to rank him as a seer, it is only because she looks upon him at the same time as a voyeur.

Making sense of Céline's behavior as a human being is actually less important than at first appears to be the case. The spectacle of a man torn by inner conflict, erupting in hate and even self-hate, may be either fascinating or distressing to the observer, especially when no effort can be detected, on the part the subject, to attain either emotional equilibrium or peace of mind. But seeking resolution to complexities where none appear to exist is the prerogative of the psychologist or in this instance, some would contend, of the psychiatrist. It is certainly not the province of the literary critic. Exploration of the intricacies of Céline's mind and the complexities of his emotional makeup surely would account for the choice of material he used and for the ways in which it is rendered in his novels. But it would not make it very much easier to tell how good a fiction writer Céline was. Similarly, we stand to learn a great deal from examination of the motives behind various transpositions and modifications brought to his own life history, when someone like Céline borrows from his experiences while writing novels. Yet the important thing, surely, is to bear in mind the following, when we are evaluating his qualities as a writer of fiction. Louis-Ferdinand Céline had no intention of telling his readers exactly how Louis Destouches had lived or was living. After all, he was in the habit of advising any critic or journalist who asked him for details about his past to invent them, asserting that history has no importance. And in his only play, L'Eglise (written in the twenties, although not published until 1933), he wrote, "For seeking out truth, you see, that's an international tradition, a most strict one, by the way; but it's about truth itself that people never agree. It's a yard and a quarter in Bragomance, a yard and three quarters in New York; it will be perhaps two yards in Geneva and it will seem all the same to be the very same yardstick that people have used" (I, 422). Assessment of Céline's accomplishment as a novelist does not begin either with fulsome praise or with violent condemnation of Destouches the man.

Turned away in 1937 from the Dispensaire de Clichy, Destouches—who had been dismissed earlier from the League of Nations medical service—fell into persecution mania before long. "I was turned out by the Communist municipality," he asserted later, "upon the orders of Dr. ... an emigrant Lithuanian Jew, and not a DOCTOR at all: an imposter, whose brother was an editor for PRAVDA, imposed on Clichy by Pravda... upon arrival appointed physician in charge... in spite of all French Laws, scarcely speaking French, set about turning out everyone who wasn't Jewish and *especially me!* who'd set the dispensary up and represented the French, the hated French!... He arrived. I had to submit my resignation."[11]

Apparently possessed by a firm determination to antagonize as many people as he could, in the end Céline had more success than he anticipated. The day came when he found himself confessing to Paul Lévy, "It's difficult to croak under total, unanimous opprobrium. *That's* the penalty, not being shot. If I'd been the Christ, being spat upon would have hurt me most."[12] One cannot help thinking, all the same, that his predicament was largely of his own making. Indeed, the idea that he fell victim to anything other than his own malevolence and self-destructive impulses seems to many observers quite untenable. After his death, Manès Sperber wrote in *Preuves,* in September of 1961: "The clamor has died down with which he glorified his hate, which was complete . . . he'd hated those he disfigured; he disfigured so as to be able to hate. . . . His hate destroyed the writer Céline long before death came to put an end to the appalling existence of a very sick Dr Destouches." Even so—and Sperber's remarks give a broad hint of this—Céline did receive more than his just desserts, as a fiction writer. He suffered from a form of injustice that still makes its effect felt upon his reputation as a novelist.


Louis Destouches was thirty-eight years old when *Voyage au bout de la nuit* came out. The book shocked several critics and many

11. Letter to Albert Paraz dated March 18, 1951. See *L'Herne,* No 3, pp. 148–49. Cf. Céline's letter to the French consul on the Isle of Jersey, dated January 29, 1938: "I was turned out from Clichy like a piece of dung. The simplest way imaginable, even worse if possible" (*L'Herne,* No 3, p. 94).

12. Letter published in *Aux Ecoutes,* December 24, 1948.

readers. All the same, its author could not be denied an impressive if unsettling talent. This same talent was to nourish *Mort à crédit*, four years later. As for the play *L'Eglise*, it survived no more than one performance, by an amateur theatrical group in Lyon. Its author was not slow or reluctant to acknowledge having no real gift for the theatre. Meanwhile his antisemitic writings were a scandal, as were his political tracts. What though of the novels he published after *Mort à crédit*? None of them was ever to enjoy the wide appeal of the first two. Céline's reputation as a writer gradually succumbed to a myth not entirely on his own fabrication.

By and large, Louis-Ferdinand Céline's claim to fame has rested on the repute brought him by qualities displayed in *Voyage au bout de la nuit* and *Mort à crédit*. Implicit in the judgment so frequently and so confidently passed on his work, inside and outside critical circles, is the conviction that Céline's art declined significantly after 1936. Relatively clearly plotted narratives, his first fictional works are seen as having given way, regrettably, to a disturbingly meandering presentation leading progressively in the direction of narrative incoherence. Céline soon found himself condemned as having sunk without a struggle into uncontrollable raving. Many commentators have been quite willing—even eager, in some cases—to associate mental and artistic decline with these unpopular tendencies. Some have gone so far, in fact, as to identify Céline's supposedly weakening grasp on his medium as a fitting sort of punishment for the monstrous—the adjective does not seem to them excessive—ideas he took pleasure in developing in nonliterary works like the tract *Les beaux draps*, published in 1941 during the German occupation of France. With mental decline presumably came a slackening of technical control, having disastrous consequences for Céline's ability as a storyteller. Thus, on the plane of professional competence, the standards he had set in writing *Voyage* seem to provide a reliable measure of subsequent collapse, visible to anyone who cares to examine, for instance, the style of the first Célinian novel and the language of the later ones. To some readers, indeed, it looks as though the only qualities Céline managed to retain unimpaired are those that made him infamous in his lifetime. In 1939 his antisemitic *L'Ecole des cadavres* was condemned and had to be withdrawn from circulation:

> That's how life goes, all mediocre. Still very fortunate to escape the extreme catastrophes that make you drop your tools—and leave you completely disarmed! My lawsuit is for L'Ecole des Cadavres—

libel—I almost got hit with public indecency—again for L'Ecole. All
in all a heavy winter—a corrida without appeal—the pack after me.

All this is on the cards—in my destiny I suppose. I'll not
change I presume.[13]

When Céline was tried in absentia for treason, in 1945, his declaration
that it gave him pleasure to see his books banned understandably was
held against him. In 1963, two years after his death, *Nord*, the last of
his novels to appear (in 1960) during his lifetime, had to be withdrawn
because of a libel suit.

That Céline should have disagreed with his hostile critics about
the value of his later novels is natural enough. We could pass over his
defense of these works as having no special significance, but for one
important fact. Speaking up for his work, Céline showed the evolution
of his fictional technique to be the result of a fundamental change in
attitude toward literature in general and toward the novel in particular.
Looking back from the year 1957, he pointed out for the benefit of
those who read *L'Express*, "In *Voyage* I still make certain sacrifices to
literature, 'good literature.' You still find well-strung-together sentences.
In my opinion from the technical viewpoint, that's a bit behind the
times." In *Arts*, the very same month, André Parinaud cited Céline as
commenting, "Today literature numbers only journalists and psy-
chiatrists. Guys that relate news items or comment on complexes.
Nothing interesting there. That's why the novel is dead." Speaking
specifically of style, Céline went on to allude to his new novel, *D'un
Château l'autre*, due for publication five months later, in November:
"I've freed myself of many clichés. Painters have abandoned subject
matter little by little." Expanding on this last remark, he explained
elsewhere, "The story, my God, is accessory. It's the style that's interesting. The painters have unburdened themselves of subject matter, a
pitcher, or a pot, or whatever, it's the way of rendering that counts."[14]
Although many readers prefer it to his other fictional works, *Voyage
au bout de la nuit*—where Céline comes closest to respect for inherited
traditions of novelistic form—is not the master work that affords us the
opportunity to judge later failures. It is, in reality, the zero point from
which Céline will invite us to measure how far he goes subsequently
with investigative experiments by which he seeks to push back the
boundaries of fiction.

In the years since Louis-Ferdinand Céline completed his own

13. Letter to Eveline Pollet dated June 2, 1938. See *L'Herne*, No 3, p. 108.
14. See Marie Chapsal, *Les Ecrivains en personne* (Paris: Julliard, 1960),
p. 73.

"journey to the end of night," widely accepted standards governing the choice and presentation of subject matter in respectable literature have come under considerable modification. Célinian writing is far less likely these days than in the past to be dismissed or censured as the self-indulgent, acrimonious outpourings of a foul-mouthed pornographer. And yet it still bears a stigma. The latter is so disfiguring that a remarkably high percentage of readers who nevertheless see something to praise in Céline's work are inclined to adopt quite a belligerently protective attitude toward it. So sensitive are they to his good name that they seem reluctant, almost afraid, to ask the public to respect for its indisputable merits the fictional universe that Céline created by means peculiarly his own.

What in fact are the merits of Céline's novels? Are they sufficient to command everyone's respect, whatever kind of man it was who wrote them? These are the fundamental questions faced in the following study of Célinian fiction. They are questions that cannot be brought into focus unless we concern ourselves more with the novelistic universe of Louis-Ferdinand Céline than with the life, emotional state, and outlook of Dr Louis Destouches.

Attempting to answer questions about the quality of Célinian writing, we actually find ourselves discussing its author's achievement as a technician of fiction. Hence the perspective from which Céline the novelist will be viewed here brings into prominence certain works commonly relegated to second rank, or placed even lower than that. Meanwhile others, generally thought to make the strongest claim upon readers' attention, while still not to be ignored or discounted, appear less deserving of consideration than critics and reading public alike have found them to be.

It is not a question of arbitrarily concentrating on Céline's less popular writings or of perversely giving them prominence over others for which he is most widely known and upon which his reputation as a novelist usually is thought to rest. Nor is it a matter of giving all his generally neglected writings uniformly close attention. No account need be taken, for instance, of the reasons behind praise of *D'un Château l'autre* by commentators like Patrick McCarthy or Henri Thomas who writes, "This great book ( and *Nord* which completes it [sic] ) is generous as only those rare books can be that go further than the personal horizon."[15] The criteria underlying a judgment of this sort, compelling though many will find them, are no more relevant to the study of the

15. "A propos *d'Un château l'autre*," *L'Herne*, No 3, p. 296. Thomas's article was written before the publication of *Rigodon* (1969) which completes the cycle of novels begun with *D'un Château l'autre* and continued in *Nord*.

mechanism of Célinian fiction than those leading some readers to condemn Céline's most famous works on moral grounds or again make certain people feel that the ideas set forth in his sociopolitical tracts are so disgraceful as to invalidate all his writings, novels included.

Within Céline's fictional universe purely polemical works do not need to detain us. Instead, we must address ourselves, first of all, to identifying the kind of subject matter to which Céline gave his exclusive attention at the beginning of his career as a writer. This is why we must start by finding where Céline's created universe is located, establishing how far it extends in which directions, and mapping its dominant features. Only after this has been done can we try to see how Céline became preoccupied little by little with style more than story, and with what consequences. In order to do this, we must look first at a book that seems to fall outside his fictional universe altogether. Written and published originally under the name of Louis Destouches, it is a doctoral dissertation defended before a committee on which his father-in-law served. It bore the unprepossessing title *La Vie et l'œuvre de Philippe Ignace Semmelweis* and, in May of 1924, earned him not only the title of doctor of medicine but a medal for excellence as well.

# PHASE ONE

PHASE ONE

# La Vie et l'oeuvre de
# Philippe Ignace Semmelweis

$B$orn in budapest, Ignaz Semmelweis went to Vienna as a law student in 1837. Soon giving up law for medicine, he went back to Hungary in 1839, transferring to the newly opened Faculty of Medicine in Budapest. Dissatisfied there, he returned once again to Vienna, to qualify in 1844. Seeing no teaching opening in the field of surgery to which he had been attracted and where he had specialized, he soon completed the required training allowing him to be appointed to the post of assistant in obstetrics.

At that time, in maternity wards all over Europe the mortality rate from puerperal fever was high. Speculating upon possible causes, Semmelweis came to the conclusion that childbed fever could be controlled and even eliminated, perhaps, if standards of scrupulous cleanliness were observed by everyone having occasion to examine maternity cases. His investigations antagonized a professor of obstetrics, Klin, in whose ward 96 percent of patients died in the month of May 1864 alone. After Semmelweis had identified the cause of puerperal infection that June, and had offered recommendations for dealing with it, Klin—who refused to implement his proposals—had him dismissed in October. Reinstated after a short while (this time as assistant to Klin's colleague Bartch), Semmelweis was dismissed a second time, in March of 1849. The Austrian Academy of Science now denied him the opportunity to have his findings evaluated objectively by an outside committee. More than this, by ministerial order (Klin was reputed to be well-connected at the Austrian court), Semmelweis was required to leave Vienna. His discovery was ridiculed everywhere, by obstetricians and surgeons alike. His proposals having wounded pride and stirred up animosity on all sides, he was calmniated and his prophylactic recommendations were derided. Referring to the acknowledged specialists of the day, Louis

Destouches remarks that they were "at once noisy and mendacious and then above all stupid and spiteful" (I, 607).

Semmelweis lived out in Budapest the difficult years following the Hungarian Revolution. Eventually he was granted an appointment at a maternity hospital, being permitted to work, part-time, during the vacation months of July and August only. He now began to write his *Etiology of Puerperal Fever,* which took him four years to complete.

Almost to a man, specialists had greeted his ideas with skepticism and downright hostility. Now the Academy of Medicine in Paris did not even bother to acknowledge receipt of a report on his work.

In 1856 Semmelweis succeeded the hospital director who had hired him only after extorting a promise that he would not press for application of his methods. In command at last, Semmelweis was still denied vindication. His instructions were deliberately ignored and his efforts were sabotaged in an attempt to discredit him for good. The number of deaths in his wards actually rose. Before long, he began to display alarming signs of mental strain. "A personality is quartered as cruelly as a body," comments Destouches, "when madness turns the wheel on his rack" (I, 617).

In 1865 Semmelweis began to hallucinate. During a brief period of lucidity he was persuaded to approve the appointment of someone to replace him at the hospital. Another attack of dementia then took possession of him. He broke into the amphitheatre where an anatomy demonstration was in progress. Seizing a scalpel, he began to slash at a cadaver. Before he could be disarmed, he had cut himself. Brought back to Vienna delirious, he was confined at once to an asylum. There, in his forty-seventh year, he died three weeks later on August 16, 1865, as a result of infection of his self-inflicted wound.

It was to reviewing this man's life and work, in an impassioned account from which the details cited above are taken, that Louis Destouches devoted his doctoral dissertation.

The chairman of Destouches's doctoral committee, Brindeau, was professor of obstetrics at the Faculty of Medicine, University of Paris. Presumably, this fact had something to do with the choice of the thesis topic. Admitting in his preface to the 1924 edition that Semmelweis' life and work furnished him with one of several subjects he might have treated, Destouches formally explained the reason for his selection. Semmelweis' career illustrated medical thought, he said, "so fine, so generous, the only truly human thought there is perhaps in the world" ( I, 577). The reason he advanced seems plausible enough. Even so, and allowing for the fact that doctoral candidates often prefer to explore unfrequented byways rather than follow well-worn paths, we may ask why Semmelweis would have been chosen over Louis Pasteur, for example. One cannot raise this question without encountering the possibility that Destouches's statement may simplify his motives somewhat. In fact, it does so to the point of concealing the particular value of *La Vie et l'œuvre de Philippe Ignace Semmelweis* for anyone interested in asking how Dr Destouches became the novelist Céline.

The purpose specified in Destouches's text—to offer a defense of the medical profession by demonstrating that professional training is essential—actually hides what appealed to him most in the career of an obscure figure from the history of medicine, misunderstood and reviled in his own time, whose contribution was to be overshadowed before long by that of Pasteur. Only coincidentally and as though inadvertently does the 1924 preface reveal what had attracted Destouches in Semmelweis' unhappy experience: "The altogether too sad hour always comes when Beauty, that absurd and superb confidence in life, gives way to Truth in the human heart." It is our role to "look this terrible Truth in the face," because "it is in this calm intimacy with their greatest secret that the pride of men pardons us least" ( I, 578).

In substance and form, comments of this kind seem more appropriately indicative of the aims of a novelist than of those to be expected in the writer of a medical dissertation. It is not surprise, then, to hear their author speak more openly when, suppressing the original introductory statement, he provided an entirely new preface with a second edition of *Semmelweis,* published in 1937, now under the name of Louis-Ferdinand Céline.

The later preface takes its point of departure from the concluding paragraph of the earlier one. It declares, "Here is the terrible story of Philippe Ignace Semmelweis" ( I, 579). Without inferring that there is something even vaguely opportunistic about Destouches's choice of subject matter in his dissertation, we still can begin by entertaining the following hypothesis. A certain predisposition, a definite orientation in thought, and a characteristic concept of human nature as well as of human relationships all make *La Vie et l'œuvre de Philippe Ignace Semmelweis* less significant by far as a chapter in the history of medicine's advance than as a reflection of an approach to life that will be distinctive of Céline in his novels.

Excusing the external signs of the book's original function as a scientific document, Céline at last made explicit in 1937 what really mattered to him. "The form has no importance," he asserted, "it is the subject matter that counts. . . . It demonstrates the danger of wishing men too much good. It's an old lesson, always young" (I, 579). The idea at the root of *Semmelweis* would be taken up and developed elsewhere in Céline's novelistic writings, through expansion and endless variation. It reflects Destouches's view of life as fundamentally futile in its maddening ironies, as posited, too, on misinterpretation and misrepresentation that combine to frustrate the individual's aspirations to happiness by making him helplessly dependent on other men, with whom daily contact can bring nothing but disappointment and suffering. "For Semmelweis," Destouches writes appositely, "as for so many other precursors, it must have been horribly painful to submit to stupidity's fancy, especially possessing a discovery so dazzling, so useful to happiness as the one he was proving daily in Klin's maternity hospital" (I, 593).

That such a book should have earned its author a medal for excellence as well as an MD degree is a reflection on the caliber of work customarily submitted in France in the form of *doctorats de médecine*, not on Destouches's deviousness or his skill in deceiving his doctoral committee.

Without going into details, Bettina Knapp has drawn attention to the "many inaccuracies, exaggerations, and omissions" to be noted in Céline's version of Semmelweis' life.[1] We notice that Céline passed over, for example, Semmelweis' marriage to a woman twenty years his junior, a loyal wife by whom he had a child who died in infancy. While there is no cause to look upon Destouches's dissertation as a work of fiction, we can characterize it as presenting a very unusual thesis indeed. The world of medicine and the nature of Semmelweis' inquiry provided an excuse for an exploration that time would show to have been of pressing concern to the writer.

Even before we come to the text of *Semmelweis*, the author's introductory statement—so much more direct in the second preface than in the first—makes clear how well its theme reflected his conception of life. Semmelweis' disastrous professional career illustrated to

---

1. Bettina L. Knapp, *Céline: Man of Hate* (University, Alabama: The University of Alabama Press, 1974), p. 14.

perfection the pessimistic assumptions upon which Céline was to erect his novels as painful commentaries on human fate, seen as stripped of all hope and at the same time as devoid of the consolation of any kind of purposefulness or impression of progress. "No doubt it was written," remarks Destouches, "that he would be unhappy with men, no doubt for people on that scale any simple human feeling becomes a weakness" (I, 587).

The striking thing about Destouches's book is that it depicts Semmelweis as a saint. This representation is far from indicative of blind idealism on the writer's part. For it has nothing to do with providing a reassuringly encouraging picture of human nature, seen in the light of selfless devotion. On the contrary, Semmelweis emerges as a saint who inescapably pays the price of saintliness in the coin of suffering, irresistibly rather than maliciously extorted by society at large. His altruism makes him fall victim, more or less submissively, to pervasive forces that bring frustration and anguish at every turn. As the second preface intimates, and as the text of *Semmelweis* consistently demonstrates, in someone who wishes to improve the lot of his fellow men Louis Destouches equated innocence unhesitatingly and unequivocally with simple-mindedness. Innocence is a defect, in other words. The spectacle of Semmelweis, an exemplary innocent persistently hounded by his colleagues, is more than a little reminiscent of that of a sickly hen, viciously pecked and mercilessly ostracized for the very weakness to which it must succumb before long. "So Semmelweis broke," insists Destouches, "there is no doubt that most of us would have succeeded out of simple prudence, out of elementary delicacy. He did not have, or took no account, it seems, of the indispensable sense of the futile laws of his time, of all times incidentally, outside which stupidity is an indomitable force" (I, 593).

Semmelweis evidently appealed to Destouches on two levels, both as innocent and as man of genius. So far as Destouches's own outlook was concerned, any supposed conflict between the two could be resolved on the plane of intractability. The latter was reflected in Semmelweis' incapacity to accept and submit to the unwritten laws by which society holds us to a life of conformity and acquiescence. In this way, the self-destructive instinct the writer identified with genius took him well past the whimsy of the Quixotic analogy. It is possible in fact to glimpse in *La Vie et l'œuvre de Philippe Ignace Semmelweis* a concept of heroism measured according to the scale of defeat, not success. Here insanity assumes its full value as an aggravated response to human destiny, but by no means an atypical one in men of superior

gifts, so Destouches would have us believe. In the case of Ignaz Semmelweis, therefore, one of the recurrent motifs of twentieth-century
western literature is awesomely paralleled, without the imaginative
shift that makes alienation so popular a motif in the work of many a
writer of our time.

Semmelweis' very distinction is shown to be the cause of his
humiliation and ultimate mental collapse. Setting him apart from the
common herd in a world ruled by mediocrity, his genius is seen as
having invited and received the punishment society's reflex of self-
defense imposes on anyone whose talent singles him out. Destouches
was quite definite in his conclusion. He gave his point of view expression through this leading question: "However high in fact one's genius
places one, however pure the truths one states, does one have the
right to be unmindful of the formidable power of absurd things?"
(I, 593).

*La Vie et l'œuvre de Philippe Ignace Semmelweis* lets us see
plainly that the pessimism underlying the novels of Céline is not merely
a convenient literary pose. Nor is it simply a fashionable one, oppor-
tunistically exploited in the interest of commercial success or pure
sensationalism. Far more significantly, pessimism is an inescapable
presupposition in Céline's depiction of human life. He would never
have been concerned just with elaborating a pessimistic theme in
anticipation of pleasing the reading public. His writing had its source
in a deep-seated conviction that treated suffering and disappointment,
like the effects of victimization, as indispensable evidence of incon-
trovertible truths. With these no argument seemed possible, for Céline
could envisage no way to escape their cruel consequences. Céline the
novelist does not argue, does not attempt to make converts, to persuade
us to adopt his standpoint in preference to any other. His writings do
no more than present testimony that, all his life long, he remained sure
can be left to speak persuasively for itself. Five months after his
release from prison, in a letter of sympathy to Eveline Pollet, recently
widowed, we find him writing on July 23, 1947, "Alas! All lives come
to a bad end."[2]

2. *L'Herne*, No 3, p. 111. Cf. "You've got to get used to snuffing it little by
little. That's life. The bench, the slave-ship and the oar." Undated letter reproduced
in Henri Mahé, *La Brinquebale avec Céline* (Paris: La Table Ronde, 1969), p. 165.

More than mere divergence of descriptive methodology, this fundamental difference in attitude toward life separates Céline from Emile Zola. Céline felt no real sympathy for Zola's novels, despite certain surface resemblances that his critics have detected in early Célinian fiction. Clearly, Céline had more in common with Guy de Maupassant's naturalism than with Zola's. This is because he and Maupassant—who ended his life insane—shared a profound certainty that life has no intrinsic meaning. Maupassant's *Sur l'eau* of 1888, a series of reflections on existence, can be read as an expansion of this statement in *Voyage au bout de la nuit:* "Maybe it's the same for everyone, anyway, as soon as you insist a bit, there's a vacuum" (I, 212). It is surely worth noting that Céline and Maupassant admired the same philosophical thinker, Schopenhauer, and that the latter's influence deeply marks Céline's fiction, just as it does the stories and novels of Maupassant.

"Nothing comes for nothing in this world," we read in the second preface to *Semmelweis.* "Everything is expiated, the good, like the bad, is paid for sooner or later. The good costs very much more, necessarily" (I, 579). *La Vie et l'œuvre de Philippe Ignace Semmelweis* illustrates that the phenomenon of expiation is a mode of suffering. The idea of redemption by way of a purification that comes with suffering was foreign to its author, incomprehensible in fact. Suffering only ridicules men. It neither elevates them nor guarantees them a sense of destiny. It brings no rewards, certainly, and no compensation either. It is, quite simply, a state of being. As such, it cannot be avoided, so long as man exists as an individual consciousness. When it does end, when an individual has completed his "journey to the end of night," the termination of suffering has proved only one thing: that yet another person has died, to no purpose.

Themes recurring in the novels of Céline so often as to betray their origin in obsession find distinct formulation in *La Vie et l'œuvre de Philippe Ignace Semmelweis.* Here they are not treated simply as hypotheses, to be advanced tentatively and handled with due caution; they are already unassailable truths. "In the History of the times," for example, "life is but an intoxication, Truth is Death" (I, 587). Even more revealing in the long run is the strange identification we sense between Semmelweis, as Louis Destouches represents him, and the man we come to know as Céline. Destouches's selection of Semmelweis to fill the role of hero–victim, falling inevitably to anyone whose gifts place him above the rest of humanity, tells us much about a mental attitude that a change of name to Louis-Ferdinand Céline really did nothing to temper. Destouches saw Semmelweis as a man dedicated to a truth no one around him could comprehend or take on trust, a man who suffered horribly for that very reason. Whether it is fitting, when we look at *Semmelweis* in the light of Céline's own unhappy life, to speak of prescience or, instead, of a form of projection, Dr Destouches's fascination with the figure of Dr Semmelweis is no less suggestive.

From time to time, a strangely prophetic note is struck in *Semmelweis*. Reading Destouches's interpretation of events, we have the impression, here and there, that some premonitory sense, above all, drew him to his subject. It is almost as though he had an inkling of his own fate, as Céline: "Those who must create admirable things could not ask of one or two particular affections the affective forces from which their formidable destiny takes fire. . . . Finally Semmelweis drew his existence from wells too generous for him to be understood very clearly by other men" (I, 587). "Every creator," we read in Céline's *Mea Culpa* (1937), "from the first word finds himself at present crushed by hate, made a laughing stock, vaporized" (III, 342).

As we watch Céline's life history unfold and notice the part that defiance of society's norms and usages plays in precipitating successive disasters, we cannot escape the feeling that Céline was driven by self-destructive impulses to prove the thesis defended in *Semmelweis*. Pasteur, after all, was a winner. Semmelweis was a loser whose defeat established beyond further question, Destouches believed, that it is not life's winners (those society approves and rewards) but its losers (castigated by the world in which they find themselves) who show us what human existence is all about.

Thus the really interesting thing about Bettina Knapp's analysis of the personality of Dr Semmelweis is that it underlines why, for Destouches, he was such a natural choice as hero–victim. Destouches's preoccupation with heroes who fail is highly significant. For he did not interpret defects in Semmelweis' character as inherent weaknesses so much as look upon them as signs of the deleterious effect of society's indifference, antagonism, and envy—all directed against a man of superior gifts. The central figure of *Voyage au bout de la nuit* will discover, in the natural course of things, it seems, that the true measure of superiority is the hate it brings down upon an individual's head.

"We must in truth point out one great defect in Semmelweis," comments Destouches, "that of being brutal in all things and especially toward himself" (I, 589). Caution recommends resisting the temptation to see the outline of a self-portrait in Destouches's account of Semmelweis' life. Still, there is evidence enough to persuade us that his interest in the Hungarian doctor was not solicited originally by disinterested dedication to scientific inquiry alone. Nor was it brought into clear focus by the high-sounding motives to which his text lays claim. If we only glance at Céline's polemical writings, we find proof of one thing, at all events. He shared some of the character defects his book attributes to Semmelweis. The only way Destouches appears to have seen himself as different from and superior to his subject is in looking at life squarely, that is, in recognizing disaster as ineluctable. In an undated letter to Eugène Dabit he once affirmed, "But I'm lucid, that's my redemption."[3]

It is well known that, his professional day behind him, Dr Louis Destouches would work late into the night, laboring over a manuscript that one day, a thousand pages long, became *Voyage au bout de la nuit.* The picture associated in many people's minds with the writing of his first piece of fiction is that of a novelistic talent of singular power, inexplicably bursting forth unannounced from the imagination of a man of medicine from whom no one had the right to expect anything of the kind. It is a picture that appeals to some literary historians, but hardly true to the facts. Even before he began to sign himself Céline, Destouches had proved fully capable of plunging into a universe made his own out of elements borrowed from the real world. From the very first, he gave signs of total commitment to a view of reality unquestionably colored by his peculiar sensitivity to the underlying violence of existence.

For Céline, objectivity in the presentation of scenes or events was to represent betrayal of the novelist's craft and of his trust as a witness to life. Hence it would be an unthinkable departure from his obligation to show things not as they are, necessarily, but the way they impressed themselves upon his sensibility. He confided in Eveline Pollet in June of 1936, "I understand only the subjective."[4] Thus the intensity marking the language and style of *La Vie et l'œuvre de Philippe Ignace Semmelweis* appears to have been adopted quite naturally, even intuitively perhaps, and certainly without reluctance,

3. *L'Herne,* No 3, p. 88.
4. *L'Herne,* No 3, p. 102. Letter dated "End of June."

strain, or sense of incongruity. It demonstrates that some of Céline's most characteristic gifts as a writer had manifested themselves almost a decade before he turned to the novel form.

To Louis-Ferdinand Céline detachment would remain always a meaningless concept and a pointless goal. Actually, respect for its principles and for the objective techniques engendered by authorial detachment would have required repudiation of his very function as a writer. Early but very clear indications of this attitude are visible in *Semmelweis*. Here the qualities that catch the eye are those that bring animation to a scene, far more often than those by which scientific facts are recorded with objectivity. In fairness, we must grant that Destouches does not deny his readers access to scientific documentation. He does prefer, nevertheless, to lead to it by the route of novelistic creation, instead of relying exclusively upon the impersonal presentation of scrupulously recorded detail. The narrative—and the nature of the material handled in *Semmelweis* is sufficiently dramatic to justify use of this word without danger of misrepresentation—is sustained by a fervor quite at odds with the aims set down in the preface. From one end of *La Vie et l'œuvre de Philippe Ignace Semmelweis* to the other, the writer's use of words testifies to his wholehearted devotion to a *vision*, a way of looking at the world, quite definitely hallucinatory at times.

"In the story of this existence," Destouches observes, apropos of Semmelweis' life, "one appears to exhaust all the expressions of misfortune. The terminology to which it is ceaselessly necessary to resort in order to accompany him in his work seems to come entirely from the heavy hangings of funerary phrases" (I, 595). Recounting events taking place the day after Semmelweis began working for Klin on February 27, 1847, Destouches tells us he was "caught up, dragged, bruised, in the dance of Death that was never to be interrupted" (I, 594). The dominant impression communicated thanks to the mode of presentation adopted in *La Vie et l'œuvre de Philippe Ignace Semmelweis* is that emotional involvement has taken over from scientific curiosity. Semmelweis' life history becomes a "calvary" (I, 588), as Destouches dwells on "the years of pitiless ordeal when the pack of enemies howled its hate at Semmelweis, hunted, banished" (I, 589). Klin is paraded before us as "the great assistant of death" and the obstruction met by Semmelweis is described as "imbecilic and enraged" (I, 593). Moreover, from the opening section, Destouches's text is marked by the staccato, nervous style, highly impressionistic in nature, for which the novels of Céline are known. One even finds numerous examples of points of suspension, the famous three dots that constitute a distinguishing formal device in the Célinian novel.

On occasion, to be sure, Destouches's writing bears witness more to good intentions than to technical expertise. "Let us wait until the day we need appears in the precinct of the Past," he suggests clumsily (I, 584). Here and there, too, the tone grates excruciatingly. Obviously, Destouches has not yet fashioned a linguistic instrument he can use with confidence and perfect assurance of touch. All in all, however, momentary lapses in *Semmelweis* only highlight the remarkable success of a narrative of sustained power. The gaucherie marring the text, now and again, reflects the inexperience of a novice storyteller who has not had time to master the basic skills of his craft. The casualty room is delineated nevertheless in quite memorable fashion. So is the lying-in hospital where, night after night, the patients' sleep is disturbed by the sound of the bell signalling the presence of a priest, come to administer the last rites to yet another victim of puerperal fever.

The surprising thing, when all is said and done, is not that the man who wrote a dissertation about Dr Semmelweis should have gone on on to write a novel, but that almost a decade separates *La Vie et l'œuvre de Philippe Ignace Semmelweis* from *Voyage au bout de la nuit*. For, in theme and treatment, the latter develops fictionally many of the virtualities that gave its predecessor its special character.

# Voyage au bout de la nuit

STRESSING THE IMPORTANCE of *La Vie et l'œuvre de Philippe Ignace Semmelweis* with respect to Céline's first experiment with fiction carries a potential danger we cannot ignore. It may foster a few suppositions entailing prejudgment of the content and form of *Voyage au bout de la nuit* (*Journey to the End of Night*) and of the manner in which it can be expected to make its impact. The result may even be an impression of confusion, as the themes of *Semmelweis* are found developing in *Voyage* with less directness than anticipated, and apparently according to a principle of selectivity to which the key is not immediately available. However, if *Voyage au bout de la nuit* seems to depart in some ways from the premises laid down in *Semmelweis,* this is for good reason.

Whereas Louis Destouches's dissertation was written from the vantage point of a sympathetic observer, a witness, *Voyage au bout de la nuit* set the pattern for all Céline's novels with its use of the first-person narrative mode. The relative detachment maintained throughout the dissertation imposed limits on the author's expression of outrage at the treatment Semmelweis received. In each of the novels he published as Louis-Ferdinand Céline, however, he entrusted narration to someone implicated as a participant in events. Indeed, the central figure in the action, the narrator invariably assumes the role of principal victim. He does not act upon events but—in this, inescapably, an antihero like Semmelweis—is carried along by them. He is quite incapable of resisting or seriously influencing the course they take, except in the most negative and thoroughly disappointing way. The best he can do, therefore, is voice a feeling of helplessness that he apparently believes his readers must share.

When François Mauriac wrote novels in the first person, he took care to dissociate himself from his narrators with an insistence that could transform a story like *Le Nœud de vipères* into the demonstration of a thesis, nourished by religious conviction. Similarly, in first-person novels like *L'Immoraliste* and *La Symphonie pastorale*, André Gide imposed an elaborate filter of irony upon the storyteller's version of what occurs. As a result, while reading Gide and Mauriac, we feel remote from events. Hence we are more sensitive and responsive than otherwise we could be to these writers' invitation to judge their characters' outlook and conduct. The contrast with Céline's method in his fiction could not be greater. Like Joyce Cary in *The Horse's Mouth*, Céline seems to identify completely with his narrators. Besides, he appears to have made no real effort to dissuade the public from confusing him with each of the central figures in his novels. In each case, we notice, the storyteller shares one of the writer's first names, the one that Destouches did not use. Furthermore, when the notoriety of his publications elicited curiosity about his private life, Céline found it to his purpose to let his principal fictional characters' attitudes, personal traits, and failings be taken for his own.[1] All in all, there results quite considerable ambiguity about his relationship to the characters who apparently speak for him. It has noteworthy implications, affecting both the content and the form of his novels.

In a private letter Céline once remarked, "Gide is a notary—I think an excellent critic—but all in prose—no trance in his work unless it be at the sight of the little Bedouin's buttocks."[2] Céline's assessment of Gide reflected his abiding conviction that authorial distance should be eliminated altogether from fiction. Distance, together with the moral inferences it invites us to draw, held no appeal for him. This is largely why many readers have found it quite natural and entirely legitimate to take for granted that Ferdinand Bardamu, narrator of *Voyage au bout de la nuit,* and the man who wrote that novel are one and the same. Hence, too, a distinct change of focus that at first glance seems to set Céline's earliest novel apart from the Destouches dissertation.

In her *Céline and his Vision*, Erika Ostrovsky calls *Semmelweis*

1. Hence the fundamental error made by critics like Wayne Booth who writes of *Voyage*, "The trap which we saw Thackeray's Barry Lyndon springing on Trollope, in spite of all Thackeray could do to make his own rejection of Barry's immorality clear, has here been sprung by a thoroughly unscrupulous man. Though Céline has attempted the traditional excuse—remember, it is my character speaking and not I—we cannot excuse him for writing a book which, if taken seriously by the reader, must corrupt him." *The Rhetoric of Fiction* (Chicago and London: University of Chicago Press, 1961), p. 383.
2. Undated letter to Ernst Bendz in *L'Herne,* No 3, p. 119.

a novel, treating it as a work of fiction. Her approach throws her into a predicament, when it comes to accounting for differences she observes between this work and *Voyage au bout de la nuit*. Alluding to a change that, she suggests, "goes beyond a simple flip of the literary coin to expose only the dark side of the same money,"[3] she ascribes it to some kind of "serious upheaval" that Destouches must have undergone between composing *Semmelweis* and writing *Voyage*. So she is led to conclude that "the active confrontation with human misery and viciousness" he went through during the 1914–18 war was somehow "reinforced and extended in the course of medical practice." This, we are to believe, explains the negative emphasis of *Voyage au bout de la nuit*, in contrast with the positive approach Destouches had adopted toward Semmelweis' exemplary fate.

Ostrovsky's explanation rests firmly on the unstated conviction that Bardamu's reaction to life in *Voyage au bout de la nuit* necessarily reflects that of Louis Destouches, and with complete fidelity. Thus any departure from the standpoint from which *Semmelweis* was written must be considered the direct consequence of a modification in the writer's outlook upon the world. Why, though, should we assume that Dr Destouches looked upon his profession and patients just the way his narrator does in *Voyage*? For one thing, this supposition commits us to endless and quite fruitless conjecture about the effect upon his attitude of something that presumably must have happened to him after *La Vie et l'œuvre de Philippe Ignace Semmelweis* came out, at a period in his life about which nothing very definite is known. For another—and this is distinctly more important—it tends to divert attention from the vital issues raised by significant differences to be noted between *Semmelweis* and *Voyage au bout de la nuit*.

Even supposing for the sake of argument that these differences owe something noteworthy to events taking place during an obscure moment in Destouches's lifetime, they still most definitely owe a lot also to strictly technical considerations governing the choice and treatment of material in *Voyage au bout de la nuit*, which is not an historical essay of any kind but a work of fiction.

Suppression of positive values that humanize *La Vie et l'œuvre de Philippe Ignace Semmelweis* is entirely consistent with Céline's narrative approach in *Voyage*, as too in his next novel, *Mort à crédit*. Except so far as Semmelweis' humiliation and suffering touch us all, the man telling about Ignaz Semmelweis had been spared direct involve-

3. Erika Ostrovsky, *Céline and his Vision* (New York: New York University Press, 1967), p. 88.

ment in the incidents he was recounting. The narrator in *Voyage au bout de la nuit* protests about what has befallen him, loudly, incessantly, and in very personal terms, all the time with sure knowledge that protest really accomplishes nothing beyond celebration of failure and defeat. Obviously, he thinks of himself as confined within the same prescribed and irremediably disastrous life pattern as everyone else. So *Voyage au bout de la nuit* reads like a *Life and Work of Ignaz Semmelweis*, as this might have been written by Semmelweis himself in humble mood, after experience of life and his fellow men had divested him of insidious idealism before it cost him his sanity.

Céline does not present *Voyage au bout de la nuit* as the diary of a general practitioner ministering to patients in a working-class district of Paris. Instead, he offers the story of an ordinary man whose sole claim to distinction is his lucidity. Bardamu is clear-sighted enough to view human existence as no more than a "journey to the end of night," an irresistible downward movement into death, completely devoid of grandeur. Hence he defines himself and human consciousness less through community feeling than by contemplating all that isolates the individual from those about him. An inevitable consequence of his viewpoint on living is his profound despair, in sharp contrast with the optimism pervading *La Peste*, Albert Camus's fictional parallel to Defoe's *A Journal of the Plague Year*, and finally validating the title that André Malraux gave his dark novel about the Spanish Civil War: *L'Espoir*. Bardamu's awareness of life deepens as he comes to know emotions that progressively cut him off from the rest of mankind. Fear and hatred soon predominate in this man whose profession we tend to associate quite naturally with love, trust, and concern for others.

Before long, though, we discover from the way he describes what has occurred that Bardamu's lucidity is actually more emotional than intellectual in origin. Indeed, Bettina Knapp goes so far as to contend that his "blanket generalizations" exhibit "no critical faculties at all" (p. 37). Bardamu's generalizations about people and about human life are impressive (or repellent, for that matter) in proportion to the emotional impact they make on the reader. Ferdinand Bardamu does not think out his situation so much as he feels it. Thus the energy he expends searching for ways to avoid the fear of death strikes Knapp as "projected outward" in the form of hate for others.

Bettina Knapp's analysis of Bardamu's temperament and of the weaknesses of his ego that vent themselves in hate presents a most interesting feature. It gives Louis-Ferdinand Céline no credit for having succeeded in studying a psychological and emotional case through the fictional character he brings before us. Instead, it encourages the belief that finding out what is wrong with Bardamu provides an accurate diagnosis of Céline's own problems. And so, just like Erika Ostrovsky and others, Bettina Knapp sees Bardamu as a mere projection of his narcissistic creator.

It takes no great penetration on the reader's part to determine that the detachment of a Henry James or a Joseph Conrad is not a quality to be found in Céline's first novel, or, for that matter, in those with which he followed *Voyage au bout de la nuit*. In *Voyage* the inexorability of the workings of fate—of that infernal machine whose efficient operation Jean Cocteau celebrated in one of his plays—is observed not from above, as it is in Thomas Hardy's novels, but from below; not from a comfortable distance, but from close up. A sign of Céline's creative powers is that, when portraying Bardamu in dreadful, sickening proximity to fate, he paints a portrait convincing enough to tempt us to take it for his own.

From the very beginning, Bardamu's version of what has taken place accords with his painful conviction that life is futile and that man is a totally defenseless creature, moved about at the bidding of forces he neither fully comprehends nor has the ability to resist. His life history grants no relief from a paralyzing fatalistic sense of the inevitable, casting man in the role of unwilling victim, taken from step to step through misery in the direction of final extinction. "Everything happens," he remarks hopelessly, "and it was my turn to become a corporal" (I, 18). "Everything took place from that moment onward, according to chance" (I, 19). From one end of *Voyage au bout de la nuit* to the other, the structure of the narrative seems to be at the mercy of the accidental, of unproductive changes in direction. These bear out Bardamu's interpretation of life as pointless and subject to the ironies of hostile chance.

Ferdinand Bardamu makes his first costly mistake when he actually invites trouble by impulsively enlisting in the army. After first-hand experience of the absurdities of war, he wanders aimlessly through life, in Africa, in the United States, and finally in France where he takes up the practice of medicine. Prodded by fatality along a road of disillusionment and anguish, he becomes the unhappy reincarnation of the Wandering Jew. Unfortunately for him, he differs from the central character in Eugène Sue's *Le Juif errant* in being denied even faint hope of salvation. All the same, he is possessed by a restlessness that sharpens his anguish. In this, he represents human kind, as described with decidedly unscientific intensity in *La Vie et l'œuvre de Philippe Ignace Semmelweis.*

Bardamu gives the opening pages of his story a touch of irony born of hindsight when relating how, as a young man not yet twenty, he fell in behind a passing regiment. Irony both protects the naiveté that was his during his youth and prepares us to see it collapse, as it must do very soon under pressure from the brutal realities of war, epitomizing all the incomprehensible forces that weigh upon human destiny. It endows the narrator's character with depth, promising an evolution in outlook, as the young man comes closer to maturity.

At the same time, there is in the text of *Voyage au bout de la nuit* the hint of another layer of irony, brought to the narrative by the presence of the novelist, to be detected behind his first-person storyteller. As we become conscious of a second level of irony, we notice how consistently throughout his life—and not only while he is still a callow youth, inclined to play at disillusionment—Bardamu is betrayed by his feelings. Céline sets and resets the trap of sentimentality to ensnare him. Try as he may, Bardamu cannot liberate himself from its effects. Thanks to its pernicious consequences, he repeatedly finds himself condemned to suffer through the experiences of others, as well as in his own misfortune.

The end of his narrative tells how Bardamu finds work in a private nursing home for the mentally ill. The director goes away for a while, "by a most miraculous stroke of luck" leaving him in charge. Bardamu, however, has no real faith in good fortune. Miracles do not last, he feels certain. Almost at once, he has the unpleasant sensation of "throwing up Destiny" (I, 340). Before much longer, he begins to receive anonymous letters accusing him of living with his long-time friend Robinson. Suspecting Robinson's ex-fiancée, Madelon, of having written these, he determines to try bringing about a reconciliation between her and Robinson. His motives, then, are the two dominant ones that rule his life: the instinct of self-preservation and uncontrollable sentimentality. Things go hideously wrong as *Voyage au bout de la nuit* reaches its climax in the death of Robinson, shot in the stomach by Madelon.

*Voyage* culminates in the inevitable arrival of death. A novel so many of its critics have condemned as sounding like the purposeless ramblings of a vulgar self-indulgent misanthropist testifies in the end to the inescapable irony of human existence. The outcome is not hap-hazard at all. It is tragic, in this sense that a major defect in Bardamu—his concern for others, the very quality Céline frequently is accused of having lacked—collaborates with self-interest to make him the instrument of fate. Until we see this, we miss the point altogether, just as we fail to detect the rigor with which Céline planned and executed his first novel. To the embarrassment of commentators who had sought to make excuses for him by referring to *Voyage au bout de la nuit* as a comic book, he was to emphasize, "The only truly nasty book among all my books is 'Voyage'... I know what I'm saying... The emotional background..."[4]


Céline was never to depart from a principle laid down in *Semmelweis*: "Man is a sentimentalist. No great emotions outside feelings" (I, 603). In a letter, regrettably undated, he once wrote to Eugène Dabit, "I also had to raise the tone frankly to the plane of delirium. Then things crash head-on, naturally."[5] Interviewed by Merry Bromberger in *L'Intransigeant* on December 9, 1932, he declared, "An autobiography, my book? It's a story to the power of three. Céline sends Bardamu into a delirium. Bardamu says what he knows about Robinson. One shouldn't see a slice of life here, but a delirium."

During his early years as a writer of fiction, Céline's model was not Gide, in the elegant posture of the master ironist. Instead, he spoke enthusiastically of "admirable Breughel."[6] To Eveline Pollet he admitted that he was "very much Breughelian by instinct."[7] And writing to Léon Daudet from Vienna, after seeing Breughel's *Madman's Feast* there, he commented, "The whole problem is nowhere else for me... . . . All my delirium goes in that direction and I have scarcely any other delights."[8] Small wonder that, with such an ideal in sight, Céline

4. See Marc Hanrez, *Céline* (Paris: Gallimard, 1961), p. 32.
5. *L'Herne*, No 3, p. 87.
6. Undated letter to Eugène Dabit, in *L'Herne*, No 3, p. 89.
7. Letter dated March 1933, in *L'Herne*, No 3, p. 97.
8. *L'Herne*, No 3, p. 92. In an undated letter to Henri Mahé, Céline reported, "I've discovered in Vienna a man after my own heart, Peter Breughel. I'll say nothing about his painting about which you [Mahé was a painter] know me to be such an expert. But the spirit! Oh! What a spirit. The madman's feast is life to me. What deliverance!" See *La Brinquebale avec Céline*, p. 58.

should have asserted during an interview conducted by Jean Guenot and Jacques Darribehaude, "The weakness of European art is being objective."[9]

"We work these days by the sensibility and no longer by analysis, all in all 'from within'" (II, 505). Céline's observation is particularly striking, when one recalls the circumstances under which he made it. It is taken from an address he delivered on October 1, 1933, at the invitation of the Society of the Friends of Emile Zola. Entitled *Hommage à Zola*, his talk was printed for the first time three days later, in the magazine *Marianne*.

On September 14, Céline had reported in a letter to Eveline Pollet that he would be speaking on Zola only as a favor to Lucien Descaves, whom he owed a favor: Descaves, Léon Daudet, and Jean Ajalbert were the only members of the Académie Goncourt who had voted for *Voyage au bout de la nuit* when the prestigious Goncourt Prize for the best novel of the year went to Guy Mazeline for *Les Loups*. "Good heavens," Céline confided, "I don't like Zola at all—so I'll speak about myself but I don't like myself much either. All this is very tiresome."[10]

Evidently, those who asked Céline to join the annual pilgrimage to Zola's country home at Médan thought they were inviting a partisan of the naturalist cause. In this, they shared a common misapprehension about his work. Writing in *Savez-vous...* in June of 1936, Daniel-Rops confidently passed the following judgment on *Voyage au bout de la nuit*: "One could not deny that there was, in *Voyage*, a quasi-demoniac power and an anguish that were touching. But there was also something else... quite a bit of shamming, faking, 'literature' of the worst kind. . . . His style was nothing other than 'écriture artiste' of a somewhat special kind." The same misunderstanding colored Charles Bourthoumieux's review of Céline's next work of fiction, *Mort à crédit*, in *La Tribune* for July 2, 1936, depicting the writer as the arch-naturalist: "Never has any novelist gone so far in naturalism, so resolutely broken with all the conventions of language and feeling that veil the repulsive realities of existence. What was the boldness of Flaubert, Baudelaire and Zola compared with the crudities of Céline?" As for an article on *Mort à crédit* by Eugène Marsan, published in *Comœdia* on May 12, 1936, it simply expanded upon its title: "Céline = Les Goncourt + Zola + Huysmans + Rictus + X": "Céline de-

9. See Jean Guénot, "Voyage au bout de la parole," in *L'Herne*, No 5, 246–67.
10. *L'Herne*, No 3, p. 101.

rives from the Goncourts in the sinuosity and picturesqueness of *l'écriture artiste*; from Zola, in crudity and desolation; from Huysmans in autobiographical or almost autobiographical character; also in the infallible attention to minute detail in his verism; finally from Rictus, as much in the lyricism as in the tartness of his slang."

Surface resemblances of this kind should not have concealed from anyone that Céline was incapable of approving the underlying optimism of Zola's outlook on the world. Zola's simple faith in the future contrasted markedly with the point of view mirrored in *Voyage au bout de la nuit* and summed up in a letter to Eveline Pollet, written September 22, 1933: "I've always had a horrible fear of the future, of the humiliation of the future. What I know of the past..."[11]

If Céline's first novel appeared to warrant Descaves's confidence, this was surely because it rested on a conviction voiced in one of Céline's letters to Dabit: "Desertion for the artist lies in leaving the concrete."[12] It did not take the author of *Voyage* long to dissipate Descaves's misapprehension, even so. True, the tone of his address was civil, conciliatory, and even perhaps a little apologetic at first. Nevertheless, because our means of gathering information have increased since Zola's day, Céline spoke of naturalism as having become impossible: "One would never be let out of prison if one recounted life as one knows it, beginning with one's own. I mean as one has understood it for the last twenty years" (II, 503). Speaking more openly in his book *Mea Culpa*, Céline would remark in 1937 that when dealing with man we must not only "see his guts" but also "his pretty little brain!..." (III, 340). What can be asked of naturalism, then, under present-day conditions?—"All and nothing. Nothing, rather, for in our day spiritual conflicts get on the nerves of the masses too much to be tolerated for long," he stated at Médan (II, 507). Lacking the faith Zola and his generation retained in progress through scientific advancement, he implied, we must expect in this day and age to see the world painted in ever darkening hues. For we live out our lives under perpetual threat of death. All in all, there can be no question of imitating Zola or of consenting to follow his lead: "We evidently have neither the gift, the strength, nor the faith that create great movements of the soul," Céline observed tactfully (II, 506). Hence his own homage to Zola sounded like a farewell, uttered on the "eve" (the allusion is to Zola's novel about the 1870 war, *La Débâcle*) "of an immense rout, another one" (II, 506).

11. *L'Herne*, No 3, p. 101.
12. Letter dated September 1, without indication of the year. See *L'Herne*, No 3, p. 88.

As well as defining his spiritual position by measuring how far he stood from Zola, Céline's speech touched upon methodological matters. It drew a brief but pertinent analogy between Zola's work and Pasteur's. Both, Céline contended, had used the same "meticulous technique of creation," sharing "the same concern for experimental probity and above all the same formidable power to demonstrate" (II, 506). Arguing that it would be too much to ask for someone comparable in our time, he asserted that no one could get away with handling the reality of the present the way Zola treated that of his day.

Later, in *Bagatelles pour un massacre* (1937), he would condemn Dos Passos, Faulkner, Lawrence, and others too for "looking back to our most out-of-date naturalists." The authors he praised now—Simenon, Aymé, Dabit, Morand, Mac Orlan—are among those that critics generally relegate to the second rank, at best. This made no difference to Céline, who affirmed, "I like even better Claude Farrère than twelve or thirteen counterfeiters" (pp. 215–16)—including, we may suppose, André Gide, author of *Les Faux-Monnayeurs*. It is significant that the writers finding favor in *Bagatelles pour un massacre* give more attention to atmosphere than to ideas in their novels. For Céline's talk at Médan advised listeners to turn to "symbols and dreams," because it is in these that we spend nine-tenths of our lives, "since nine-tenths of existence, that is, of living pleasure, is unknown to us or forbidden" (II, 503–504). In short, for Louis-Ferdinand Céline the art of fiction resided in working "by the sensibility" while equating symbols and dreams with "the concrete."

To see how these ideas affected Céline as a practicing novelist, we can begin with an important early section of *Voyage au bout de la nuit*. It details Bardamu's experiences during the First World War.

Ferdinand soon has reached the firm conclusion that it is from his fellow men that he has most to fear. Early on, his account concentrates on this major theme of *La Vie et l'œuvre de Philippe Ignace Semmelweis*. It reveals him to be anything but a brute. Basically, he is an idealist, deeply hurt by evidence all around him that forces him little by little to recognize and acknowledge the painful truth about mankind. From his sense of hurt erupts explosive protest, taking a variety of forms.

Bardamu ends up blaming mankind because he sees the world

as man-made and holds humanity responsible for each individual's suffering. One cannot understand this attitude fully without first having reviewed the process of disillusionment by which war educates young Bardamu. This process is radically different from the one that comes close to placing warfare among the rites of passage, in Stephen Crane's *The Red Badge of Courage*. Soon it becomes evident that Céline believed the novelist has no right to sentimentalize the experience of war, from whatever perspective, and for whatever motive. The lyricism with which Henri de Montherlant imbued his *La Relève du matin* is totally absent from *Voyage au bout de la nuit*. The latter depicts war in violent contrast with the picture presented by Roland Dorgelès in his emotional *Les Croix de bois*. Georges Duhamel, in his *Vie des martyres*, and especially Henri Barbusse in *Le Feu* come closer to sharing the point of view on the 1914–18 war adopted in *Voyage*, where military conflict is shown to be simply monstrous. From the outset, Bardamu's experiences assume nightmarish features. He finds in war a symbol of the hideousness of life, touched up with shades of the grotesque.

War quickly convinces Bardamu to look upon fear as natural in any intelligent individual. It helps him see in fact that fear is an eminently healthy state. To his mind, those unaffected by terror, like the colonel with whom he finds himself caught under fire, must be insane. Heroism is without meaning, because unwarranted by circumstance. Heroes end up dead, duly having paid a fair price for their bravery. In death, the colonel, his belly ripped open, seems to embrace, in an ironically fraternal gesture, a common soldier whose head has been blown off. Blood bubbles in the soldier's neck "like jam in a cooking pot" (I, 15).

Beneath the apparent naturalistic objectivity of these descriptions lies horror, captured in cruel images that at first sight suggest only callous indifference on the writer's part. "It's difficult to get to essentials even so far as war's concerned," Bradamu will assert before long, "fancy puts up a long resistance" (I, 36). Shells are still falling all around when he leaves the scene, "pretty happy," as he puts it, to have "such a fine pretext for fucking off" (I, 15).

Bardamu's subsequent suspiciously negative attitude toward life can be traced to his firm determination—fruit of bitter experience—never again to be a willing accomplice in his own destiny, the way he was when he walked into an army barracks, found the gates had closed quietly behind him, and realized too late that he and the other new recruits "were done for, like rats" (I, 10). Still, the negative solution to life at which Ferdinand Bardamu finally arrives will never be more than a totally ineffectual attempt to avoid the penalty for living—an adjustment to life, more or less. With something less than perfect logic, he will come in time to look upon the dead colonel as really better off than he, after all: the officer could have saved his own life, had he not insisted on being a hero.

What eventually begins to obsess Bardamu is this: there are certain forms of absurdity in human life he cannot escape, whatever he does and wherever he goes. His early contact with war has brought him face-to-face with the monstrous, the supposedly unnatural. The horrible discovery Céline reserves for him later is that the monstrous is not unnatural at all. This is why, looking back, Bardamu likens what he saw at the Front to the loss of sexual innocence. Enraged, he will resort to throwing the monstrous back in men's faces, in protest, as he recounts his unedifying life history. For man can find dignity, in Bardamu's estimation, only in protesting his fate. The more loudly and violently he utters his cry of protest, the more clearly he will assert his inner sense of dignity, at the risk of letting his vulgarity appear intended to undermine dignity and destroy it altogether.

Not surprisingly, Bardamu's sanity has been endangered by his wartime experiences. He now finds himself placed under observation in a military hospital. Insanity has become the reverse of the coin on which war defaces the obverse side. Bardamu already knows his form of insanity is incurable, by the way, even though he is released eventually. Its roots sink into fear. "Long live madmen and cowards," he exclaims (I, 50). In the meantime, he has found more evidence of sanity in hospitals, among fellow patients, than outside. Here, at least, the only form of madness he encounters is one he can handle: the patriotism mouthed by the attending staff. In fact, he and the other patients vie with one another in responding to the patriotic claptrap they hear daily with far-fetched tales of their own gallantry. These culminate farcically in a performance, at the Comédie Française, of an epic poem written by an earnest young scribbler in honor of Ferdinand Bardamu's heroism.

Later on, Bardamu's life will have come full circle when he accepts a position in a private nursing home for the mentally ill, with little pay, but passable food and good beds, not to mention this bonus: "You could also screw the nurses" (I, 302). Where once he was among those supervised, now he watches in his turn, yet with no feeling of superiority over his charges. "A madman," he knows, "that's only the ordinary ideas of man but shut up tight in a head." Reflection leads him to conclude, now, that there are no more than two realizations of the depth of the human temperament: war and illness, "those two infinite nightmares."

Finally invalided out of the army, Bardamu embarks for Africa. On board ship, he soon learns he cannot escape contact with the fundamentally evil nature of men. "One is never fearful enough," he infers (I, 85). Everyone else is traveling at government or company expense. As the only paying passenger, like the ship's Jonah, Bardamu is regarded with deep suspicion and finds himself accused of everything from spying to sodomy. He is treated as a hunted man, already guilty. "Of what? When men's hate carries no risk, their stupidity is soon convinced, motives come all on their own" (I, 87). "The crowd is sadistic and cowardly and envious and destructive," Céline concurs in a letter to his secretary, Marie Canavaggia, written May 20, 1936. "It has to be given the feeling of sacking and pillaging and of reducing things to pulp. Otherwise nothing doing" (II, 720). Man, he observes in *Mea Culpa,* has only one tyrant: himself. "Man is human about as much as a hen flies. When it gets a hard blow in the gut, when a car sends it flying, it really goes up as high as the roof, but it starts over again in the mud, pecking away once more at droppings" (III, 345–46).

To prove his point, Bardamu makes no attempt to disabuse those aboard ship who have the wrong idea about him. Instead he acts in ways he knows will appear suspect. He provokes antagonisms that will unmask those around him for the dangerous, vicious creatures they are. He voluntarily takes on the role of scapegoat for which, like Semmelweis, he is well fitted.

No man to turn the other cheek—Christian charity has no place in his life—Bardamu speaks of the male passengers without affection or indulgence as malaria-ridden, alcoholic, and syphilitic, eczema eating at their paunches and crab-lice in their pubic hair. As for their wives, they are no more than "impatient vaginas." One woman in particular strikes him as looking forward to seeing him manhandled as eagerly as she would to being raped by a gorilla.

Naturally, Ferdinand Bardamu does not attempt to set himself above the rest of mankind. He feels no need to singularize himself, to claim the superiority that is the hero's privilege. On the contrary, what he freely admits about himself is proof enough that he regards himself as no better (but no worse) than anyone else. Other people may be malevolent; he himself is deceitful and hypocritical. He learns to shirk his responsibilities wherever he sees an advantage in doing so. When he takes up the study of medicine it is because he believes that being a doctor will give him an advantage over the sick, whose dependence on his professional knowledge promises him some release from the menace they represent as human beings.

Hate being the last resort of a cowardly victim of society's cruelty, Bardamu returns hatred for hatred aboard the *Amiral Bragueton.* Turning society's methods back upon the embodiment of its coercive authority—a military man who threatens him, after donning full dress uniform for the occasion—during a mockingly humorous scene Bardamu makes an impassioned appeal to patriotism, so as to escape a beating. With appropriate references to military glory, he turns to full account his hard-won title of war veteran, embraces his enemy in a show of comradeship, and then at the first safe opportunity slips over the ship's side.

For Bardamu, Africa—the dark continent which takes him, like Conrad's Kurtz, to the heart of darkness—is characterized by its smell, "its heavy mixture of moist earth, crotch and ground saffron" (I, 134). The concrete takes on symbolic value as he sees the jungle at night as "an enormous railroad station of love, without light, full to bursting point," while whole trees are "bloated with mutilated erections, with horror" (I, 125). To Ferdinand, we begin to realize, the world experienced directly is a world distorted by disgust, fear, sickness, and unavoidable suffering. Hence his smile is often very much like a rictus of pain, as when he mentions the natives who, in the absence of gazelles, eat at least one grandmother a week.

Abandoning his post in the bush—since the war, self-preservation is the only code by which he intends to live—Bardamu is foolish enough to trust a Roman Catholic priest. The latter sells him to the captain of a Spanish slave galley, bound for New York. With no risk of losing their jobs and with retirement guaranteed at the age of sixty-two, the other slaves have no complaints. Indeed, they do their utmost to dissuade Ferdinand when he announces his intention of jumping ship, while it is in quarantine in New York harbor.

Having learned to count fleas with unusual efficiency on the voyage over, Bardamu wants to put his talent to use. He proposes to place his statistical skill at the service of a country that lives by statistics. He is hired immediately, to work in the Shower Section on Ellis Island, under someone called Maj. Mischief. Once on the job, he demonstrates how competently he can separate Spanish fleas from Polish ones, to say nothing of his gift for identifying Crimean crab-lice and Peruvian itch. "This was work, you can see, at once monumental and meticulous" (I, 141). In the Land of Opportunity (and the Free), promotion soon rewards Bardamu's diligence. The man above him earns an important appointment, as flea counter for prospectors' dogs in Alaska. His departure leaves an opening. Permitted now to carry vital statistics to New York City, Ferdinand Bardamu unhesitatingly betrays the trust placed in him. He never returns to Ellis Island.

In *Voyage au bout de la nuit* the narrative swings continually like this between the horrible and the farcical, as Céline brings our scale of values under hostile scrutiny. Frequently, the limits of naturalism are left far behind, as a sensibility acutely responsive to an alien environment is permitted total liberty to communicate its impressions without being submitted to any obligation to distinguish the normal from the abnormal, the realistic from the demonic.

Very often Céline's anguished evocation of the urban landscape in which he situates the action of *Voyage* has the quality of suffused misery we associate with the descriptive method used by Henry Céard in *Une belle journée* and more especially in *Terrains à vendre au bord de la mer*. They seem reminiscent, too, of Huysmans' descriptions in *Croquis parisiens* ("Nature is interesting only when sick and woe-begone," comments Huysmans in one text from this volume, dedicated to Céard), though they display none of the studied sophistication of detail that betrays Huysmans' interest in painting. Above all, the picture Céline provides of the working-class districts of the Zone spares us the condescension for the lower social orders so typical of the Goncourts in their novels. We never find in Célinian writing intrusive evidence of the presence of the self-conscious observer, displaying his skill through what the Goncourts Brothers revealingly termed "l'écriture artiste." In Céline's first novel we witness something far more original than the spectacle of the self-congratulating artist with words, seeking and finding proof of his own talent, as the Goncourts did in their *Germinie Lacerteux*.

A scene taking place in a men's subway toilet promises to be worthy of *L'Assommoir* or *Les Sœurs Vatard*. However, it exceeds the limits within which both Zola and Huysmans confined description, overspilling the bounds imposed on them by the naturalist esthetic. Without warning, Bardamu finds himself in an underworld that contrasts alarmingly with the New York streets above. He looks about him in a sort of empty swimming pool, lit by a wan light shining on "men unbuttoned among their odors, quite crimson from pushing out their dirty business in front of everyone, with barbarous cries" (I, 145).

The humor that touches Céline's description is certainly Gargantuan. Yet it does not simply reflect the uncomplicated pleasure that Rabelais took in natural functions. The crowd cheers the performers on, "as at a football game." In this "fecal cavern," men appear to find some sort of liberation at the prospect of "dropping their guts in tumultuous company" (I, 145). With the stall doors hanging from broken hinges, it is possible to socialize. In "terrific intestinal familiarity," those waiting for seats encourage "the rectal workers" with slaps on the shoulder, while threatening the constipated with "ingenious tortures." The odor makes Bardamu so afraid that he soon withdraws to the relative safety of the street.

True-to-life details are exaggerated beyond measure, but never in a way calculated to reconcile man to living. In his uninhibited exploration of the monstrous potential of observable reality, Céline succeeds in painting a picture he is far from content to keep within recognizable proportions. In his own words, it is "delirium" that best describes what follows from the head-on crash of external reality and exacerbated imagination. Thus his description of the subterranean world of defecation sets the tone for his evocation of New York City, charged with feelings of loneliness, fear, hostility, and anguish, for which even Bardamu's sojourn in Africa has not prepared him adequately. Despite the fascination of rich women's legs and the consolation of 42nd Street movies, he speaks of a lassitude aggravated by his stay in New York, "that chancre of the world" (I, 150). He utters his *De Profundis* from the window of his room atop the Laugh Calvin Hotel, crying "Help" to a city from which no answer comes. "That's the great modern miracle," observes Céline in *Mea Culpa*, "A gigantic, cosmic fatuity" (III, 342).

Albert Camus contends in *Le Mythe de Sisyphe* that we must believe Sisyphus was happy in his fate. Céline counters in *Mea Culpa*, "The great pretension to happiness, that's the enormous imposture! That's the one that complicates all of life! That makes people so venomous, scoundrels, unfit to drink. There's no happiness in existence, only more or less great unhappiness" (III, 342). In *Voyage au bout de la nuit* he shows how Bardamu, thrown back by loneliness on his own resources, finds them pitiably inadequate. Wondering how we can find the strength to follow our daily routine, making repeated abortive attempts to escape "crushing necessity," while succeeding only in convincing ourselves that destiny is "insurmountable," Bardamu concludes that we must "fall at the bottom of the wall" every morning, "beneath the anguish of that next day, always more precarious, more sordid" (I, 148). Even worse, when we lack the courage to put an end to everything, we have to be resigned to knowing ourselves a little better each day. Self-examination leads directly to self-disgust, in Bardamu's case, as well as to the firm conviction that life is worthless.

The phrase expressing this disheartening belief, "Des haricots, la vie" (I, 155), establishes a significantly depressing link between Bardamu's dreary existence in New York and his later life pattern back in Europe.

From his window overlooking a courtyard, Bardamu, now a doctor in France, can observe the private lives of neighborhood families. Also he can hear what takes place in one apartment lying out of his line of vision. Familiarity with a scene recurring there has made it possible for his imagination to supply all the horrible details.

Making up after a quarrel, a husband and wife begin exciting themselves sexually by tying their little daughter to a bed. About ten years old, judging by her voice, the child utters cries like those of a mouse caught in a trap, as her parents swear at her so ferociously that she pleads with the woman to hit her instead. When she has been beaten until she can howl no longer, the adults, now sufficiently stimulated, copulate up against the kitchen sink. And Ferdinand Bardamu sits listening. "I couldn't have eaten my haricot beans while that was going on," he confesses. "I couldn't close the window either. I was good for nothing. I couldn't do nothing. I just went on listening like always, everywhere" (I, 196), finding in the horrifying incident a perverse source of strength to sink even lower.

*Voyage au bout de la nuit* portrays man as imprisoned by time in the flesh. Time, the dominant factor in human life, is a purely negative inexorable force, here, universally making its dreadful effects felt in progressive decay and degradation. Meanwhile, the inner crumbling of man's hopes and ambitions is externalized in a physical decline that cripples the individual, deprives him of self-respect, and has but one outcome for everyone. As Céline interprets existence, it is not death but life itself that is the great leveler. Interviewed by Marc Hanrez in March of 1959, he agreed with the latter's statement, "Therefore, in your opinion, a lucid thought is an eschatological thought essentially."[13] For Louis-Ferdinand Céline, however, eschatology was less the anticipation of death than the invalidation of human activity, measured by the scale of death. And so Bardamu can look for no peace in contemplating the regular rhythm of the life cycle. In his later years, Zola, for one, took comfort and found release from existential dread in the thought that life renews itself from death. Céline, however, could never see any reason to acquiesce in man's destiny. He looked upon life as a bloody struggle, having one outcome only, never for a moment in doubt.

In Céline's fiction, existential anguish does not find expression in abstract discussion of man's fate. His method was as different from Aldous Huxley's as it was from Simone de Beauvoir's. Anguish is implicit, in *Voyage au bout de la nuit,* in the emphasis given physical aspects of human life that generate disgust and horror. Man is presented here in his physicality, and therefore is condemned to death through life. The Cartesian image is degraded, as mankind is plunged helplessly into the contingent. Something other than the dignity of being privileged to think out their situation in the universe emerges as common to all men. The fundamental unifying feature of human existence is shown to be biological. The only form of good luck mentioned in *Voyage* is that of a man, known to the police under the "terrible pseudonym" of Balthazar, blessed with "a terrific penis" that makes him especially popular with the ladies (I, 263). More typically, insistence on physical attributes and on their inevitable decline helps Céline strip away the veneer that society and cultural pretensions give our relationship with other people. "You have to learn," warns Bardamu, "to recognize in the toilet the smell of each of the neighbors on your floor, that's convenient" (I, 261).

Meanwhile, individual consciousness is denied the consolation of being able to differentiate itself from the experience of the common herd. The plane on which Céline allows us to be sensitive to our relations with those around us gives no one the prospect of escaping nausea and self-disgust. Idealism and any elevation of thought and aspiration are

13. See the interview reproduced in Hanrez, *Céline,* p. 277.

eliminated from the start. Bardamu sees "the great fatigue of existence" in the enormous trouble we take to stay twenty, forty, or more, "so as not to be simply, profoundly ourselves, that is, foul, atrocious, absurd" (I, 304). Nietzsche's superman gives way, necessarily and invariably, to the universal subman.

The contrast is clear and instructive between the horribly passive role in which Bardamu is cast by human fatality and the active part played in life by the revolutionary Kyo, in André Malraux's *La Condition humaine*. While in jail, Kyo responds to the spectacle of human degradation—of one man's dependence on another—by demonstrating an ennobling sense of dignity. Pointless though it may be for him to allow himself deliberately to be struck by a prison guard, this act affirms the dignified status of every individual. As for Bardamu, even in the security of his own home he is paralyzed by the very humanitarian feelings that render him powerless to turn away callously from someone else's suffering. This experience calls forth no elevating or consoling reflections on life. Quite to the contrary, it repeats a lesson that always throws Bardamu back upon his own inadequacy, so reaffirming man's defeat instead of proclaiming his greatness. Fostering increased sympathy for others, sometimes no less revolting than he himself, disgust will sharpen his suffering through the misery he sees everywhere about him. Underlying every experience is mental and emotional torture, because "I never managed to feel completely innocent of the misfortunes that occurred" (I, 204).

In all this, the recurrent image of darkness is not merely an esthetic device, used to give the narrative a certain tonality. Bardamu is a nocturnal creature. He obviously links what is most essential in human existence with darkness and negativity, rather than with daylight and the positive forces of sunshine. Speaking of a movie-house where the foyer lights seem to undress people, he complains, "You couldn't speak to one another of personal business in that entry, it was like the very opposite of darkness" (I, 257). There are clear indications in Bardamu's account that his persistence, his tenacity where life is concerned, comes from adjustment to the misery of existence, suggested by his familiarity with darkness. He even argues that, just as "one cannot live a second without pleasure," so it is very difficult to "really know sorrow" (I, 256). A masochistic thread is palpable in the texture of his story. The sadism he sees as ruling the human heart has its counterpart in submission. Thus the examples by which he teaches the lessons he wants us to learn are brutal, shocking, and revealing, like the one concerning a mother who masturbates continually while her child is dying of meningitis: she cannot be made to stop even after the child has succumbed.

The medical cases on which Dr Bardamu reports are always of the same nature. As attending physician, he finds himself a helpless spectator before terminal agony, before a little boy's meningitis, the butchery of illegal abortion, and a difficult typhoid case that his colleagues have the good sense to avoid. And so, as we hear his recitative of failure and recurrent disaster, we are led to ask ourselves why things happen the way they do, in *Voyage au bout de la nuit.*

Céline was not tempted to try following the example set by Franz Kafka, concealing the underlying reason for human misfortune in order to stress men's uncomprehending dependence on forces they can never explain. Indeed, like other major French novelists of the thirties and forties, Céline gave those forces weighing on man's destiny a name that has become even more popular since he began writing. He called it the absurd. All the same, it was not by bowing to fashion that he displayed originality in his fiction. One distinguishing feature of his novelistic writing is the interpretation it proposes of the sources of the absurd and of the ways the absurd has of manifesting itself in human affairs. At every turn, we are conscious of a contrast between Céline's outlook and that of his better liked and far more limited contemporary, Malraux. There are moments in fact when *Voyage au bout de la nuit* seems to have been written as a riposte to Malraux's *Les Conquérants* (1928), in *Bagatelles pour un massacre* ironically called a masterpiece, "so far as I can judge" (p. 215).

During the period when he wrote his first novels, Malraux looked upon action as the pathway to salvation for man. His predilection for the adventure story testified to a conception of human existence that gave the man of action a very positive role in life's drama. Céline would have none of this. He portrayed man in *Voyage au bout de la nuit* as stumbling through life without hope of redemption of any kind. And so, in this novel action is no more than a token of the irony of man's fate, while adventure is but "a shabby enterprise in practical living" (I, 261).

Céline began writing fiction with a point of view radically different from that of contemporary French novelists for whom he expressed only contempt. *Voyage au bout de la nuit* proposes no constructive maxims by which man may hope to order his life and make positive sense of existence. Céline offered neither an encouraging ideology nor an elevating one. He never was to stop regarding man as "too petty, weak and futile to ever be anything other than a pretentious nick-knack, quickly outmoded."[14] In *Le Mythe de Sisyphe* Camus extends his readers at least the possibility of reassuring reconciliation with an absurd universe. In contrast, when Céline warned that we must teach ourselves to consider men worse than they in fact are, he was asserting the helplessness and hopelessness of each individual's fate. "The cult of the hero," we read in *Bagatelles pour un massacre*, "is the cult of good luck" (I, 138).

In his way, and despite the criticism of Malraux's faith in adventure implied in *La Nausée*, Jean-Paul Sartre shares Malraux's confidence in the grandeur of man, manifest in the individual's aggressive response to the world where he finds himself. Similarly, one can look on Camus's *La Peste* and even Hemingway's *The Old Man and the Sea* for that matter as proof of the vitality of the optimism at the root of Malraux's novels. From the first, however, Céline's writings represented hope as capable only of making man a dupe, an unsuspecting accomplice in his own downfall through prolonged misery and renewed suffering into final oblivion. In *La Vie et l'œuvre de Philippe Ignace Semmelweis* we find the statement, "However high in fact one's genius places one, however pure the truths one states, does one have the right to be unmindful of the formidable power of absurd things? (I, 593). Logically, *Voyage au bout de la nuit* next shows us life as no better than a succession of false starts, by definition abortive. Picking one's way through existence, Bardamu says, calls for the same circumspection as is needed for "finding your way about in a piss-house you don't know" (I, 263).

Camus opened his essay on the myth of Sisyphus with the confident declaration that suicide poses the only philosophical question that matters. This text and most of Camus's best known works all point in the same direction, to the same answer: that man must find a solution to life in ways other than that of self-elimination. The moral and ethical code of post-Nietszchean society, Camus taught, calls for rejection of suicide on the grounds of self-respect, rather than on the basis of religious dogma. Man becomes his own Messiah. Trust in himself and in his beneficent liberty to act positively comforts him in a hostile

14. Letter to Ernst Bendz, dated simply "the 8th," in *L'Herne*, No 3, p. 128.

universe that repeatedly—and so very fortunately—throws him back upon his own perfectly adequate resources. Thus, like Malraux's or Sartre's, Camus's popularity, especially among the young, grows out of the postromantic elevation of individual man as capable of surpassing his fellows when the need presents itself, and therefore as fully able to rise above common human destiny. This is why, reassuringly but somewhat paradoxically, Malraux's novels equate humanism with heroism.

Céline, whose Bardamu refers to youth as "only young after the fashion of boils because of the pus that hurts from the inside and swells them up" (I, 277), has no such promise to extend. Camus may well have spoken for others as well as for himself, when depicting the absurd in *Le Mythe de Sisyphe* as affecting all of life, perhaps, yet as exterior to man and located in the universe itself. To Céline, far more disturbingly, the absurd was not merely a feature of living in this world. He saw it, distressingly, as the very essence of being. For this reason his main characters resemble Ferdinand Bardamu in being denied the energy that Malraux treats as the blessed compensation granted mankind for being cast adrift in life. The positive aspects of Camus's sense of the absurd, and of Sartre's too, lie fruitfully in man's gift for turning his energy outward to combat everything in the world about him that otherwise could oppress and overcome him. Céline had no comparable optimistic solution to propose to the ever-present problem of survival in a hostile world. For, in his eyes, it is not the universe but man himself that is absurd. So what passes for energy within us works against our happiness. Meanwhile, the precious sense of the absurd as functioning as a spur to action is lacking in Bardamu. He carries within the seeds of his own failure, inevitably nurturing these as he follows the road to extinction.

While Malraux's heroes are motivated by a profound and compelling need to live up to their self-esteem, Céline puts up no serious argument against Ferdinand's motives for surrendering self-respect: "That feeling always seemed to me," Bardamu confides, "very much above my station, a thousand times too expensive for my means" (I, 312). To Céline, the fatal flaw of existence—of what Malraux termed the human condition—is inherent in man himself, not merely implicit in his situation. The bleakness of outlook, the total lack of favorable perspective marking all Céline's novels—these are not the effect and fault of the world outside but, like man's inhumanity to man, a projection of the basic nature of mankind.

Malraux and Camus assure us that the absurd must be and can

be confronted by positive action leading to transcendence of human fate, liberated from fatality, and its transformation into destiny. They feel confident in relaying this encouraging message because they look upon the absurd as an external phenomenon that man finds the strength within himself to combat and defeat. For Céline, on the other hand, the absurd is more insidious, quite inescapable in its effects. Man carries with him into this world the forces that will bring about the collapse of his aspirations, invalidating all supposedly positive effort, draining every gesture of meaning, and calling the life force itself into question. And yet we see in *Voyage au bout de la nuit* that Bardamu cannot give up on life, cannot let go. As a result, his suffering is compounded by successive disappointments we would expect his pessimism to spare him: his failure to persuade the husband of a woman hemorrhaging in childbirth to have her admitted to a hospital, for instance. What is more, Bardamu is eternally harassed by guilt. We see its consequences when reading the incident centered on a rabbit hutch.

      The episode involves Robinson, whom Bardamu met for the first time in Flanders during the war, whom he subsequently found to have been his predecessor in the African jungle from which he soon would run away, whom he anticipated meeting by chance in the New World (and actually did run into while in Detroit), and who lives now not far away, on the outskirts of Paris. If there is something unpredictable yet strangely inevitable about the way Robinson reappears from time to time in Bardamu's account, Céline leaves us in no doubt about the attraction he holds for the narrator. It is as though Robinson embodies an energy and a positive attitude to life that Ferdinand knows to be lacking in himself. In fact, Céline once confided to his secretary, "Bardamu? He's not me, he's my double. But so is Robinson."
      Bardamu looks upon his friend as having what he calls a "weakness" for independence (I, 237). The circumstances under which this man left Africa, his illegal status in the United States, and so on, make of Robinson an outlaw figure, well suited by his "weakness" to enter into an agreement with a couple of neighbors to kill the husband's mother. He plans to build a rabbit hutch and bobby-trap it, so it will explode and dispose of the old woman, who tends the animals. Informed of the plan, Dr Bardamu has two reasons above and beyond friendship for not informing the police. First, standard morality means

no more to him now than in the past: he sees no cause to turn Robinson over to justice. Second, Robinson's plan is not original, by any means. It is one already used before and about which he first heard from Bardamu himself.

Shifting about in its cage while the trap is being set, one of the rabbits triggers the mechanism. The latter goes off in Robinson's face, instead of Madame Henrouille's. Temporarily blinded, Robinson becomes an unwelcome, unpaying guest in the house where the old woman, who witnessed the accident and has put two and two together, is reinvigorated and now feels she is going to live forever.

Fate has play out a cruel comedy, illustrating that it has no more respect for the strong than for the weak. Admired by Bardamu for his self-reliance, Robinson has become helplessly dependent on others. The light has gone out, for him, years before the night of death will settle in. After trying to console him, Bardamu reports, "He was crying. He'd arrived at the end, him too. There was nothing more one could say to him. There's a moment when you're quite alone and you've arrived at the end of everything that can happen to you. It's the end of the world" (I, 240–41). As for Bardamu himself, he confides, "I wasn't proud of myself. It isn't that I'd done anything positively criminal. No. But I felt guilty anyway. Most of all I was guilty, when you come right down to it, of wanting the whole business to go on" (I, 243). A little later he comments, "Here, on this point, we're much more unfortunate than shit, this mad devotion to persevering in our state constitutes the incredible torture."

Despite his conviction that movement brings no relief from suffering, Bardamu seems to regard moving on as his only defense against destiny. Although he warns, "Mustn't hope to leave your sorrow anyplace along the way," before long he is feeling restless again. Just as he slipped over the side of the *Amiral Bragueton* one night off the African coast, so now he slips away from his apartment in Garenne-Rancy, abandoning his practice and deserting his patients without a twinge of conscience.

Céline's dreadful concept of the absurd as an inner drive, gathering strength perversely from human aspirations, from optimistic impulses, and even from simple inattentiveness, blights existence for

Bardamu. In *Voyage au bout de la nuit* Ferdinand finds himself time
after time drawn by human nature into complicity in his own disillusionment, in the degradation that marks his progress (the word
can have only an ironic function, here) along the road to death. On
the crucial question of the exercise of meaningful choice through action,
Céline's views differ radically from Malraux's, or Camus's, or Sartre's,
or Beauvoir's and with crippling consequences for Bardamu's life. The
other writers mentioned consider the fundamental importance of restless inquiry to be at the origin of responsible living. Their attitude to
the world reflects positive and consoling assumptions: that a fruitful
choice can be made and that the possibility always exists, thereafter,
of adopting a line of conduct that will compensate fully for the anguish
of having to choose. In Céline's first novel, what approximates to choice
really comes down to nothing better than man's involuntary participation in his own defeat. Hence action becomes an essentially and
irresistibly negative factor. Total inactivity remains unattainable, nevertheless, because restlessness keeps man on the move, sending him
further and further among his "dirty road" (I, 254).

Ferdinand Bardamu enjoys a momentary glimpse of possible
contentment when, in reaction against the heavy responsibilities of
medical practice, he becomes a theatre extra. After only four months
of relative calm, however, he feels compelled to resume his journeying.
Listening to nude English girls sing a love song (three performances
a day, while he is on stage dressed as an English policeman), he hears
none of the comforting indications of permanence and stability that
Roquentin, narrator of Sartre's *La Nausée,* finds in the popular tune
*Some of These Days* while struggling with existential nausea. Instead,
guilt surfaces in Bardamu's consciousness at the memory of Robinson's
plight. More important, he lets us see that he still has not learned his
lesson from life, when he decides to go back to Rancy to inquire how
Robinson is getting on, working down in Toulouse as Madame Henrouille's assistant at a macabre tourist attraction. Retrospectively,
Bardamu will assess his own foolishness without a trace of indulgence:
"And that indeed was the imprudence I committed. You don't stay on
your guard long enough! You don't know you've got there and yet
you're already right in the dirty regions of the night. . . . There's
no end to it afterward" (I, 271).

Thinking this will give him a couple of weeks' relaxation,
Bardamu decides to pay Robinson a visit: "the devil has all sorts of
tricks to tempt you! You'll never get to know them all," he points out,
after relating how a priest came to offer him a loan so he could go to

Toulouse (I, 277). By the time he returns to Paris, he has had sexual intercourse with Robinson's fiancée, Madelon. Subsequently, he muses, "The fancy takes you all the same to go a bit further to know if you'll have the strength to find your reason again, all the same, among the debris. It quickly turns to vice, reason does, like good humor and sleep in neurasthenia. There's nothing else to think about but your reason. No more bets can be put down. The party's over" (I, 311).

Even now, Bardamu has not learned to master his sentimental impulses. He arranges an outing to an amusement park. Here he, his girl friend of the moment, and Robinson and Madelon find themselves in an ambience very different indeed from that of the Luna Park in Raymond Queneau's *Pierrot mon ami.* Things go from bad to worse. Finally, on the way home, Robinson turns to Madelon: "Well, everything repels me, disgusts me now!... Not only you!... Everything!... The sentimental tricks you want to play, shall I tell you what they're like? They're like making love in a shit-house! Get it now?... All the feelings you scrape together so I'll stay shacked up with you strike me as insults if you want to know!..." (I, 360). Madelon's reaction leaves Robinson dying on a table in the asylum, while Bardamu reflects, "We're short of just about everything we'd need to help someone die. . . . You've lost confidence along the way. You've pushed it, worried it, the pity you still had, carefully to the bottom of your body like a dirty pill. You've shoved pity right to the end of the intestine with the shit. That's the best place for it you say" (I, 363).

We know Ferdinand Bardamu is plagued by an ever-present sense of impending catastrophe, closely linked with an abiding awareness of his own inadequacy. Since disappointment and failure are merely proof of his inability to cope with life, it is no surprise to learn he takes the path leading to the Seine, instead of following the two men carrying Robinson's body to the police station. It is only to be expected, also, that his continued incapacity to face responsibility brings neither comfort nor feeling of release. He derives no consolation of any kind from looking at the river and thinking of the ocean into which it flows. "It's no good trying to lose yourself to be able to find yourself facing life again, I simply found it again everywhere. I turned back on myself. Dragging myself around was over for me" (I, 365). At this point, he realizes fully how much further in life Robinson went than he himself has gone. After all, Robinson did work out a criminal plan to give himself a fresh start, "a superb thought altogether stronger than death," comments Ferdinand (I, 366), in a phrase that brings to mind Maupassant's title for a novel expressing agonized obsession with death, *Fort comme la mort*. His own ideas, Bardamu has to acknowledge, are "little candles," flickering throughout a lifetime "in a very horrible abominable universe."

If anything, the conclusion Louis-Ferdinand Céline drew from life in *Voyage au bout de la nuit* was even more disenchanted than Bardamu's. In fact, he did not hesitate to proclaim everyone's stupidity in not understanding the meaning of his story. "Here it is! It's love about which we still dare not speak in this hell as if one could compose quatrains in a slaughterhouse. Love impossible today." Thus, in an effort to escape love and himself, Léon Robinson tries to be "heroic after his fashion," without really knowing how to be a hero. "At the end, in the taxi, he finds how. He tells Madelon it isn't she but the whole universe that disgusts him. He says so the best way he can and he dies for it" (I, 744).

Céline acted quite consistently with the viewpoint he had adopted in *Voyage au bout de la nuit* when he spoke in a letter to Milton Hindus, dated October 1, 1947, of writers like Malraux as being "rotten with general ideas, vast concepts, remedies for the human race."[15] The very next day, addressing the same correspondent, he was ridiculing Sartre, "that pope." For Louis-Ferdinand Céline had no panacea, no guarantees or recommended remedy for the ills besetting mankind. He considered the human condition irremediable and life an inoperable disease.

15. *L'Herne*, No 5, p. 98.

# Mort à crédit

FROM HIS FIRST NOVEL ONWARD, Louis-Ferdinand Céline had something special to offer and was fully aware of this. In *La Vie et l'œuvre de Philippe Ignace Semmelweis* he had declared, "Great works are those that reveal our genius, great men are those that give it form" (I, 603). At the end of his career, in an interview granted Pierre Audinet appearing in *Les Nouvelles littéraires* on July 6, 1961, just five days after his death, he scoffed once more at those who "bring a message," and exclaimed, "Why do I write? I'll tell you: to make the others unreadable."

In view of his opinion of those about him, one cannot suppose Céline was astonished at finding the critics too obtuse to understand *Voyage au bout de la nuit.* After all, Semmelweis' life history was adequate proof, for him, that incomprehension and hostility present the individual endowed with superior talents an accurate measurement of his gifts. The ambiguous responses he often made to those who questioned him, to say nothing of his half-truths and outright falsehoods, leave us with the feeling that Céline deliberately sowed confusion and encouraged misinterpretation of his work, in order to give more weight to his contention that greatness draws misapprehension and is penalized by ostracism. On November 28, 1947, he wrote in a letter to Milton Hindus, "In truth, Sartre, Camus, Miller, etc.... . . . are really furious to know I'm still alive; they aren't gifted those snots—They lack an *Inner Dream.*"[1]

Only extreme perversity could make it possible for the work of any artist to find momentum in the firm assurance that he will never be understood or truly appreciated. It is not surprising, therefore, that, viewed in conjunction with his emphasis in *Semmelweis* on great men's obligation to give form to our genius, Céline's pointed reference to an *"Inner Dream"* betrays a need for recognition having deeper sources

1. *L'Herne*, No 5, p. 101.

than the sardonic pleasure he derived from putting journalists off the scent.

Céline's efforts as a novelist were directed at externalizing an inner dream of a delirious nature. It was in relation to this ambition above all that he wished to see *Voyage au bout de la nuit* evaluated. When no one came forward to assess it in the terms he deemed appropriate, the novelist himself passed judgment on the book in a private letter to Eveline Pollet, written September 14, 1933: "But I've never reread it and never will reread it. I find the whole thing tedious and sickeningly flat. It's odd how that barn-storming in the end takes the reader's fancy. I think he feels the urge to do likewise. Everything lies in *that*. Anyway we don't know ourselves very well. We're covered with civilized garbage."[2]

The silence into which Céline lapsed after the appearance of *Voyage* indicates how sincere was his statement to Mme Pollet. Seriously dissatisfied with his first novel, he evidently was determined to experiment no more with fiction until he had found a way to eliminate the faults that had bred both tedium and flatness. And so for several years his readers appeared to have reason to consider Louis-Ferdinand Céline a one-book man from whom nothing more was to be expected.

This conclusion might seem quite natural to any reader of *Voyage* who took time to wonder which way Céline might head, now, as a novelist. He could not change direction, supposedly, without repudiating his first piece of fiction. He appeared to have followed one route obstinately and clear-sightedly to the very end. And he seemed temperamentally unfitted to explore any other, or even to want to try doing so. Would not a return to the themes developed in *Voyage au bout de la nuit*, meanwhile, carry the risk of repetitiveness? And in any case, having drawn so freely (or so it seemed) upon his own experiences when writing his first novel, had he not used up all his narrative resources at one time, leaving himself with nothing more to say? These questions were raised in a review of Céline's second novel, *Mort à crédit* (1936), appearing in *Le Merle blanc* on May 30, 1936. Here Châtelain-Tailhade took the opportunty to quote from a letter written him by the novelist after his public homage to Zola: "I could people a whole asylum with my memories." Meanwhile, reviewing the book in *Paris-Match* on May 13, Noël Sabord reminded his readers of something Céline had said after *Voyage au bout de la nuit*: "These six

2. *L'Herne*, No 3, p. 101.

hundred pages I've taken from more than fifty thousand, and I've more than a hundred thousand others at your service. I'll make you something like a cathedral out of them, all my own; but give me time to put them in order."

Bringing out *Mort à crédit* finally on May 12 of the year 1936, Céline seemed to give a very direct, perfectly simple answer to those who had been wondering what his next novel would be like. At first glance anyway, his new title seemed a frank admission of his intention to treat the very same themes as before, this time by presenting human existence as "death on credit." Writing his new work (even longer than its predecessor), he presumably had turned once again to the same subject matter—his own life history—to concentrate now on reviving memories of childhood and adolescence. In short, the heading Sabord chose for his review in *Paris-Match* relieved all those who had detested *Voyage au bout de la nuit* of any qualm of conscience about declining even to open *Mort à crédit*: "Defying grammar and honesty, L.-F. Céline pursues in *Mort à crédit* his interminable *Voyage au bout de la nuit*." From its very first page, *Mort à crédit* was destined to be misinterpreted. In the long run, it was to occasion numerous fundamental misconceptions about Destouches the man and about Céline the novelist.

Noting that a certain timidity or shyness had led Céline to hide himself partly behind Bardamu in *Voyage*, Ramon Fernandez contended in *Marianne* (May 27, 1936) that everything leads us to believe the author is telling his own story, now, "bequeathing his memories to posterity." Even with the qualifying assertion that these memories were representative ones, Fernandez still unequivocally invited full identification of Ferdinand's character and outlook on life with his creator's. Doing the same thing, in his review of the novel in *Le Figaro* (May 9, 1936), L'Homme qui rit had spoken of "scatological obsession" as apparently a "morbid defect" in its author. As for the reviewer who on June 11 signed his notice in *Candide* with the initials J. F., he showed how dangerously far it is possible to go, when one has started from such a premise: "Obviously we are dealing with a maniac," said this commentator, one of several too squeamish to quote from the text of *Mort à crédit*. "Mr Louis-Ferdinand Céline is perhaps, in private life, a worthy medical man, full of reserve, restraint and formal dignity. Perhaps his books serve as an indispensable outlet for a repressed temperament. But then one regrets that he has not brought his case before his eminent colleague Freud or at least that he has not been content to set down his public-convenience reverie in a notebook reserved for his own delectation."

Like *Voyage au bout de la nuit*, Céline's *Mort à crédit* is a first-person narrative, recounted by a doctor of medicine. He has the same first name as Bardamu and does not divulge his last name, even to the police. Marcel Lapierre, who had reviewed *Voyage* in *Le Progrès de Bordeaux* on November 26, 1932, treated Ferdinand as "no doubt the Bardamu of *Voyage au bout de la nuit*," when reviewing Céline's second novel for *Le Peuple* on June 3, 1936. Louis Laloy confidently asserted in *L'Ere nouvelle* (May 28, 1936) that readers recognize the narrator of *Mort à crédit* as the very same person who narrated *Voyage*. Another reviewer, Eugène Marsan, was more cautious in one respect. In *Comœdia* on May 12, 1936, he spoke only of a resemblance between Ferdinand and Bardamu. He was far less guarded, however, in his remarks about Ferdinand's relationship to his creator: "He resembles Céline like a brother."

Seeking where the truth lies, we can begin with the commonly held assumption that the narrator of *Mort à crédit* is none other than Ferdinand Bardamu, devoting himself in middle age to supplying details of his formative years, passed over in *Voyage au bout de la nuit*. This basic supposition is open to dispute.

Ferdinand's story in *Mort à crédit* ends with his decision to enlist. He reaches this decision for reasons and under circumstances very different indeed from those that brought Bardamu into the army at the beginning of *Voyage*. Presumably, then, chronologically speaking, the sequel to *Mort à crédit* is not the novel Céline published immediately before it, but *Casse-pipe*, an account of life in the prewar French cavalry of which nothing was known publicly until 1948. Furthermore, the main protagonist's character and attitude to life differ noticeably from Bardamu's, in *Mort à crédit*.

His profession brought Ferdinand Bardamu into daily contact with human nature. With one or two exceptions only seeming to prove the rule, he found people to be selfish, cruel, and basically sordid. Yet his idealism was never quite consumed by disillusionment. He never came to look upon medicine the way the narrator of *Mort à crédit* does, as "that shit" (II, 5). Supposing it was once present in his nature, humanitarianism has been drained from Ferdinand, who declares categorically, "Philanthropists piss me off" (II, 9). Suspicion, fear, contempt, and hate are the cardinal points of his relationship with his fellow men (and women). He realizes only too well how "terrible" it is to have lost faith, but he sees no real hope of reviving his own confidence in people, in his job, or even in life itself.

After telling of the burn marks ("That's the poker," he sees at once) on the thighs of a woman who has bullied him with her pleading into coming to examine her sick child, Ferdinand hurries away as soon as he can, although quite sure that she and her drunken husband are only waiting to see the back of him before beginning to fight once again. Not merely abiding by Bardamu's policy of nonintervention, Ferdinand displays downright callousness: "Let him shove his poker right up her asshole," he says. "That'll straighten her out, the bitch! That'll teach her to disturb me!" (II, 7). Ferdinand never misses a chance to affirm his detestation of those who come to him for help. He feels resentment more than the mistrust in which Bardamu held those around him, and makes no secret of it. He says he is thinking of sending his patients to the slaughterhouse to drink warm blood. "I really don't know no more what I could do to disgust them" (II, 6). Is this an early sign that—for some particular reason we can expect to hear revealed before long—Ferdinand had been provoked by momentary anger to take refuge in a ridiculously violent fantasy? We soon find it is not. Instead, it is an important clue to Ferdinand's usual behavior and to the tone he will give his reminiscences.

Ferdinand's need to disgust his readers reflects an irresistible impulse to keep the world at a safe distance while paying people back for all the misery they have caused him. His resentment is not the result of momentary pique. It is fostered by inability to hold out against his patients' persistence: although cursing the woman who appeals to him to examine her child when she meets him on the street, Ferdinand still accompanies her to where she lives. His anger at those who cry out for help comes from rage at seeing them look to *him* to change the pattern of life, to improve a situation he regards as beyond hope. "Just as soon as an enterprise begins to get off the ground," he observes, "it finds itself 'ipso facto' on the receiving end of a thousand hostile, sneaky, subtle, tireless plots!... You can't deny it!... Tragic fatality penetrates its very fibers..." (II, 376). To see any plan through to a successful conclusion, we have to rely on some miracle, he is convinced. Meanwhile practice of a profession for which he is spiritually, emotionally, and mentally unsuited casts Ferdinand in the painfully uncomfortable role of helpless witness to human destiny. As he himself stresses, it makes him testify to degradation, by telling stories other people do not like to hear.

In spite of what we know so far, it still might be argued that one can consider Ferdinand to be Bardamu, older and consequently more embittered. So it would seem to matter little, in the end, whether Céline actually took care to differentiate his storyteller in *Mort à crédit* from the one in *Voyage au bout de la nuit*. It is true, of course, that observations made by Ferdinand at the beginning of the second novel do not contribute anything really new to the picture painted by Bardamu in the first. As *Mort à crédit* opens, the tone of the narrative is muted, resigned, as though Ferdinand has no fight left in him. His concierge has just passed away and death is a presence from the first. Nothing he has to say at this point in his life contradicts or departs from the conclusions set forth in *Voyage* or, indeed, in a letter from Louis-Ferdinand Céline to Eveline Pollet, written on June 2, 1939: "Serious man must be an undertaker's mute or simply a corpse."[3] It is clear that Céline was not going to revise his opinion of life in *Mort à crédit,* that he continued to see man the way he later described him to Marc Hanrez, as having to "go to bed in his coffin every night."[4]

What, though, about the title of *Mort à crédit*? Beyond any question, it catches the imagination. A moment's reflection reveals, however, that the thought of buying death on the installment plan, as though we had signed some purchase agreement, is far more emotional than rational in appeal. Do we really enter into a contract, as we would to be sure to have something we cannot afford immediately? This would turn death into some sort of luxury product, or a necessity we feel compelled to acquire, even though it is beyond our means. *Mort à crédit* displays an ambivalent attitude toward death, since Ferdinand intimates that he looks upon it as a release from life. In his very first paragraph, he remarks pointedly, "Soon I'll be old. And it will be over at last" (II, 5).

Why not resort to suicide then? In his *Les Noyers de l'Altenburg* André Malraux, son of a suicide, extolled suicide as a profoundly responsible and therefore admirable act. Céline disagreed, though not for moral reasons. The suicide leaves a distressing mess for other people to clean up (after des Pereires has shot himself, revolting details of the process fill several pages of *Mort à crédit*). More important still, the act of self-elimination is not complete until the last hurdle—dying—is behind us. After telling how he and an acquaintance, Metitpois, have been discussing the best way to die, Ferdinand describes the other

3. *L'Herne,* No 3, p. 108.
4. "Conversation avec Louis-Ferdinand Céline," in Hanrez, *Céline,* p. 277. Interview dating from 1959.

man's death as two seconds of stoicism followed by eighteen minutes of "howling like a polecat." Metitpois ends up under the piano in the drawing room: "The small arteries of the mycardium when they burst one by one, that's no ordinary harp... It's a pity no one don't get over angina pectoris. There'd be wisdom and genius enough for everyone" (II, 16).

Death is no victory. It is just the final proof of the futility of life. This fact above all resolves the apparent inconsistencies in Céline's title. When anything is bought on credit, interest charges have to be paid. *Mort à crédit* emphasizes that we pay now and die later. The finance charges on death, meanwhile, are levied against the living: Ferdinand pitilessly reports on his father's physical decline and describes the collapse of Courtial des Pereires's ambitions and illusions. No man in his right mind wants to buy death on the installment plan, but everybody has to do so, all the same. Thus Céline's *Mort à crédit* stands in the same relationship to Flaubert's *L'Education sentimentale* as *Semmelweis* does to his *Bouvard et Pécuchet*.

Life is a *farce*—to take the word in the sense that, following the practice of his native Normandy, Guy de Maupassant understood it when writing many of his short stories. That is to say, life is a practical joke, cruelly played at someone's expense, without regard for the suffering it may bring him. In *Mort à crédit*, the joke is on mankind, and played by death. Events may be touched by comedy, of course. But the comic simply highlights, never quite concealing, the underlying misery of man's role as victim in a situation that, try as he may, he cannot fully control or turn to advantage. "I rejoice in the grotesque," Céline explained to Léon Daudet, "only on the confines of death."[5]

Young Ferdinand learns this from harsh experience: the gradual process that inevitably turns a life into a death is illuminated by the malevolence of those about us. We must pay off our installments in suffering and pain, living in a general atmosphere of spitefulness until death is ours. His education in living (while *Voyage* is Céline's answer to Maupassant's *Bel-Ami*, his *Mort à crédit* is *Une Vie, Notre Cœur*, and *Fort comme la mort* all in one) has not instilled resignation in Ferdinand. Far from it, he finds himself in complete agreement with Dylan Thomas, who advised, "Do not go gentle into that good night / Old age should burn and rave at close of day." Entrusting the narration of *Mort à crédit* to a man already in his middle years, Céline extends him no hope of any mode of salvation through literature, the transcrip-

5. Letter probably written in December 1932. See *L'Herne*, No 3, p. 92.

tion of lived experience, such as Jean-Paul Sartre offers Roquentin in
*La Nausée,* or Michel Butor gives Léon Delmont in *La Modification.*
Viewing his life in retrospect, Ferdinand does not share with the narrators of Gide's ironic tales an aspiration to self-justification. And self-
redemption is as far from his mind as self-revelation. Ferdinand's
account of what has happened to him is an act of aggression, directed
in rage against all who may read it.

Referring to those to whom he might write to report the death
of Madame Bérenge, his concierge, Ferdinand comments, "They've
changed souls, the better to betray, to forget, to speak always of something else..." (II, 5). Very soon he is explaining, "Me I could speak
out all my hate. I know. I'll do so later if they don't come back. I
prefer to tell stories. I'll tell such tales that they'll come back just to kill
me, from the four corners of the earth. Then it'll be all over with and
I'll be well satisfied" (II, 6).

In *Voyage au bout de la nuit* Bardamu did not give his readers
the opportunity to think the world any different from the way he described it. In contrast, reporting that his cousin Gustin Saboyat
(another doctor, as it happens) frequently advises him to change his
manner as a storyteller because "It isn't always dirty in life," Ferdinand
confesses very willingly in *Mort à crédit,* "My case has a bit of mania
about it, some partiality" (II, 8). Nowhere could this partiality show
more clearly than in the account he proceeds to give of his early life in
the bosom of his family.

*Mort à crédit* reads like Alain Fournier's *Le Grand Meaulnes,* as
it might have been written by someone in whom nostalgia for childhood has been transformed by dementia into horror. In comparison
with Céline's novel, Jules Renard's *Poil de carotte* sounds like a bed-
time story.

Taking Ferdinand to be interviewed for his first job, his mother,
Clémence, feels duty bound to itemize all the boy's character weaknesses and urges a prospective employer to make him "feel ashamed"
(II, 98). Disheartening as it is, her pessimistic assessment of their son's
capabilities radiates confidence, next to her husband's. In the father's
opinion, "I already had too many dirty instincts I'd picked up

someplace!..." (II, 102). To Auguste, indeed, the vices of his son Ferdinand tie in with his own blighted hopes and "the worst misfortunes of Destiny," so he can see no hope of saving the boy. "As for me," Ferdinand interjects, "I no longer knew how to atone... Some children are untouchables."

When caught wasting time, relating parts of his favorite legend to a fellow employee, Ferdinand is dismissed from his first place of employment. Now he has to face his father. At first, Auguste's reaction to the news evidences remarkable restraint: "So you're even more unnatural, more sly, more abject than I imagined, Ferdinand" (II, 108). Once over the surprise, however, he begins to catalog his son's faults in earnest, one by one. "He could see himself persecuted by a carnival of monsters," including Jews and especially Free Masons. "He got so worked up in that deluge he forgot me in the end" (II, 110). As for Clémence, she feels sure their son will end on the scaffold. The boy's own feelings about what he has done show him in agreement with their opinion that he is beyond redemption: "I myself was utterly crushed, I searched deep down in myself, looking for what immense vices, what unheard-of depravities I could be capable of one day?... I couldn't find them very easily... I was undecided. I found crowds of them, I wasn't sure of nothing..." (II, 108).

Finding a second job proves more difficult. It takes so long that Clémence "wondered after all if it didn't show on my face that I was a bad little character, a good-for-nothing scamp" (II, 113). Auguste, though, "didn't even have no doubts no more... For a long time he'd been sure. . . . He hadn't been to school for nothing, he knew how to make comparisons, draw conclusions" (II, 114). Before long, Clémence has drawn a few conclusions too, coming to look on Ferdinand as "a heartless child, a selfish monster, wayward, a scatter-brained little brute" (II, 204).

The emphasis that, as an adult, Ferdinand places on his immunity to altruism is just one indication of a systematic inversion characterizing his picture of humanity. In his experience, maternal love gave way to serious misgivings and paternal love became undisguised hate. Permanently soured by resentment, meanwhile, filial affection was replaced by open antagonism. As a child, Ferdinand continued to fill his pants, long after this was tolerable in a small boy. He was always stinking and disgusting. Far from trying to merit his parents' love, as he grew up he acted persistently in ways that defied them to cherish him. And now, looking back over his life at home, Ferdinand has to confess:

Thinking it over in the end, always and ceaselessly, I almost admit my father was in the right... I realized from experience... that I wasn't worth nothing at all... I had disastrous leanings... I was very clutsy and very lazy... I didn't deserve their great kindness... the terrible sacrifices... I felt quite unworthy there, purulent all over, all worm-eaten... I can see alright what I ought to have done and I put up a desperate fight, but I succeeded less and less... I wasn't improving with age. (II, 214)

In Ferdinand the romantic image of the hero, superior in a world of mediocrity, is inverted. Living in an environment of pettiness, vulgarity, and cruelty, he learns to see himself as the lowest of the low. He is a victim in situations of dependency—at home or as a youthful employee who cannot hold down a job for long. He is more than ready, though, to take advantage when the opportunity presents itself. By reason of age the biggest boy at Meanwell College in Rochester, where his parents have sent him to learn a foreign language he obstinately refuses to learn, he turns nasty.

Ferdinand complains of never having reached the sublime. "And I found myself in spite of everything, despite all the sermons, still more unhappy than any of the other lousy guys, than all the others put together!... It was stinking selfishness. I was only interested in my own blighted hopes and I found them there, all horrible, I stank of them worse than an old decaying brie cheese" (II, 314). Emotionally crippled, persuaded of his own worthlessness, he finally decides to join up.

As we read of all that happened to Ferdinand while he was still an adolescent, it becomes apparent that, by the time he is old enough to enlist, he has learned more about life than Bardamu has done at the beginning of *Voyage au bout de la nuit*. There is little likelihood he would have been duped by momentary enthusiasm into joining the army. Moreover, if Ferdinand is not Bardamu, he certainly is not Louis Destouches's double either.

Factual details drawn from the novelist's own life are twisted in *Mort à crédit*, where their distortion cannot be ascribed simply to lapses of memory. Anyone undertaking to compare the description of the Passage des Bérésinas, where Ferdinand's mother has her shop, and the Passage Choiseul, where Destouches spent his childhood, is wasting his time. And, needless to say, there is nothing in the work of Zola or Huysmans to compare with the Passage Ferdinand describes. So far does its description go beyond naturalist representation that the storyteller himself insists the Passage is "unbelievable," a stinking hole that kills people off slowly but surely among the odors of dog droppings and leaking gas (II, 47). Measuring the description of this place, where— apparently against all odds—the young boy grew up, beside reality is as futile as undertaking to check against one's own recollections of being seasick the account given by Ferdinand, when he recalls a trip across the English Channel.

It comes as no great surprise to readers acquainted with *Voyage au bout de la nuit* that Céline lets his narrator's version of events plumb the depths of vulgarity. Still, there is something in *Mort à crédit* for which his earlier novel offers no true precedent. For instance, vomiting affords Ferdinand an opportunity he accepts with alacrity, as he describes people retching and itemizes stomach content in a running commentary on the suffering of helpless victims of seasickness: "A passenger implores pardon... He howls to heaven that he's empty!... He strains himself!... He brings up a raspberry even so!..." (II, 89). As passengers in first and second class vomit down on those traveling third, among whom are Ferdinand and Clémence, an incongruously comic note is struck. Its effect is not to diminish the disgust generated by numerous revolting details (the wind blowing someone else's vomit into Ferdinand's mouth, for instance, and the ensuing "exchange" with another passenger). Rather, it sets the whole scene beyond the limits of lived experience, which in consequence ceases to offer an adequate measure by which events can be assessed. Céline takes us on to something that very definitely exceeds naturalism in its scope and implications.

What, now, of the way Ferdinand depicts life at home? Does it signify some deeply felt urge, provoking the novelist to take revenge on his own parents, to strike back at them? This question is especially intriguing, for we know that Louis Destouches's parents were very different in nature and conduct from Ferdinand's. No evidence furnished by persons close to the novelist indicates or allows us to infer that the Destouches couple's affectionate and indeed indulgent attitude toward their somewhat rebellious son inspired in him either terror or abiding hatred. Does this mean, then, that we are obligated to probe deeper? Are we to conclude, as a result, that the only acceptable reason for blatant modification of the truth of lived experience in *Mort à crédit*'s picture of home life is to be sought in certain ineradicable pathological influences, entirely beyond the writer's conscious control? To some readers, this hypothesis is not only quite plausible, but really persuasive. Encouraged by early signs of mythomania in Louis-Ferdinand Céline, a number of them have not hesitated, when examining the text of his second novel, to infer that he was truly possessed, a man driven by quite irresistible inner forces. To them, *Mort à crédit* appears as a public confession that Céline was dominated by a vengeful spirit, playing havoc with truth. Hence they see this work of fiction as bringing supposedly well-deserved discredit on his reputation, not only as a writer but as a human being as well.

Looked at this way, *Mort à crédit* appears to reflect entirely reprehensible motives. These may inspire pity in some. In others, the only possible response is positive disgust. The novel seems, at worst, an inexcusably disgraceful act of betrayal and, at best, a disastrously unfortunate essay in confessional fiction. Either way, judgment is sure to be clouded by factors so strongly emotional that many readers feel little inclination to look farther, when evaluating *Mort à crédit*. So involved are they with their personal reaction to its evocation of Ferdinand's home life that they do not wonder whether they have interpreted Céline's motivation correctly. What if, though, far from writing solely under the hypnosis of hate for his parents, L.-F. Céline remained in full command of his medium when composing his second novel? We have only to ask this to find ourselves considering this piece of fiction from an angle that gives us quite a different perspective on his purpose and ambition in writing *Mort à crédit* and on the technical means adopted to achieve these.

*Mort à crédit* may be divided into two unequal parts. Relatively brief, the first is a sort of preamble giving an impression of Ferdinand's life as an adult and of his mature outlook on existence. The second, vastly longer, reanimates the years extending from his earliest recollections up to the moment when, contemplating giving military life a try, he stands on the threshold of manhood. A *zeitroman*, this is an ironic *bildungsroman*: Céline demonstrates with harsh insistence that the child is father to the man.

Summing up *Mort à crédit*, David Hayman speaks of it as "the reminiscences of a sick and tormented man of his impoverished and harassed childhood and adolescence, reminiscences born of hallucination brought on by fever."[6] Such a résumé is less faithful to the truth than it sounds. Ferdinand does begin to tell of his childhood while fever confines him to his room. He even notes, "When fever stretches about, life becomes soft like a boozer's belly... You sink in an eddy of guts" (II, 26). But the important thing is this. The account he offers of growing up at the turn of the century is no less hallucinated and hallucinatory when his bout of fever has subsided. Mention of fever excuses nothing, here, and is not meant to do so. In fact, Ferdinand avows, "It's run behind me, madness has... twenty-two years and more. That's a fine thing. It's tried fifteen hundred sounds, an immense hubbub [Ferdinand is alluding to a buzzing in his ears, the same famous buzzing sound that Céline claimed to hear all his life—as a result of having been trepanned, he said], but I've been delirious quicker than it has. I've screwed it, I've had my way with it at the 'finish line' " (II, 23). An attack of fever early in the novel is not to be taken as excusing the way Ferdinand remembers things—even as a schoolboy, he tells us with characteristic vulgarity, he wiped his asshole on memories (II, 188)—it merely pitches his narrative on a certain tone.

Delirium marks Céline's second work of fiction even more than his first. *Mort à crédit* shows how sincere were his criticisms of naturalism in his 1933 talk at Médan. It demonstrates the inadequacy of the naturalist method for treating reality the way he chose to deal with it. "You are only too right," he observed in a letter to Elie Faure, "so far as the essence of man is concerned. One has to place oneself deliberately in a nightmare state to come close to the true tone!"[7] In his second novel the border between true-to-life detail, caricature, and unfettered imaginative flights has no permanence. It appears at best as a tenuous dividing line, with no serious claim on the attention of a writer who doubts its esthetic usefulness.

Recounting his story, Ferdinand consistently violates two fundamental tenets of the naturalist code: impartiality and objectivity. It is easy enough, of course, to identify passages evoking scenes that take their coloration from fever. Some of these remind us of Bardamu's confession that, during an attack of malaria and amoebic dysentery (from which he suffered, just like Destouches), he could not tell the real from the absurd, and lived in a twilight world. It is not difficult to see when and where Ferdinand enters that same world. Making love

6. David Hayman, *Louis-Ferdinand Céline* (New York and London: Columbia University Press, 1965), p. 31.

7. See the undated [1932] letter in *L'Herne*, No 5, p. 48.

in the Bois de Boulogne, he and Mireille draw a crowd. An orgy follows, before the mob marches up to the Arc de Triomphe and eventually has to be dispersed on the Place de la Concorde by no less than twenty-five thousand policemen. Isolating such incidents, however— detaching them from the novel as extraneous elements, the way Bardamu allowed his readers to do in *Voyage*—leads to very wrong deductions about *Mort à crédit*.

Making sure the narrator of this novel acknowledges how much his life has been touched by delirium and dementia, Louis-Ferdinand Céline takes his stand at a considerable distance from the naturalists. Measured by the yardstick of nineteenth-century French naturalism, the story told in *Mort à crédit* lacks acceptable proportion. Stepping repeatedly outside prescribed limits, Ferdinand is always going too far in what he has to say and in his manner of narration. Even more than *Voyage au bout de la nuit*, this novel is the product of an imagination that finds expression through visual effects. Gestures, externalizing acutely felt emotions, are exaggerated to the limit of credibility and beyond. Typically, things are not perceived in normal perspective and dimension. During an attack of fever, Ferdinand sees a man's hat as impossibly oversized, its brim "so vast that a velodrome..." (II, 25). The interesting thing is that the hat belongs to someone the narrator knows, Léonce Poitrat, employed as an accountant at the clinic where Ferdinand works. Even when describing the man while not in the grip of fever, Ferdinand still affirms that Poitrat has an erection "hard as thirty-six biceps" (II, 25).

True detail is often no more than a stepping-stone to antinaturalist effect in *Mort à crédit*. When fever makes Ferdinand describe his mother's legs, seen when she raises her skirt to run, they are so hairy (reminding him of a spider) that they become entangled in one another and she is rolled along on a bobbin. The ludicrousness of touches like these, defying acceptance as faithful to reality, is a sign to the readers that he is being taken into a domain Céline began to make his own when writing *Mort à crédit*. Letters addressed to Hindus in 1947 illuminate both the creative process itself and the motivation behind its implementation.

On September 2, Céline explained, "What throws me into a rage, you see, is the insensitivity of men—the malady of the world is insensitivity —To get out of that obsession I set about things the best I can—"[8] On July 7 he responded to a query, "The relationship between reality and

8. *L'Herne*, No 5, p. 94 .

my writings? My God, real objective life is impossible for me, unbearable—I go mad with it, into a rage, so dreadful does it seem to me, and therefore I transpose it as I dream and go along... I suppose it's more or less the general malady of the world called *poetry*... In me it must be a bit more lively, stubborn, than in other people."[9] Questioning him, Hindus presumably was feigning incomprehension in the hope of hearing him amplify an aside in a letter dated March 30, where Céline bemoaned his situation in Denmark: "but you know I am much more of a poet than a prose writer and I write only to transpose . . . ."[10] Fortunately, the vagueness of the words "poet" and "poetry" is counterbalanced by stress upon transposition as the key to intention and method. Louis-Ferdinand Céline, whose storyteller introduces into *Mort à crédit* scraps of a legend about a king called Krogold, commented on May 29, "I am a Celt, above all a *bardic dreamer*—I can recount legends like having a piss, with a facility that disgusts me, scenarios, ballets as many as you like [his collection of texts published in 1959 under the title *Ballets sans musique, sans personne, sans rien* testifies to this facility], telling tales is really my gift—I've submitted it to realism in a spirit of hate for the spitefulness of men—in combative spirit—but in reality my music is legend . . . ."[11]

Céline made no secret of the fact that in his fiction transposition of reality followed upon the intervention of imagination, granted total freedom to modify the raw material furnished by the everyday world. He expected, so he declared in a letter to Hindus on May 15, 1947, to be acknowledged one day as having rendered the French language more sensitive, more emotional, and less confined by academicism, "through a knack consisting (less easy than it seems) in a monolog of spoken but TRANSCRIBED intimacy—That immediate spontaneous transposition is the trick—In reality it is a return to the spontaneous poetry of the savage."[12]

Céline's concept of the role of the novelist in transposing the real rested firmly on a clear idea of the fiction writer's function. "I want to be charmed, bewitched," he informed Hindus in a letter dated simply the 12th, "—I don't want to be instructed! 54 years of life and what a life—27 of daily medical practice have taught me too much raw reality—I want realism to be made to 'sing' for me—anything that

9. *L'Herne*, No 5, p. 84.
10. *L'Herne*, No 5, p. 72.
11. *L'Herne*, No 5, p. 76.
12. *L'Herne*, No 5, p. 75.

doesn't sing for me is shit."[13] This statement casts light on another, made a little later in the same letter: "French literature is scarcely ever delirious—it is lyrical reluctantly—no lyricism between Villon and Chénier! 4 centuries!" Lamenting the absence of delirium in the literature of France, Céline—whose preface to Guignol's band confessed that he could not bring himself to read other books ("I find them rough drafts, not written, still-born..." [II, 518])—commented, "I'm not speaking of surrealism which is a fabrication, intentional, conventional delirium, a simulation without an echo, without a heart—nothing at all—Sartre, Camus, Guilloux and a thousand others fall into that fabrication—Green, etc." In a long postscript, he returned to the same theme: "Ah! I want to be enchanted—Harpagon reasons too much in my opinion, Volpone enchants me. . . . Be delirious if you like, but be delirious JUST RIGHT, watch out. Being delirious just right has to go to the core of man of his soul not his head—All the Sartre, Camus and Green delirium comes from the head and even Le Grand Meaulnes... So highly spoken of... Goat droppings" (p. 81).

The principles summarized here clearly had a greater influence on Mort à crédit than on Voyage au bout de la nuit. In his new novel, Céline set out to oblige readers to see transposition of reality as something more than a side effect of the fever periodically confining Ferdinand to his bed. Not content with allowing his narrator, whether sick or well, the same kind of exaggeration in descriptive detail, Céline placed him in situations that can only be termed delirious by nature. They are borrowed from the world Ferdinand knew as a child, a world dominated by the frightening presence of his father.

We find no image in Mort à crédit comparable to that of night, recurrent in Voyage au bout de la nuit. Indeed, formal structure is altogether more relaxed in this novel than in its predecessor. Its author holds the reins less tightly, letting plot meander so that it develops through stages he makes no visible effort to keep within realistic bounds. Ferdinand's association with Des Pereires takes up more space in his narrative than any other episode, incidentally. After Des Pereires's death, the ending comes quickly, as though the narrator wishes to have done, now, with the story of his youth.

13. L'Herne, No 5, p. 80.

There is another difference, an even more important one. Most of the time, Bardamu appeared content to let events speak for themselves. Ferdinand's narrative though, generates horror as much by the manner in which it relates as by the incidents themselves. "A style," Céline will remark in *Bagatelles pour un massacre*, "is an emotion first, before anything else, above everything else" (p. 164). In *Mort à crédit*, at all events, the abnormal is heightened by emotion, in a narrative characterized by distortion calculated to make things look larger than life. Action takes place on the periphery of everyday experience, and the novelist often lets it slip past the boundaries of reality into the grotesque, the insane even. The reader finds himself witnessing scenes that cannot be assessed adequately by reference to life as he knows it. Animal images paint humanity red in tooth and claw. Under impetus from anger, encounters between characters turn into so many bull-fights: "With furious people," Ferdinand remarks, "it's straight-forward... it's a question of corridas... Jumping the railing before they make a hole in your guts" (II, 318).

In *Mort à crédit*, life breaks down into episodes of explosive emotional force. Recollection in tranquillity has no meaning when Ferdinand reminisces. He concentrates on sharply defined events, recalled with such intensity that, in retrospect, they quite often assume mythical dimensions. Life is stripped of any semblance of coherence. We are given glimpses of savagery at the very opposite pole from Proust's privileged moments, reconciling man with time through memory. Memory becomes a source of torture for Ferdinand and brings no sense of fulfillment. It confronts him with the monstrous, in himself as well as in others.

His father is subject to uncontrollable awe-inspiring rages that figure prominently in the story. Describing one spasm of anger, Ferdinand reports, "He couldn't get out of the nightmare no more... . . . He couldn't tell truth from imagination no more" (II, 361). Such moments of delirium create particularly interesting situations because Ferdinand, too, lacks the ability to recognize and respect the limits of reality when recreating them. In short, he falls into a trance of the kind that Céline suggested André Gide never experienced as a writer.

Time after time, Auguste explodes into physical violence when he finds he has exhausted his powers of vituperation. The shift from verbal to physical brutality is typical in the following scene:

He began to yell that I was flaying him alive, and my mother too, that I was his complete dishonor, his irremediable shame, that I was

responsible for everything! For the worst mischief! In the past as in
the future! That I was driving him to suicide! That I was a murderer
of an absolutely unparalleled kind!... He didn't explain why...
He was whistling, blowing so much steam he created a cloud between us... . . . He was carrying the chest of drawers away... The
shop was very small... No place for somebody in a rage... He stumbles
over the umbrella stand... He knocks the two vases over. (II, 224)

Whenever Auguste is provoked by ungovernable wrath to acts
of extreme violence, Clémence submits—somewhat less than stoically, it
is true—to treatment that would kill or maim someone of normal
physical resistance. Seeking a parallel for what goes on between this
married couple, we discover it is not to be found where one might
expect it—in the scene from Zola's *La Bête humaine*, for instance, during which Roubaud beats his wife unmercifully. Roubaud's reaction to
the news that his wife became an old man's mistress before reaching
the age of consent has a distinctly cathartic quality. In contrast, there
is always a crazy disproportion between crime and punishment at the
hands of Ferdinand's father. His brutal behavior departs from the
tradition of literary naturalism respected in Maxence Van der Meersch's
*Invasion 14*, for example. We are reminded more readily of a marionette
show built around the character of Polichinelle, Petrouchka, or Hans-
wurt: the *guigol*, in fact. Ferdinand's parents put us in mind of Punch
and Judy.

At times, incidentally, the very profusion of detail has an effect
that would weaken a naturalist novel. It tends to blur the picture. On
these occasions especially, we face something quite different from the
functional brutality of a Zola, or of Van der Meersch's description of
the execution of a wartime spy. No doubt, the tradition of theatrical
farce with its onstage beatings has left its mark on *Mort à crédit*. At no
time, however, does Céline release his characters so completely from
physical reality as to let his readers' imagination find refuge in a fantasy
world where, as in cartoon films, violence is merely comic. In this
novel, paroxysm is the starting point for scenes of violence. Such situations can attain their climax, therefore, only in disintegration of the
limitations of realistic representation.

The news that a well-to-do client has stolen a handkerchief from
his wife's stock throws Auguste into a fit of rage. "He bellows, he
charges, he explodes, he's going to bombard the cooking" (II, 44).
Imploring Heaven's forgiveness on her knees, Clémence tells Ferdinand

to run for it. From his bedroom, he hears her howling and making noises that indicate she is stifling:

> I go down again just for a look... he's dragging her along the stairs. She's hanging on. She's squeezing him around the neck. That's what saves her. He breaks loose... He knocks her down. She goes ass over tip... She goes bumping down the stairs... Soft bumps... She gets up at the bottom... Then *he* shoves off. He beats it through the shop... He goes off outside... She manages to get to her feet. She goes back up to the kitchen. She's got blood on her hair. She washes over the sink... She's crying... She's choking... She sweeps up all the broken stuff... (II, 45)

Céline's own analysis of his method—a kind of impressionism of which he claimed to be the sole inventor—reveals how this passage was put together, and with what purpose: "I follow emotion alright with words and I don't let it have time to dress up in sentences... I catch it all raw or rather all poetic—for the core of Man in spite of everything is poetry—reasoning is learned."[14] Like so many resembling it, this half-page is calculatedly disjointed in appearance. Once a certain pitch of tension has been reached, we are granted no relief from violence. Perhaps only when it is past do we glimpse the full implications of what we have seen: a son powerless to stand up to his father and too callous to try comforting his mother when the danger is past.

The care taken in structuring this little scenario points up one noteworthy feature of Céline's narrative technique. The effect is too firmly controlled to leave the impression that negligence on the writer's part explains why the whole incident strains the bounds of credibility. Time and again in *Mort à crédit*, Céline demonstrates the following: where human relations erupt in dementia, failure is catastrophic, and man's confrontation with living is cataclysmic, credibility is no valid criterion for evaluating accompanying violence. Credibility, at all events, is not permitted to lay down boundaries within which descriptive skill will be exercised.

Looking at the page on which Ferdinand recalls visiting the great Paris Exhibition as a small child, we find evidence of respect for the usages of fictional verisimilitude. Céline has limited himself to recording reality just as his character would have seen it. The picture is

14. *L'Herne*, No 5, p. 73.

fragmented and gives prominence to things that would have impressed themselves on a little boy: being trampled underfoot, trudging through dust so thick he can barely see, and suffering from intolerable thirst. Details like these give a ring of truth to Ferdinand's recollections, this time. Rather different, though, are the descriptions of his father's physical appearance in moments of anger. Even allowing for the impressionability of a small child, readers must find Ferdinand's words evocative in quite a different way, as he speaks of Auguste, pop-eyed with rage, as visibly swelling so much "his jacket was splitting everyplace" (II, 44). The current is overloaded, and realism is short-circuited.

Angered at the suggestion that their son be sent to school in England, Auguste becomes furious when Clémence pleads with him to calm down, for fear he will kill himself:

> He breaks loose, the shock sends him off the deep end, he knocks my mother Clémence over. Now he's on his feet again, bawling again... He hadn't thought of that... Death! Son of a bitch... His death!... Now he's off again into a fine trance... He gives his all... He perks up!... He throws himself at the sink again... He wants a drink. Ta ra! Wham!... Off he goes!... He caroms about! He goes sprawling... He dives into the buffet... He bounces off into the sideboard... He's bent his schnozz... He tries to steady himself... Every damn thing falls on our mugs... All the crockery, the implements, the standard lamp... It's a cascade... an avalanche... We're left buried underneath... Can't see one another no more... (II, 145)

Ferdinand's narrative reveals the characteristics we notice here whenever he has occasion to recall how his father behaved during fits of wild temper and how Auguste's conduct affected the rest of the family. At such times, readers of *Mort à crédit* see everyday reality surpassed. The storyteller's account so transposes events that exaggeration touches both action and reaction. Obviously, Auguste is demented with rage, and Clémence and Ferdinand are similarly carried away by fear. Turning from the fever-ridden visions recorded by Ferdinand the adult to his recollections of his terror-ridden home when he was a child, we have not left fantasy behind. As Ferdinand tells what it was like to grow up in his parents' shop in the Passage des Bérésinas, reality is contaminated by fantasy or, we might say, is heightened by it. In this account of life past and present, Céline has taken care to avoid any impression of rupture that would set the delirium of fever off by itself.

While Auguste is mistreating his wife for letting someone steal a lace handkerchief, a neighbor stands at her window "to get a better laugh out of it" (II, 44). Madame Méhon's amusement brings to mind an earlier incident of quite a different kind.

After inviting little Ferdinand into her bedroom for candy, a client had lain down, thrown back her robe to display her pubis, and, in a tone more tender than he had ever heard before, invited him to "suck there" (II, 38). All that had kept him from complying, he recalls, is that the maid was standing by, scarcely able to control her laughter. At first, laughter seems hardly a firm enough link between two apparently quite unrelated scenes. Before Ferdinand's story has continued much longer, however, we notice that manifestations of violence and eroticism are placed consistently on the same plane in *Mort à crédit*. Their proximity reveals a connection between them, deep enough to bring to light something important about the narrator's character and some significant features of Céline's fictional technique.

Ferdinand is considerably less discreet about his sex life than Bardamu was. Céline's first novel, without pretending that physical love has no part in his relationship with women, lets us see Bardamu emphasizing over everything else his emotional dependence on the opposite sex. On the other hand, Ferdinand gives early warning: "I fuck too much, I ain't got a good reputation" (II, 9). Sex obviously has been an important factor in his life, and since before he was old enough to understand fully what was going on. Little by little, it helps teach him a great deal about living, more by far than it seems to have taught Bardamu.

Questioned about Bardamu's affection for an American woman, Céline once defined love as follows: "It's a feeling, it's an act, my God! quite bestial—and, naturally, bestial it has to be! Warding it off with little flowers seems to me crass. Bad taste, precisely, is putting flowers where none are really needed. . . . You go into a delirium (coitus is a delirium): to rationalize that delirium with precise verbal manoeuvers seems to me very silly."[15] Insisting that love is a physical act demanded by nature for the purpose of reproduction, Céline remained true to the view expressed by Bardamu, that love is "the infinite brought within the capacity of poodles" (I, 18).

Consideration of the treatment accorded sex in Céline's first two novels leads to an interesting discovery. It is *Mort à crédit*, not *Voyage au bout de la nuit*, that expands on this definition, which would have sounded more natural coming from Ferdinand than from Bardamu. When we ask why this should be so, a perfectly satisfactory answer seems to be the one provided by Céline himself in a letter written to

15. Hanrez, *Céline*, p. 275.

Eveline Pollet in April of 1933: "The difficult thing is finding the irresistible tone. The rest follows all by itself."[16] Once accustomed to the
tone selected for *Mort à crédit*, we can see nothing inappropriate in
the stress placed on man's bestiality, as much during scenes of sexual
encounter as during moments of physical violence. Brutality apparently
sets the right tone, whether Ferdinand is talking about beatings or
about love making.

It seems so logical for Céline to have used brutal sex to maintain
the desired tone in his second novel that we may easily fail to notice
one small detail. When she laughs at the fight taking place in
Ferdinand's home, Madame Méhon is not directly involved. The maid
laughing while her mistress is making sexual advances to a little boy
is similarly detached, a mere spectator. It is from the safe vantage point
of their hiding place atop the kitchen stove that Ferdinand and his
friend Robert laugh until they hurt, as a fellow employee, Antoine, his
erect penis bumping against everything, blunders about, looking for
the butter he needs to be able to sodomize their boss's wife. While
Ferdinand is directly engaged in sexual activity, however, he has a
very different perspective on the whole process. When his turn comes
to be in bed with Madame Gorloge one day, he finds the experience
quite terrifying.

Ferdinand's anxiety is aggravated by his naiveté about sex—he
is a virgin—and even more by Madame Gorloge's gigantic size. Made
to perform cunnilingus on her, he had to fight for his life under her
enormous, crushing breasts. Her vagina appears to him as an engulfing
maw. Being raped by this woman is a sharp lesson in the predatory
nature of humankind. The demands she makes upon Ferdinand cast
him in the passive, frightening role of victim. Afterward, while she is
urinating, he seizes his chance to run away. He will not escape so
easily, all the same. He discovers almost at once that she has stolen
from his pocket a piece of jewelry he was supposed to have delivered to
one of his firm's clients. Her action will cost him his job, and this misfortune, of course, will send his father into yet another homicidal rage.

Responding to sexual advances (to Ferdinand Madame Gorloge
is a "vampire" [II, 132], as too is gentle Nora Merrywin, wife of the
headmaster of Meanwell College [II, 177]) and participating in the
sex act are no more than reflexes of self-defense. To the narrator of
*Mort à crédit* they bring much less pleasure than anguish.

Just off the cross-Channel ferry, he finds a young girl called
Gwendoline a voracious sex partner, the personification of the *vagina*

16. *L'Herne*, No 3, p. 97.

*dentata*: "She tries to gobble me up!" (II, 156). Even under the best of circumstances, coitus is hard work: "I couldn't go on!...," Ferdinand comments, likening himself to a shying horse (II, 133). Tenderness has no place in his recital of sexual engagements. Sex is no less a menace to this victim of other people's desires than being beaten by an incensed father. Surviving the sex act is, to Ferdinand, much like hanging on to life while Auguste is hitting him. "She pulls me out of the debris... I come back to the surface...," he reports after being forced to kiss Madame Gorloge's vulva. "I got like a coating on my eyes, I'm slimy to the eyebrows..." (II, 132). Like those occasions during which his father loses all self-control, direct participation in sex is, for youthful Ferdinand, a form of unequal combat in which he is predictably the weaker protagonist. He speaks of caresses just as he does of blows, telling us that they fall in "an avalanche." He refers to sexual activity the way he does to brutal beatings, as so many "corridas," in which— no less to his amazement than to his relief—nobody is quite unfortunate enough to end up dead or crippled.

Sex brings no consolation of any kind, no sense of release. It is a heightened form of terror, that is all. After joining him in the boys' dormitory for an act of unadorned sexual aggression during which Ferdinand feels buried and strangled under "an avalanche of tenderness" (II, 197), Nora Merrywin, suddenly conscience-stricken, abruptly breaks away from him. Leaving the school building, out of her mind with guilt, she goes down to the river and drowns herself. As is the case during bullfights, we realize, it is the threat of death that gives the ritual of sex its meaning in *Mort à crédit*. Ferdinand's sexual contacts revitalize the cliché that represents sex as a form of death and likens the ecstasy of orgasm to dying.

When *Mort à crédit* first appeared it was evident that certain cuts had been made in Céline's text. The novelist had agreed to these only on condition the typesetter be instructed not to close up the lines, so that blank spaces would show where words and phrases had been excised. Even some of those critics who claimed to have too much respect for their readers' susceptibilities (to say nothing of their own) to deign to quote at all from the novel did not refrain from dwelling on this suggestive feature of Céline's new piece of fiction. In 1936 almost

all who commented in print agreed that the published text was shocking. Many of them found it hard to imagine what could have been so
much more disgusting as to merit censorship. A few concluded that
censorship in fact was merely a hoax on this occasion, designed to en-
tice the reader's imagination to supply additional details that the writer,
his inventiveness presumably exhausted, could not provide for himself.
Discussing *Mort à crédit* in *Les Nouvelles littéraires* on May 12, René
Lalou summed up the main objection voiced by the majority of critics
when he wrote, "Whether by the way they are printed or simply called
to mind, these famous obscenities seem too often stuck on to the story."

Lalou's criticism was a serious one. It came close to relegating
Céline to the category of novelists who, like Octave Mirbeau in *Le
Jardin des supplices,* set out quite deliberately to appeal to prurient
inclinations and who write accordingly. Only examination of the full
text can show how much attention Lalou's objection deserves.

After bringing him to ejaculation on her stomach, Madame
Gorloge throws herself on Ferdinand. Then, the 1936 version of *Mort à
crédit* makes abundantly clear, she proceeds to fellate him. The uncut
text confirms this, leaving little to the imagination: "She jumps on my
acorn like a greedy thing... She sucks the whole lot in... She's giving
herself a treat... She likes that, the sauce... 'Oh! how good it is, your
little come!...'" (II, 723). Details comparable with these were suppressed from the original version of the scene in which Madame
Gorloge and Antoine play leading roles. Reinstated in the text, they
deepen its vulgarity and at the same time paint the situation in even
more monstrous shades.

In doing this, however, the censored details do not divert the
novel from its course, however briefly. Nor do they create a set piece,
valuable most of all to someone assembling an anthology for the benefit
of people who seek sexual stimulation through literature. On the contrary, they contribute directly to animating scenes where they take a
place that Céline was justified in regarding as theirs by right. They
sound titillating only to a reader whose response to them prevents him
from appreciating their role in maintaining the delirious atmosphere in
which sexual activity occurs in *Mort à crédit.* The additional descriptive details insist upon the essential fact that Madame Gorloge and
Antoine couple like rutting animals, in the grip of a purely physiological
compulsion that rules out consideration and tenderness for the partner,
as well as all vestiges of human dignity: "He was rummaging in her
slit" (II, 722). Deprived of the spectator's feeling of security, Ferdinand
reluctantly engages in the bestial horror of sex, without experiencing

any pleasure: "It's red, it's drooling, it's juicy, my eyes are full of it... She makes me lick it... It moves under my tongue... It's dripping... It looks like a dog's mouth" (II, 722).

Viewed in context, the missing words that aroused so much conjecture when *Mort à crédit* appeared confirm that Céline's writing is neither prurient nor suggestive in intent. If this were the case, then his treatment of Ferdinand's masturbatory practices would be far less significant than it is.

Ferdinand appears to have enjoyed onanism for as long as he can remember. It is very difficult to estimate his age at the time of his earliest memories, but he seems to have been a sexually precocious little fellow. Unburdened by guilt feelings, he indulges in auroeroticism in all sorts of circumstances, even a storm at sea arousing him to activity. Yet he does not usually share his sexual fantasies with his readers. In this respect, Céline's handling of sex displays noteworthy reticence. Use of the first-person mode in *Mort à crédit* could have been taken as an excuse for recording sexual confidences. Céline evidently preferred not to take advantage of a guaranteed source of sensationalism. In this, he created with *Mort à crédit* a novel that stands in sharp contrast with Raymond Guérin's *L'Apprenti,* a third-person narrative that does not stop short of detailing the masturbatory daydreams of its central character, to whom Guérin never comes so close as to forget to call him, formally, Monsieur Hermès.

Like the beatings and the sex act with a partner, even masturbation can be indelibly marked by terrorism, when circumstances render the individual helplessly dependent on someone else. This happens when, to punish a retarded child for incurring penalties during a soccer game, the other boarders at Meanwell College first beat him with belts (stifling his cries, if he gets too noisy, by laying a mattress over him and stamping on it). Then they masturbate him until he can ejaculate no more and cannot even stand on his feet. Only when practiced for his own satisfaction, and in the safety guaranteed by privacy, can onanism give Ferdinand what *he* asks of it.

At no time in his life has Ferdinand felt capable of trusting women enough to love any of them. His widowed mother (who now speaks of her late husband as a veritable saint) comes into his room while he is undergoing an attack of fever. He seizes the opportunity to lift her skirt so that he can vomit on her calves. A confirmed misogynist from boyhood up, at Meanwell College he classifies Nora with all other women as "dung" (II, 167), while yet centering his thoughts on her as he masturbates night and morning. Only on the frequent occasions when he escapes into onanist daydreams can he dominate women and be as violent with them as he is masterful. There is a well-defined contrast, therefore, between the way he treats Nora in the one fantasy he places on record and the way he submits to her in terror, the night she finally slips into his bed.

Practiced in the security of solitude, onanism represents for Ferdinand a way of rectifying the world, of giving it proportions and an order that are in keeping with his private desires. Thus masturbation is an integral and significant feature of Ferdinand's early life. It is a direct expression of his profound need to change his destiny in a world ruled by violence and predatory sexuality, where he is alternately victim and pariah.

In *Voyage au bout de la nuit* Bardamu was spared the madness that signalled Semmelweis' final collapse beneath the unbearable weight of the world's hostility. But in *Mort à crédit*, Ferdinand has lived under the menace of insanity for as long as he can remember, first at home, in enforced proximity to a father subject to crazy rages, and then, after attaining adulthood, as a victim of recurrent attacks of fever. In addition, "fever or not, I still have such a buzzing in both ears that it can't teach me much more" (II, 23).

The circumstances under which he grew up, and those under which he has lived since, account for the tone Ferdinand gives his narrative, touched everywhere by frenzy. In *Mort à crédit* details are accumulated with far less respect for the sober pattern of external reality than in *Voyage au bout de la nuit*. For it is not only the nature of events related but the impact they have had on the sensibility registering them that brings Ferdinand's story much closer to delirium than Bardamu's. All the same, it seems perfectly appropriate to link *Mort à crédit* and *Voyage*, so long as one goes on attempting to situate Céline's fiction in relation to the naturalist tradition. To be more exact, among the Célinian novels it is *Voyage au bout de la nuit* and *Mort à crédit* that come closest to respecting the traditional view of fiction for which, in France, naturalism has represented the norm since the nineteenth century. In consequence, departures from naturalist criteria— more noticeable and less excusable, apparently, in the second novel than in the first—seem to be merely unfortunate breaches of convention, committed by a writer who therefore must be judged guilty of having lost control, here and there.

Considering *Mort à crédit* by supposedly reliable inherited standards for fictional transposition of reality, traditionalist readers find, or think they find, enough that is reassuringly familiar to compensate for more or less disturbingly innovative features. And so, viewing the novels Céline published in the thirties in the light of the naturalist esthetic, they fail to acknowledge *Mort à crédit*'s originality as an exploratory work of fiction. In this novel, rather than attempting to repeat *Voyage au bout de la nuit* or to prolong it by several hundred pages, Céline was trying to go beyond the earlier work, in an effort to remedy the weaknesses he had detected in his first experiment with narrative form.

Technically speaking, in *Mort à crédit* Céline began to take a road that would lead him to his highly distinctive later novels. Looking at the latter, critics have displayed remarkable unanimity in judging them to be deplorable proof that Céline's talent declined after 1936. All agree that his fictional writings slipped their moorings after *Mort à crédit*, drifting willy nilly on a sea of chaotic emotions, liberated by terror and hate, at the expense, naturally, of narrative unity. So confidently do they condemn Céline's later novelistic effort that they do not appear to have paused to ask themselves whether he might not have set out deliberately—aware of what he was risking—upon oceans he knew as well as anyone else to be uncharted. Certainly, they fail to appreciate that Céline was heading for new waters from the moment he began writing *Mort à crédit*.

If we are to believe Céline himself, Denoël (who had published both *Voyage* and *Mort à crédit*) did not understand the first volume of *Guignol's band*, the next of Céline's novels to appear. Denoël was not to be alone in feeling puzzled. The critics' inability to come to terms with this 1944 novel was less a sign of hostility from all sides, for which Céline himself inclined to take it, than proof that the full significance of *Mort à crédit* had eluded them.

# PHASE TWO

# Casse-pipe

W HEN HIS WRITINGS are examined in order of appearance, a simple comparison of publication dates gives rise to a seriously misleading impression of Louis-Ferdinand Céline's activities after *Mort à crédit* came out. For several years, apparently, other concerns kept his attention off the novel. In consequence, reflecting on his supposed abandonment of the fictional mode, sympathetic readers of his first two novels (those of them, anyway, who had not been alienated by the character and tone of nonfictional works he had published meanwhile) might well have interpreted his behavior as Noël Sabord had encouraged his readers to do in his review of *Mort à crédit* for *Paris-Match*: "That must leave the worker, with no help, no 'ghost writer,' no 'apprentice,' an immense fatigue, but also a vast and profound satisfaction! Lying down now, if he is allowed to rest, he can look at his work with complacency: it is unique, and there are people all around it."

However, Céline was not content to rest on his laurels. He did return to the novel form, finally bringing out the first volume of *Guignol's band* in 1944. But at some point in time after the appearance of *Mort à crédit*, his attitude toward novel writing underwent sufficient modification to alarm his faithful publisher, Robert Denoël. "But say," he exclaimed in Célinian style—according to the preface to *Guignol's band*, at all events—"I don't understand anything in it! ah! but it's terrible! Not possible! I don't see anything but brawling in your book! It's not even a book! we're headed straight for disaster! Neither head nor tail!" (II, 517).

Putting two and two together at this stage, one risks making five or even six, unless account is taken of another fictional work altogether. This is a novel that still remained unfinished at the time when Céline felt it wise to flee the country in 1944. It was never completed.

Only its first chapter appeared in print, in the Summer 1948 issue of the *Cahiers de la Pléiade*, under the inaccurate title *Le Casse-pipe*.

In Jean A. Ducourneau's estimation, Céline started work on *Casse-pipe* (*Kick the Bucket*) as early as 1936. It certainly was begun before *Guignol's band I*. Thus, even if it took Céline longer than Ducourneau thinks to settle down to writing a new novel, it would be a mistake to believe that some significantly long pause followed *Mort à crédit* before its author again turned to fiction. Even more important, Denoël would have found *Casse-pipe* hardly less disconcerting than *Guignol's band I*, had Céline been able to submit a complete manuscript before leaving France via Germany for exile in Scandinavia.

When, after publishing in his own name an apologia for *Mort à crédit*, Robert Denoël complained (in whatever terms) that he could make neither head nor tail of *Guignol's band I*, we can safely assume he was protesting against one feature above all of Céline's technique in this novel. It appeared to signal the lamentable collapse or near-collapse of solid narrative structure. Had he been acquainted with no more of *Casse-pipe* than the first two chapters that have come down to us, he surely would have appreciated one very important fact. *Guignol's band I* does not read the way it does simply because, over the years, its author somehow had lost his touch, and so was incapable of controlling his material on the process of putting it down on paper.

In the perspective of Céline's evolution as a novelist, *Casse-pipe* stands out as important. For in this uncompleted story, the relationship between content and treatment takes on a special character that can be described roughly as follows: the manner of telling the tale counts for more than the narrative itself.

Actually, though, the distinctive emphasis given *Casse-pipe* does less than it seems to do to mark a really new departure for Céline as a fiction writer. An apparent paradox in *Voyage au bout de la nuit* disappears when we appreciate that its author insisted on not being taken for a novelist of ideas because he wanted to direct attention to the following. His use of a distinctive mode of presentation implied a concept of life altogether his own and related to an equally individualized mode of expression. It is significant, in this connection, that over the years he never ceased stressing the value he continued to attach to slang.

From the beginning of his career as a novelist, Céline's use of slang struck readers as one of the most controversial aspects of his writing. For the most part, response from among the critics was less than favorable, when indeed it was not openly hostile. In one regard at least, those who reacted negatively were merely reiterating objections raised nearly a half-century earlier to Emile Zola's novel in slang, *L'Assommoir*. In 1877 *L'Assommoir* appeared to many to be an unacceptable experiment in verbal sensationalism. The writer seemed to have surrendered the benefits of esthetic distance when allowing his anonymous narrator to speak the very same language as the working-class characters whose lives he was describing. In 1932, *Voyage au bout de la nuit* gave a similar impression, especially to readers who asked themselves why Bardamu, a man of some education, should write as though he had had little or no instruction. Granted, it was Céline's privilege as a writer of fiction to entrust narrative responsibility to someone who had had a miserable time of it his whole life long. Why, though, let Bardamu (like Ferdinand in *Mort à crédit*) express himself so coarsely that he seemed at times quite satisfied with playing variations on the word "shit," in a text where words like *s'emmerder, emmerder, emmerdant,* and so on abound? And why did Céline feel it necessary—or even consider it permissible—to introduce into his novel speech patterns that, in their fidelity to colloquial language of the most informal kind, regularly violated the basic rules of French grammar?

At first the answer seemed perfectly simple, though, in some readers' opinion, hardly sufficient to warrant the vulgarity it released. It appeared that *Voyage* was to be assessed in light of the naturalist tradition extending back, as everyone could see, right to *L'Assommoir*. So far as Céline could be assumed to feel justified in introducing verbal excesses and eccentricities into his first two novels, naturalist esthetics gave him all the authority he could need. Hence the public were free to take or leave what he had written according to their sympathy or distaste for naturalism in fiction. Soon, however, new reservations began to take shape. Upon closer examination, sentence structure in *Voyage au bout de la nuit* and *Mort à crédit*—presumed to typify the writer's concern to capture authentic patterns of familiar speech—proved to be less faithful to everyday spoken French than had been supposed. These novels of Céline's appeared no longer excusable on the grounds that they had been written the way people express themselves at a certain level of society. Deprived of support in day-to-day usage, the language Céline had chosen to use seemed open to attack. Those who disapproved now condemned it as contrived. Calling Céline's style literary, his critics implied that it was artificial because it was not modeled closely enough on popular speech. Not one of them showed any inclination to admit that, approaching language as he did and arranging the elements of the sentence according to a strongly developed rhythmic sense, Céline aspired to achieve in his novels a mode of expression he was only too glad to acknowledge to be literary.

The next step—closer scrutiny of the vocabulary Céline borrowed from colloquial speech—brought to light discoveries it seemed fair to interpret in exactly the same misleading way. At this point, the critics' estimate of his work began to persuade Céline that he could not look to commentators in newspapers and magazines to explain his purpose and its consequences for fiction. Mistrust developed early in Céline and soon blossomed into derisive contempt.

One certainly loses sight of essentials in *Mort à crédit* if one follows the lead given by Marcel Lapierre, reviewing it in *Le Peuple* on June 3, 1936. This observer found Céline guilty of anachronism because he used slang words not in circulation as early as the period in which the novel is set. Citing Emile Chautard as an authority on French slang makes sense here only to someone who mistakenly believes that in *Voyage* and *Mort à crédit* Céline tried seriously to respect the limits of a given historical period. Had this been the case, then both of these fictional works would invite judgment—just like *Les Rougon-Macquart,* Zola's "natural and social history of a family under the Second Empire"—on the clearly defined basis of historical accuracy. Yet Céline forcefully rejected such limitations in a statement to the newspaper *Arts.* Under the heading, "L'Argot est né de la haine. Il n'existe pas," he declared on February 16, 1957, "No, slang isn't made up with a glossary, but with images of hate, it's hate that makes slang."

Working with a glossary differs radically from writing under the impulse of hate. The one approach betokens concern for some degree of objectivity at least, while the other is unequivocally subjective. To the extent that the narrative technique of *Mort à crédit* departs from the norm established in *Voyage au bout de la nuit,* it does so at the expense of vestigial respect for the constraints of external reality (objective truth) and to the advantage of subjectivity. From *Mort à crédit* onward, narrative truth in Céline's work will be conditioned far more by the narrator's sensibility than by historical or pseudohistorical fact, to which even in *Voyage* Bardamu is less submissive than many readers take for granted. In other words, in the work of Louis-Ferdinand Céline, stylistic impressionism does not serve the same function at all as in the novels of Zola or Huysmans, or in those where the Goncourts indulge their taste for *l'écriture artiste.*

Céline did not entrust impressionism with responsibility for mediating between his public and the physical world about them, so increasing awareness of its beauty or ugliness. The role of impressionism in his novels is to catch and hold subjective response, rather than reflect objective truth. In a letter to Hindus, Céline explained on May 15, 1947, "You have to get down into the nervous system, into the emotion and stay there till you reach your goal."[1]

Céline the novelist exercised strict control over slang out of devotion to the following central ambition: "The trick," as he explained to Hindus, "lies in imposing on spoken language a certain deformation such that once written down, being read, IT SEEMS to the reader that you're speaking in his ear." What matters is that, to Céline's mind, spoken language "in reality *doesn't give* this impression *at all*," when recorded stenographically. Instead, a degree of distortion is required for desired results, a veritable "little harmonic *tour de force*."

Writing earlier to the same correspondent, Céline had insisted on April 16 upon the fact that spoken language in literature calls for something more than mere stenography. Also he had stressed the fundamental need for appropriate "deformation." He had pointed out that this is obtained by "a transposition of each work which is never altogether the one expected a little surprise." In that April letter he had commented too, "What happens is what would take place with a stick plunged into water, so that it seems straight you have before thrusting it into water to break it slightly if I can put it that way you have to twist it in advance." Spoken language has to be twisted in the same manner, he asserted. "It's a sort of poetry that gives the best spell—*the impression, the magic, the dynamism*—and then too you have to choose your subject" (p. 73). Taking up the image of the broken stick once again on May 15, he insisted that one must not "*break* [it] *too much*—just what's needed." He now assured Hindus that all this has nothing to do with Henry Miller's "verbal boldness." For his own aim was very different: "To resensitize the language, to let it throb more than it reasons—THAT WAS MY GOAL."[2]

The prime target remains the same in *Mort à crédit* as in *Voyage*. Even so, reading Céline's second novel we become conscious of changing priorities that set it at some distance from his first. Certain

1. *L'Herne*, No 5, p. 75.
2. *L'Herne*, No 5, p. 73. Letter dated "the 16th" [April 1947].

noteworthy modifications in perspective point in the direction where we shall find *Casse-pipe* before long.

*Voyage au bout de la nuit* offers a steady succession of distressing events. It is an inexorable advance into suffering, hypnotically observed and carefully recorded. With *Mort à crédit* Célinian narrative form begins to break down into disconnected impressions, each individually acute and sharply rendered. Often disordered in their presentation, these show existence losing its appearance of coherence. Continuity fades, as the fortuitous becomes the dominant characteristic of life's pattern. In rendering human existence this way, Céline has started along the road that will bring him eventually—by way of *Casse-pipe*—to *Guignol's band*, leading him to preface the latter with remarks like, "Transpose or it's death" and, "You'll write 'telegraphic' or you won't write no more at all" (II, 519).

Unable to grasp what lay behind certain visible signs that Céline was bringing his purpose into clearer focus, several reviewers of *Mort à crédit* remarked that they felt cheated. "We expected much of Mr Céline," declared Jacques Debû-Bridel in *La Concorde* on June 3, 1936, "our disappointment is all the keener." Writing in *L'Action française* one week later, Robert Brasillach concurred. Beneath the dissatisfaction voiced by observers like these, we can trace the source of their disappointment. Evidently, the latter stemmed directly from their inability to comprehend that Louis-Ferdinand Céline was not bending his energies to modeling a novelistic universe upon day-to-day reality, after the example set by late-nineteenth-century novelists. Thus, for example, condemning the "obsession" and "convulsions" he found therein, Debû-Bridel argued that *Mort à crédit* "rarely attains the real."

The implications of such a criticism are clear and apparently unassailable. It would seem that Céline's second work of fiction failed because it did not measure up against observable reality. The criteria upon which such a judgment rests are easy to identify. They are the ones by which, since the nineteenth century, it has been customary in occidental literature to praise one writer of fiction as capable of rendering reality well and to condemn another as lacking the skill necessary for doing so. Attention goes first to subject matter, the real world about us. Then the mode of presentation adopted by the novelist is assessed on the basis of its adequacy in giving a faithful (or at least credible) impression of the physical world where we live, of what Debû-Bridel termed quite simply "the real." At this point, it does not seem essential or even appropriate to differentiate the process of perception from that of rendition. This is because the realistic tradition in fiction encourages the public to look upon perception as saluting the familiar (or even the exotic, for that matter) and, in consequence, to treat rendition as adequate only so long as it evokes reality with an acceptable degree of fidelity.

In short, those to whom being faithful to objective reality is the sole admissible criterion for credibility in fiction inevitably must find Céline lacking as a novelist. Without a twinge of conscience Brasillach could comment, "If Mr Céline were to relate for us his heroes' adventures simply and clearly, in the language dear to him, we could believe in these. The madness he mixes in accentuates the altogether literary and almost gratuitous character of what he says." Viewed this way, Céline looks guilty of violating fundamental rules of realistic representation, whenever—and this begins to happen very noticeably in *Mort à crédit*—he gives more attention to the way he treats his material than to subject matter itself. If what he commits to paper now seems gratuitous, lacking in a reassuring air of *necessity,* this is for the following reason. In *Mort à crédit* the substance of Célinian fiction begins to lose its power to convince realist-minded readers that it is strictly true to life. Thus to the extent that it overspills conventional limits for fiction, it appears undeserving of a stylist's attention.

Moreover, the way Céline writes does not seem to everyone to merit the dignity of the word *style.* With complete self-confidence, Brasillach complained, "One does not write to create such an artificial, false world, even decked out in the colors of reality." And L'Homme qui rit's comments clearly anticipated the objections ascribed to Robert Denoël apropos of *Guignol's band I.* In *Le Figaro* (May 9, 1936) he greeted *Mort à crédit* with the words, "It remains to be seen to what degree this writer without compare is master of what we really have to call his art." The ambiguity of these phrases soon gave way to sharp criticism of "a rhythm that seems intentional sometimes, but is also the one that impresses itself on the expression of a waking nightmare, of an intoned delirium." Michel Beaujour takes this criticism to its logical conclusion in his evaluation of Céline's second novel. Here, he asserts, Céline "perfects the style of delirium, and for this very reason commits suicide as a novelist."[3]

---

3. Michel Beaujour, "La Quête du délire," *L'Herne,* No 3, p. 284.

Beaujour's argument runs as follows. "But alas, we know very well that after 1936 appears a new Céline. Totalitarian, he knows everything, explains everything; supremely peremptory, without a chink in his armor: a swine" (p. 285). One might think Beaujour has Céline's polemical writings in mind. Yet his remarks reflect the conviction that, with *Mort à crédit* behind him, Céline had completed "his quest for total delirium." Hence, Beaujour contends, he had stopped being "fraternal and easy of access" because he had become "like his characters," understanding, now "the trick to delirium." What is more, "Having cut himself off from the incoherence of *Mort à crédit* by humor," Céline "suddenly accepts responsibility for all incoherence, in that very way justifying all his ridiculous characters," and even becoming one of them himself.

Not everyone would agree with Beaujour's observation in a footnote that, after *Mort à crédit* came out, Céline remained a writer easy of access only to people "locked up in mediocre paranoias." All the same, his comment summarizes fairly accurately the views held by many of those who consider Céline's later fiction evidence of declining talent, erecting the scaffolding of their criticism on the belief that Céline was a novelist who went astray because he lost his grip on reality.

All who follow Beaujour's line of argument draw their deduction about Céline from the same premise and as a result fall into the same error. Their interpretation depicts the novelist as a man who inevitably fell victim not only to insidious technical weaknesses but also to emotional inadequacies having a disastrous effect on his outlook upon the world. For them, he is a writer who, after making an impressive start in fiction, lost command of himself as well as of his medium. They picture him as a man who succumbed to the magnetic attraction of impulses and irresistible compulsions that were to have a totally destructive effect upon his art. In short, they do not seem to have paused to ask whether Louis-Ferdinand Céline might not have ended up writing the very kind of novels he wanted to write.

This question does not deserve to be raised merely because it offers some faint hope of finding a defense for the indefensible. Over the years, Céline's treatment of the fictional mode came to reflect a change of viewpoint, one that took him away from the assumptions of naturalist esthetics earlier than most readers think.

In *Bagatelles pour un massacre* Céline admitted to owing much to Henri Barbusse and Léon Daudet's *Le Rêve éveillé* (p. 216). So far as Barbusse' influence goes, he is usually thought to have been indebted primarily to the Prix Goncourt war novel *Le Feu*, in *Voyage au bout de la nuit*. And yet the evolution of his art discernible already in *Mort à crédit* causes us to wonder whether he was not alluding, a year later in *Bagatelles*, to Barbusse' novel of alienation and voyeuristic sexuality, *L'Enfer*.

Colin Wilson opens a study called *The Outsider* with an analysis of *L'Enfer*, commenting, "Barbusse has suggested that it is the fact that his hero *sees deeper* that makes him an Outsider; at the same time, he states that he has 'no special genius, no message to bestow,' etc."[4] The parallel with similar statements by Céline does not seem altogether fortuitous. After all, Louis-Ferdinand Céline has more in common with William S. Burroughs than with Honoré de Balzac. And whereas Burroughs incontestably owes something to the example set by Céline, the author of *Guignol's band* owes very little indeed to Balzac.

The first-person narrator of Barbusse' *L'Enfer* asks what is the nature of Truth. Céline's answer came in a brief letter to Ernst Bendz: "This is a universe *à la* Hieronymus Bosch. Torture and fun! Lies they don't even talk of any more! There is no truth! They've killed it, sold it, gobbled it up..."[5] Made privately to someone who had his confidence, this remark obviously was provoked by Céline's bitterness over his enemies' malicious exaggeration and slander during the years he spent in Denmark. Hence it would be unwise to treat this statement as meant to apply on the broad scale of esthetic theory. All the same, Céline, who had expressed admiration for Breughel during his early years as a novelist, wrote to Hindus one day in 1947, "Hieronymus Bosch, the painter, surpasses Breughel by far in my opinion he dares more—similarly Villon better than Bruant so gifted however and in the same vein, of the same race—"[6] There is plenty of evidence in the surviving manuscript fragments of *Casse-pipe* to suggest that Céline's growing affection for Bosch began to manifest itself with tangible consequences after *Mort à crédit*, in the book that was to have been its sequel.

4. Colin Wilson, *The Outsider* (*An Inquiry into the nature of the sickness of mankind in the mid-twentieth century*), (London: Gollancz, 1956), p. 14.
5. Letter dated "the 30th." *L'Herne*, No 3, p. 124.
6. Letter dated "the 12th." *L'Herne*, No 5, p. 81. Mahé states that it was he who introduced Céline to the work of Bosch, during a visit they paid to the National Gallery on a trip to London. See *La Brinquebale avec Céline*, p. 59.

As in *Voyage* and *Mort à crédit,* Céline turned to his own past life for the material to be used in *Casse-pipe.* However, no more than in the preceding novels or in those to come after did he attempt to authenticate *Casse-pipe* by trying to set the stamp of lived experience upon its contents. The naturalist concept of fiction as a "slice of life" had no abiding merit in Céline's eyes. He persisted in looking upon novel writing as a process of intentional deformation. Despite the impression all his novels give—and were meant to give—of having gushed forth spontaneously from recollections of the past, heightened by a fevered imagination, for Céline the procedure of deformation was an exhaustingly laborious one, carried out with close attention to detail and long-term effect. The essence of creativity, he was convinced, is not to be sought in painstaking devotion to factual details. Instead, it lies in practicing a form of transposition by which only skillful evocation in words can permit the writer to make of reality whatever he wishes.

The difficulty with *Casse-pipe* is this. We do not have access to enough of the novel to be confident we know exactly what Céline wanted to make of the reality of life in the French cavalry for the regular soldier during the years immediately before the 1914 war. One does not have to read half a page, though, before realizing that he had no wish at all to emulate Georges Courteline's success in *Les Gaîtés de l'escadron* and *Le Train de 8 h. 47.* But recognizing that earning popularity with a farcical novel about military life held no appeal for Céline advances us no distance at all. Hardly more enlightening is comparison with *Les Soirées de Médan* where Zola and his disciples subjected the 1870 War to ironic mockery, designed to contrast with the sentimentality of Alphonse Daudet's patriotic *Contes du Lundi,* equalled in Céline's day by Louis Aragon's *Servitude et grandeur des Français,* published the year after *Guignol's band I.*

We are told that the only two sections of *Casse-pipe* known to exist open the novel. The fact that Céline entrusted the manuscript of the second fragment to his secretary seems to indicate he had developed it beyond the stage of preliminary or early draft. Still, this second chapter is very much shorter than the first, is made up of a succession of unrelated segments that could bear expansion, and ends very abruptly. It is hard to believe it complete in its present form. Moreover, we have no firm assurance that Céline would have denied himself the right to review and revise this section thoroughly, before allowing it to pass into print in its designated place in the definitive text.[7] Any estimate of Céline's long-range intentions in *Casse-pipe* and of the importance of this piece of fiction in relation to the evolution of his art is necessarily tentative, and must be considered no more than provisional.

"I had the ambition—before I turned back in 1923 and saw the inadequacy of my Seven Pillars in the cold light of revision—to write a real book."[8] These words at the beginning of the chapter titled "An Explanation" in T. E. Lawrence's *The Mint* reveal the motives that prompted their author to place his "depot notes" on record as an account of his experiences after enlistment in the Royal Air Force under an assumed name. From this ambition resulted a book profoundly different from *Casse-pipe* in a variety of ways. One suspects that Lawrence sought in military life a special kind of companionship, the feeling of shared experience he missed after returning to England from the Arabian desert. What *Casse-pipe* has to say leaves us doubting that Lawrence would have found even a glimmer of companionship in a peacetime French cavalry regiment. Fights break out in hallways and men hang themselves in closets. Céline's narrator, a new recruit, is assigned to an old sweat, supposed to show him the ropes. Unfortunately, this *ancien*, Le Croach, is afflicted with flatulence capable of "fantastic squalls of gas" that keep everyone at a distance of at least fifteen feet (II, 498).

Readers notice at once that a fundamental difference between *Casse-pipe* and *The Mint* has to do with the manner in which they recreate daily life for the enlisted man. It is not just that Lawrence may be said to have tried to be more factual. The really important factor comes to light when the style adopted in *The Mint* is examined next to the language of *Casse-pipe*. Lawrence's reveals a characteristic detachment (or air of detachment) with which he tried to evoke the spectacle of barrack-room and parade ground life. In *Casse-pipe*, Céline's spokesman is a long way from the same detachment. In fact, the beginning of this novel owes its distinctive features to one feature above all. With acute and sometimes brutal fidelity, it seems to render the impressions of a raw recruit considerably younger than Lawrence was in 1922, infinitely less experienced in life and in dealing with men.

As in *Mort à crédit*, the narrator is Ferdinand. He begins his

7. The marked similarity between two paragraphs, three pages apart (II, 493 and II, 495), indicates clearly that Céline did not subject his second chapter (considerably shorter than the first) to final revision.

8. T. E. Lawrence, *The Mint* (London: Jonathan Cape, 1955), p. 165.

account of a new phase in his life by describing how, after joining up, he reported to his unit for duty. At first, he stands at the center of an ever-widening circle of emotions released by horror, a sense of being threatened, and outright fear. We have to wait for a few lines surviving from a later chapter to discover that the young man finally adapts well enough to his new environment to earn promotion to the rank of corporal, so getting the chance to become, in his turn, the terror of all new recruits.

The emphasis placed on the disgusting and the revolting, by which Céline's writings commonly are thought to betray their dependence on the esthetics of naturalism, characterizes *Casse-pipe* from the start. The guard room appears to Ferdinand a lair in which resting soldiers wallow like animals and those returning from making the rounds are so many "grinning wet bears" (II, 451). Colors give the locale an unsettling quality that brings to mind the painting of Soutine or Bacon. With the exception of one that appears "rather greenish" (II, 450), all the men's heads are red, crimson, in fact. Revealing rotten teeth like those of old horses, their mouths yawn and are said to be "enormous ovens." Céline draws a sharp contrast between these cavalry men and their magnificent plumed helmets, symbols of the glamor of military life, on a shelf above the corporal of the guard's head. This small detail of visible reality seems touched, like everything else in *Casse-pipe*, by a form of gigantism. Ferdinand sees the helmet plumes as "swollen," looking like "enormous manes dragging behind" (II, 450). The row of helmets does no more to convince us the novelist wants to depict the scene with objective accuracy than does his supposedly naturalistic attention to repellent olfactory impressions.

The guard room is characterized by a strong, harsh stink of flesh (or "meat," as Ferdinand calls it), of urine, chewing tobacco, "silent farts," and stale coffee. In every corner lurks a hint of "something stale like dead rat" (II, 449). Céline's brand of verbal impressionism takes readers beyond the point where they can measure his narrator's responses to life against those they themselves have had. Who could verify—or would want to try doing so—Ferdinand's assertion that there is also, in this place, a "taste of horse-dung"? In *Casse-pipe* Louis-Ferdinand Céline exceeds the limitations set by naturalism, at the very moment when he seems most willing to abide by them. He prolongs our sense of the horror of reality beyond direct experience of life's disgusting aspects, without for all that affording us access to the escape hatch of the fanciful.

At the same time, though, reality is approached from another angle altogether in *Casse-pipe*. As Ferdinand's squad is being marched off through a rain storm, outside the guard room conditions are no less alarming than he found them a few moments before. The men are "drowned, swept away, brought back furiously by the surge, shoved upright again by the squalls" (II, 459). Being with his companions, who so intimidated him upon arrival, does not make Ferdinand feel protected in any way. The squad is dwarfed by the "enormous décor" rising to the sky above the barracks, "all black, rumbling, all swollen, monsters with a formidable whisper... these are the fears that come from the leaves... from the night moving about..." Aggravated by the ridicule and unsympathetic laughter to which he continues to be subjected, the anguish of insecurity prompts Ferdinand to use over again the adjectives "swollen" and "enormous." They become keys to an exacerbated sense of the real that mirrors his sense of alarming disorientation. The latter stands between him and attainment of an orderly arrangement of his impressions of the environment where he finds himself, still an alien figure in his civilian clothes. Aiming to recapture his reactions, he will resort to a kind of short-hand, typical of the presentation we associate with later Célinian novels: he writes "telegraphic," as Céline puts it. A momentary stop in one of the wind-swept stables brings the notation, "All the rafters flying about... A wild hubbub... Bam... Dam... Vrang... It doesn't stop rattling... ransacking the manger... the boards. A real furious menagerie" (II, 459).

Many details that catch the reader's attention, now, are like the one representing the rafters as flying about in the wind during a moment of menacing cosmic upheaval. They are so exaggerated as to be incontestably antirealistic in effect. Their presence in Ferdinand's account is explained in exactly the same way as that of details by which the limits of naturalist description are expanded. Whatever direction it takes in *Casse-pipe*, description expresses response in the

sensibility of an impressionable young man, reacting on its own terms
to a situation and an environment disconcertingly, distressingly unfamiliar. Neither the fever induced by momentary indisposition nor
that brought on periodically by disease explains the tone set at the
beginning of *Casse-pipe*. Here delirium comes from the spectacle of
reality itself. Objective truth is just the starting point for the exercise of
descriptive talent, nor its ultimate goal. Meanwhile, given the perspective selected, exaggeration and distortion become logically, in this
novel, the means by which the writer will attain the deformation he
deems necessary. In the stable, urine falls from above, "but not a rain
of it... a waterfall... piss on every floor... It came in a funny down-
pour. So I wouldn't duck the shower, they shoved me several times,
those frightful men, under the spray... They wanted me to be soaked
through and through by it, for it to baptise me good. Real fountain
jets under all the windows upstairs... It pissed down in spurts, in
bursting splashes... in squalls..." (II,465).

Nature's disturbed state outside has its counterpart in the horses'
restlessness in the stables. "A storm of horses in a fury from one end of
the place to the other. All the tackle, the hardware, the wood, the
swinging-bails in the dance... A menagerie blowing up a gale..."
(II, 465). The corporal of the guard has forgotten the password and
does not dare approach the sentry on duty at the powder magazine for
fear of being shot. While he is pondering what to do, his men take
refuge in another stable. Here the horses in their stalls are so active
that no one can make himself heard without raising his voice above
"squalls, flying rushes, right into the swinging-bails, real tornadoes of
snorting, smashing, enraged livestock... Not a break, not the slightest
pause, a frightful, ferocious racket, a catastrophe of crazy nags. Rumps
and shadows jumped around, boomed again and again terrible in
squalls, such mettlesomeness, so high that it smashed the cross-bars"
(II, 468).

Violence in men and animals and turmoil in nature itself come
together in the hallucinating opening section of *Casse-pipe*. The horses
may be taken to represent, as they do for Bettina Knapp, "unbridled
instincts in their rawest, most vicious, and bellicose forms" (p. 88).
But before they represent anything at all, they claim our attention as
creatures of elemental violence ("squalls," "tornadoes," "catastrophe")
that frighten the new recruit: "In the background of darkness is
the threat, the whole whirlwind of animals...," says Ferdinand (II,
465), who feels he is witnessing "a real mares' Sabbath" (II, 477).

Reading what he has to tell, we wonder why he joined the cavalry instead of the infantry, or better still the navy.

At moments, Céline's images do appear to afford some relief from the atmosphere of anxious tension created at the beginning of *Casse-pipe*. Thus, in the stable Ferdinand observes two men going from stall to stall. "They punctured the darkness with their lanterns. Butterflies, you'd have said. They had wings of light. They came back this way and that. Fairylike, their frolic" (II, 474). Yet these men are collecting horse-droppings and piling them in a heap so mountainous that—hiding behind it with the rest of the squad—Ferdinand fears being buried alive under it. The men cleaning out the stalls only *seem* to resemble butterflies. The menace Ferdinand feels as the fruit of their labors enlarges the pile of dung is very real: "We are smashed in our hole, drowned, reduced to pulp under the avalanche" (II, 477). He and his companions crawl out, "shitting our pants," only to find that the horses are tearing strips of "meat" from one another.

Back in the guard room, with its "strong, unbelievable odor, enough to knock you down, dead rat, rotten eggs, old urine" (II, 484), efforts to determine the password of the day continue. The chapter comes to a close before anyone has occasion to use it.

It would be premature to judge the plot of *Casse-pipe* on the evidence furnished by its opening chapter. All the same, this section appears to indicate that Céline's interest goes first to something other than plot. The narrative thread is too slender to hold the pages together all by itself. At this stage, the novelist seems well content to rely for thematic unity on Ferdinand's encounter with ungovernable brutal forces that turn men into bears and elephants, transforming cavalry horses into savage beasts.

The second chapter of *Casse-pipe* was not made public until 1958, when Robert Poulet published it in the fourteenth issue of *Tribune libre*. At first, it builds on the foundation laid in the initial chapter, recounting Ferdinand's induction into military life. How closely does Ferdinand's existence at this moment in life resemble that of Louis Destouches in the 12th Cuirassiers? Asking this and wondering whether Destouches's reaction to enlistment is reflected in Ferdinand's do not take us very far. As Céline explained during an interview granted Jean Guenot and Jacques Darribehaude, "Well, you know... experience is a bull's eye lantern that lights up the person carrying it... and uncommunicable."[9] Given the novelist's commitment to the principle of transposition in fiction, any attempt to measure Ferdinand's feelings against his creator's and the accuracy of what he tells us against verifiable fact is scarcely likely to be fruitful. *Casse-pipe* must be read for what it is: Ferdinand's emotionally subjective version of military life, not a sober record of Destouches's impressions of the peacetime army.

In the second section of his account, Ferdinand starts reviewing past events in dual focus. Telling of one of the officers in his squadron, he changes narrative viewpoint just long enough to recall how, later on, during the war, he came upon Lt Portat des Oncelles lying wounded, propped against a milestone. By and large, though, Ferdinand seems to prefer reviewing past events in chronological sequence, beginning with the period of basic training he had to undergo. He emphasizes that things are as fresh (hence as agonizing) in his mind as when they happened. The passage of time has done nothing to sweeten his recollections, to mitigate their horror, or to generate some feeling of detachment from them.

The content of the second section of *Casse-pipe* falls into two categories of information. First, Ferdinand describes aspects of the training he received as a raw recruit. Second, he offers a series of vignettes, portraying some of the men among whom he lived at the time. Possibly, this section might have been expanded in the end to make two separate chapters. As it stands, it takes its unity not from what Ferdinand describes, but from the way he tells everything.

One can scarcely speak of what Ferdinand says about those he knew as a soldier as characterizing them. As though wishing to defend himself on this score, he points out on one occasion how difficult it is to appreciate, after all these years, who was "the biggest dummy of all the noncoms" (II, 494). And yet the passage of time seems to be no obstacle at all to reporting verbatim things he heard said while in training. *Casse-pipe* stresses dialog over narration, as the means by which the story is brought to life.

Everyone whose words Ferdinand notes down speaks exactly the same violent slang. Monotony of speech indicates they all live shut up in the same circumscribed world. In a situation where individuality

9. *L'Herne*, No 3, p. 189.

has been eliminated systematically there is not even a hint of independence in the ideas expressed through speech or in the feelings underlying what men say to one another. At the level on which Ferdinand exists, everybody in *Casse-pipe* shares the same repetitive pattern of life. It would have been inconsistent to portray one of them the way Céline made Robinson emerge from the crowd as a loner in *Voyage au bout de la nuit* and later caused the idiosyncratic genius des Pereires to stand out in *Mort à crédit*.

Only in external appearance did the soldiers Ferdinand came to know differ from one another enough for him to recall a few of them. These were men with physical characteristics so bizarre that they would be memorable wherever he met them, and after no matter how many years. For instance, Le Croach's flatulence is not his only distinguishing feature. His face too repelled people, "a real ugly one, forbidding, jaws so thick, broad, swollen, full, lubberly like seas-slugs, and then on the edge great scabs, pustules that he scratched raw" (II, 498). As for Corporal Le Maheu, Ferdinand remembers him as a martyr to boils, covered in pus, lancing his own furuncles with a knife ("Pflac!"), and dressing them with straw, chevril, and garlic, ceremoniously applied. "Lads! lads! Here's another truffle coming through on the edge of my asshole!" he would cry to the recruits, "Tomorrow it'll be ripe! The rookie that bursts it for me! Excuse me! that's got a sweet tooth! I'm candy! I've spoken! To my boot the bird that's giving himself a treat! Who? Who's signing up?" (II, 496).

As a "fartomaniac," Le Croach was awe-inspiring, Ferdinand assures us. "He astounded" (II, 498). Even the man's horse was affected by his performance: "it snorted something horrible." Coloring everything Ferdinand has to say about Le Croach, exaggeration leaves its imprint no less deeply on his account of the training he underwent to become a cavalryman.

When Ferdinand talks of learning to ride a horse, the second section of *Casse-pipe* takes up again major themes introduced in the first chapter. Céline's technique now is the same as it was earlier. Strict confinement of narrative perspective within the limits of subjective impression shows emotional and mental anguish being rendered more acute by physical discomfort. Fear is aggravated by the risk to which

Ferdinand feels subjected on horseback. All sense of permanence and stability is dissipated. Astride his mount, he recalls, he had the impression of being "ground alive." Writing in the historic present, he reports, "I'm rolled a bit, stuffed in strips, flattened to a powder. I evaporate" (II, 495). His account is so subjectivized that the standards of realistic accuracy give way before anxiety, emotional disorientation, and terror. The threat of physical danger expands into fear of extinction, of being carried away. And this goes with the image of the whirlwind—the horse astride which he is compelled to execute prescribed manoeuvers. An inescapable sense of the impermanence of life gives added emphasis to fugitive impressions, hastily noted in their brutal impact, without elaborate development: "I'm caught up in the squall, in a trampling thunder, in the lightning of horseshoes" (II, 495).

"Lengthways, sideways, crossways, I moved, me Ferdinand Beelzebub, between the legs of my nag... at every pace... walk... trot... charge... more than half unseated... hanging on wrong way up... I shook my ass to a jelly..." (II, 494). Initially, Ferdinand's recollections are distinct enough to be reported in the past tense, in quite an orderly, consecutive fashion. Soon, however, he is resorting to a kind of shorthand that reinforces the impression of immediacy created by his use of the historic present: "Wiped out! Panic! Up in the air! Up high! The beams! The abyss! The pit of vertigo!" Reliving the experience, he is so terrified that his horse seems to be jumping higher than the roof-tops and he receives bumps "enough to make you vomit up the sky!" Realistic parallels are no longer adequate to capture his feelings. At this juncture, images of cosmic upheaval return, summoned up by the narrator's inner disturbance: he speaks of "the furious sea wrong side up" and a storm that is "enough to cause a stampede." It all adds up to a "dreadful spectacle," as Ferdinand freely acknowledges something his version of events has made clear. He cannot recall what happened to him without "raving." He confesses, "I still reel at the memory" (II, 495).

Among Louis-Ferdinand Céline's letters to Eugène Dabit (all undated, but written before Dabit left with Gide on a trip to the U.S.S.R., where he died suddenly in 1936) is a particularly interesting one. Referring to his correspondent's novel *Villa Oasis*, Céline made this revealing comment, "It's a work book, I mean a book whose tone forces one to work, it catalyzes all the confused feelings of a certain environment."[10] He went on to remark that *Villa Oasis* "represents a tone it is indispensable not to forget, to go, if possible, further."

The formal manner in which Céline addressed Dabit indicates that this was one of his first letters to the author of *Hôtel du Nord*. The two writers were already on more familiar terms, however, when Céline announced on another occasion that he had finished his current project—evidently *Mort à crédit*. There are indications that he had tried to attain, in this novel, the tone he admired in *Villa Oasis*. And there seems no doubt at all that his enthusiasm for Dabit's work helped clarify the goals he set himself when beginning *Casse-pipe*.

It was not simply an impulse to aggravate the critics that led Louis-Ferdinand Céline to acknowledge publicly the affection he felt for the work of Aymé, Dabit, Farrère, Mac Orlan, Morand, and Simenon. The little we know of *Casse-pipe* is sufficient to persuade us of his sincerity in praising novelists like these, to whom evoking an environment, creating an atmosphere, and achieving a certain narrative tone were more important than interpreting the mysteries of human destiny. He found such novelists infinitely preferable to those he condemned in a letter to Lucien Descaves as being "carried along by nothing" and "short on Dream."[11]

By the time he began work on *Casse-pipe*, Céline had arrived at certain fundamental conclusions about the art of fiction. He had decided it could be practiced only by a novelist like himself, with the good fortune not to be "short on Dream" and therefore capable, as he put it, of "flying." We do not know exactly how far his flight would have taken him in *Casse-pipe*. For an impression of the range that fidelity to his inner dream granted Céline the novelist, we have only to look, though, at *Guignol's band*.

10. *L'Herne,* No 3, p. 85.
11. Letter dated April 20, 1947. *L'Herne,* No 3, p. 115.

# Guignol's band

T HE FOUR YEARS *Mort à crédit* was in the making fell during a period when Louis-Ferdinand Céline published only one text, his play *L'Eglise*. In comparison with the eight years extending from *Mort à crédit* to *Guignol's band*, this was, for him, a time of notable discretion. After the appearance of his second piece of fiction, the polemicist in Céline appeared to have taken over from the novelist. In 1937 he brought out both *Mea Culpa* and *Bagatelles pour un massacre*, following them a year later with *L'Ecole des cadavres*, soon condemned by the courts and consequently withdrawn from circulation. In 1941 Denoël published Céline's third racist, pacifist pamphlet, *Les beaux draps*. *Guignol's band* came out finally in 1944, just three months before the Allied invasion of Normandy convinced Céline that it would be prudent to leave France for Germany. Twelve months after its appearance, he was arrested in Copenhagen.

It would be foolish to ignore the influence of Céline's violently polemical activities—which had earned him the reputation for being a Collaborator—upon the reception accorded his third published novel, when it came out during the German occupation of France. Anticipating the public's hostility and characteristically taking perverse pleasure in it, Céline exclaimed in his preface, "I piss everybody off" (II, 517). All the same, we should be unwise to attribute solely to the writer's unpopularity among French people his lack of success with *Guignol's band*, both initially and in the long run. Milton Hindus, who prides himself on his objectivity, places the novel among Céline's secondary works.[1]

1. Milton Hindus, "The Recent Revival of Céline: A Consideration," *Mosaic* 6, 3 (Spring 1973), p. 63. Cf. McCarthy's comment that *Guignol's band* is "ultimately unsuccessful" (p. 219).

Those who read the first installment in 1944 heard louder than ever before the "apparently artless scream" that Rima Drell Reck identifies as "the sound of Céline's novels."[2] In *Voyage au bout de la nuit* and *Mort à crédit* the tone had not been so consistently shrill and had never sounded quite so aggressive. More important, to many of Céline's readers, it had never seemed so offensively artless in the preceding novels as it did now. Bettina Knapp's response to the first volume of *Guignol's band* faithfully reflects their reaction: "In none of the descriptions involving fights or antagonisms does the sequence ever become balanced or evolve into a whole composition. The images are made up of glaring, harsh, explosive tones, with cacophonies and atonal notes constantly infusing a macabre, disturbing and nerve-racking noise into the whole" (p. 140).

His *Hommage à Zola* had made it perfectly obvious that Céline looked upon twentieth-century Europe as doomed. Time and again in his correspondence during the thirties he referred to impending cataclysm. This imminent collapse of western culture appeared to him the inevitable consequence of Adolph Hitler's rise to power and of the marked degeneration of European society. So when, after the outbreak of the Second World War, he again raised his voice as a novelist, it could only be to celebrate disaster. In a world fallen into chaos, he would not speak up with the hope and purpose of making sense of things, of imposing comforting order and meaning on current events. A cursory glance at any page of *Guignol's band* reveals a text that erupts everywhere in points of suspension and exclamation marks. At times, sentences appear to have difficulty surviving whole, and sense seems to be losing a life-and-death struggle with the absence of form. In short, Céline's concept of how to write either has crumbled or has developed so dramatically since *Mort à crédit* that it must look, indeed, to many people as though he can no longer write at all. No one is more convinced of this than Bettina Knapp, who comments on the first volume of *Guignol's band*, "Endless passages of words are piled one upon the other in meaningless sequence, disconnected and entangled. Lucidity is virtually nonexistent. This lack of vision gives rise to a narrowing of consciousness and to extreme suggestibility. A series of clang-reactions occurs—superficial verbal and motor associations, repetition of 'stimulus-words,' constant distractions, all indicating a kind of regression

2. Rima Drell Reck, *Literature and Responsibility: The French Novelist in the Twentieth Century* (Baton Rouge: Louisiana State University Press, 1969), p. 192. McCarthy calls the second volume of *Guignol's band* "even more chaotic" than the first. Summarizing the novel as a whole, he excuses himself, "This summary is not very coherent, but neither is *Guignol's band*" (p. 218).

into an infantile world, an archaic realm of raw, undifferentiated instinct" (p. 141).

Even when commentators do not agree with Knapp's Jungian reading of Céline's work, they still share the view expressed by David O'Connell, who interprets the opening pages of *Guignol's band I* as "the confused ravings of a besieged mind."[3] By and large, critics have been far more inclined to treat *Guignol's band* as a document primarily of interest to a psychiatrist than as a work of fiction in which Louis-Ferdinand Céline began building on foundations laid in *Casse-pipe*.

Still pursuing his inner dream, Céline began giving expression, now, to an increasingly original conception of novelistic form. In *Guignol's band* he applied once again, and with increasing assurance, techniques tried out before in the manuscript of *Casse-pipe*. And so in a statement that is more a take-it-or-leave-it challenge than an apology, the narrator of *Guignol's band I* declares, "I traverse like an old nag, I flounder about as I frolic, I realize, I'm not telling things in the right order, tough luck! You'll excuse me just a bit, dallying on the way back, digressing without rhyme or reason, jabbering about my friends instead of showing you things!..." (II, 538).

Like the novels written before it, *Guignol's band* is based very loosely on the experience of Louis Destouches, who had been sent to England for several months in 1915 before he finally was invalided out of the French Army, a decorated veteran, honorably discharged. Considered together, the two published parts of this novel make up Céline's longest fictional work. Even so, it covers but a short period of a few months. Within that temporal span, it concentrates less on the inexorable and depressing passage of time—dominating *Voyage au bout de la nuit*—than on moments of lived experience, caught in a few memorable scenes. Setting the pattern for J. P. Donleavy's novels, these scenes for the most part play comic variations on the theme of ineluctable catastrophe.

The background facts are these, according to the testimony of Georges Geoffroy, Céline's co-worker in the French Passport Office in

3. David O'Connell, *Louis-Ferdinand Céline* (Boston: Twayne, 1976), p. 119.

London.[4] Destouches spent a considerable amount of his free time in Soho, where he was able to satisfy his appetite for women. In addition, "We had occasion to see—besides people of very good standing—many bizarre and shady individuals that delighted Louis Destouches, who enjoyed observing people and getting to know them to listen to them talk and study them." However, says Geoffroy, "During all that time, Louis never spoke to me of writing and I never saw him take a single note."

In the plotting of *Guignol's band* the principle of deformation and transposition underlying the Célinian method is enlighteningly and unambiguously applied. The effect of transposition is clearly discernible upon a story in which Céline does not claim to be offering historical truth and does not rely on verifiable fact to lend credence to his tale. Instead, he borrows from, elaborates upon, and wherever necessary distorts his past life in the interest of narrative intensity. In *Guignol's band* the man telling how he, his friends, and acquaintances lived during the First World War is not a respectable citizen, observing the low life of a foreign capital with detached curiosity. He is himself one of those expatriate marginal figures whose *modus vivendi* in the British capital during wartime provides the backdrop for the novel. Appropriately, the title of Céline's book brings to mind the activities of a French anarchist gang very much in the public eye during 1912–13, *la bande à Bonnot*. "Luckily there are some free men!...," exclaims the narrator who, instead of helping the war effort by working in a munitions factory, prefers—like his friend Cascade (twenty years in the prostitution business)—to take care of the girls patriotic fellow pimps leave behind when they return to France to enlist.[5]

Little by little, the reader manages to identify the storyteller as the same Ferdinand who recounted his childhood and adolescence earlier, in *Mort à crédit*. A twenty-two-year-old veteran who has been invalided out of the army, Ferdinand has made his way to London. As his tale begins some time during the Great War, he is living among a group of French pimps and their protégées, nervously avoiding contact with the police, since his papers are not in order. The pariah figure of *Mort à crédit* has developed into an outlaw, the only kind of person in modern society, apparently, who can aspire to true freedom.

The dramatic high point of the first volume of reminiscences is

4. Georges Geoffroy, "Céline en Angleterre," *L'Herne*, No 3, 11–12.
5. Mahé reports that Céline asked to be introduced to "un homme de Londres," that is, a pimp. See *La Brinquebale avec Céline*, p. 125. Mahé was able to oblige.

Ferdinand's account of how he and an anarchist acquaintance, Borokrom, happened to kill a pawnbroker named Van Claben. *Guignol's band I* does not end with this incident, though. Subsequently, while hiding from the police, Ferdinand meets up with a strange visionary called Sosthène de Rodiencourt ("All great dreams are born in London, young man!" [II, 684]) in whose company he decides to leave for Tibet. Hoping to finance the trip, Sosthène consults the London *Times*, seeking a partnership that will bring a quick return on any investment. As the first installment of *Guignol's band* comes to an end, he and Ferdinand board a bus to pay a call on Col. J. F. C. O'Collogham, who is looking for someone to join him in an enterprise that Sosthène regards as promising: inventing a new gas mask for the British War Office.

The second volume of the novel begins with a description of life in the O'Collogham household, where experiments with a new mask are being conducted. The results prove to be less than encouraging. Sosthène and O'Collogham reduce the laboratory to a shambles when their masks turn out to be ineffective against a gas called "Ferocious 92," invented by a teacher of botany and harpsichord who dabbles in chemistry as a hobby. For Ferdinand, however, the experience provides the opportunity to meet the colonel's fourteen-year-old niece, Virginia. He falls in love with her, associating the prospect of living out his life by her side with the disappearance of the nightmare of his past existence. Escape, he evidently comes to realize, offers itself through love. Virginia becomes Ferdinand's "totem," his "soul," his "salvation" (II, 109). Whereas *Mort à crédit* was a novel of hate, *Guignol's band,* despite its atmosphere of violence and imminent disaster, is a novel of love. Ferdinand duly makes Virginia pregnant before she reaches the age of consent, thus giving himself yet another reason to keep out of the reach of the law. Then this installment of Céline's novel comes inconclusively to a halt. Accompanied by Sosthène and Virginia, Ferdinand fails to complete arrangements to board ship (illegally, of course) for the River Plate, and renews contact with his old friends, one of whom—known as Mille-Pattes (Centipede)—has told the young man, "Nobody goes to Tibet!... Nobody goes there, you big dummy!..." (III, 123).

Within this loose narrative framework, *Guignol's band* presents a number of familiar features and enough innovative elements to set it apart from the Célinian novels published before it.

This story does not evidence a fundamental change in Céline's outlook on life. The narrator of the opening section in the first installment is, apparently, either someone other than Ferdinand, or a Ferdinand who has forgotten what his father did for a living, or again a Ferdinand who chooses quite simply to lie about it. He speaks as Bardamu might have done: "My old man who'd been in the 1870 war, who was a cabinet-maker in Bezons, he always used to tell me: 'Kid! Watch out for buses!'... *He's* the one who ended up under the 'Courcelles' bus! See where being careful gets you!... Catastrophe!..." (II, 538). He notes further, "We started out in life with parental advice. It didn't hold up against existence. We've fallen into piles of shit each more horrible than the last" (II, 529).

In *Voyage au bout de la nuit* and *Mort à crédit* it was essentially one person's life that gave focus to Céline's interpretation of human destiny. The beginning of *Guignol's band* introduces a new note in testifying to global destruction, collapse, and violence. Its central images illustrate the same phenomenon—explosion. The first lines read, "Braoum!... Vraoum!... There are the grand ruins... The whole street caving in along the water's edge!... It's Orleans tumbling down and thunder in the Grand Café!..." (II, 521). The novelist's view of life as soured by blighted hopes and aborted ambitions proves to have been singularly prophetic. Events taking place in France in 1939 and 1940 merely have confirmed on the broadest scale intuitions illustrated earlier in the lives of Bardamu and the adolescent Ferdinand.

Writing *Guignol's band* after the fall of France, Céline had every encouragement to open his new novel with an hallucinating picture of catastrophe and to elaborate on key phrases in the text like, "We are rotten calamity" (II, 521), "It's a saraband of dread" (II, 522), and "The dung heap is in delirium" (II, 522). With boundless energy, he now set about describing the *débâcle* he had foreseen at Médan in 1933. In a section of less than a dozen pages, he gave a harrowing account of an attack by German dive bombers, witnessed by his narrator when (like Dr Destouches, in 1940) driving an ambulance along a French road jammed with refugees.

If the world has learned anything since 1914, there is no indication of it in the opening pages of *Guignol's band I*. Indeed, the early description of the colonel's death in *Voyage au bout de la nuit* has its counterpart in that of a woman who has fallen victim to a machine-gun bullet. Here erotic association—disturbingly out of place—underscores the monstrosity of what we are made to visualize: "The lady who's taken one in the back embraces a sheep, lying there, goes squirming under the axles, with him, crawls and convulses... a bit further on... grimaces, falls, topples over arms outstretched!... groans... stops moving!..." (II, 522).

The irony to which patriotism is subjected in *Voyage* is present too in *Guignol's band*. A bomb severely damages a bridge. Among those hurled into the water below is a colonel in the Zouaves. "He's succumbing beneath the weight of the dead! goes to the bottom... 'Vive la France!' he cried in the end... overcome under the heap of corpses" (II, 523). Again, as in *Voyage*, horror is measured by the effect events have on the very young: "A baby comes into view on the front of a blazing truck. He's roasted, done to a turn... 'Good God!... Good God!... Shit!... It's not fair!...' This is the father in a sweat close by... He says *that*..." (II, 523).

*Guignol's band I* does not only demonstrate the continuity of Céline's thinking on the topic of war, misplaced loyalty, and the cruelty of fate. It takes us beyond *Voyage au bout de la nuit* in a direction to which *Casse-pipe* has pointed the way less equivocally than *Mort à crédit*.

Louis-Ferdinand Céline has not ceased to "rejoice in the grotesque on the confines of death": The ambulance, his narrator reports, "our ship of grace on the largest pavingstones balks, is driven off course, wobbles, is sent spinning, loses all its bolts, rams a flock of sheep, comes to rest in the middle of bullocks, stallions, poultry... an armored car smashes it up the ass... 'Brouang!...' With the impact it fricassees two tricycles, a nun, a policeman..." (III, 522). And there is more, too, than this Rabelaisian enumeration. The opening section of *Guignol's band I* draws us into a crazy world unhinged by total war.

Before the first paragraph is over, even the stability associated with gravitational pull has disappeared. "A pedestal table flies and cleaves the air!... A marble bird!... spins, smashes the window opposite into a thousand pieces! A whole room of furniture teeters, bursts from the casements, scatters in a rain of fire!" (II, 521). Before long, "It's the turn of a baby carriage that finds itself carried away over our heads!... a little soldier lolls in the bottom! his legs hanging outside in shreds... dripping juice..." (II, 522). And finally the narrator himself has his turn:

The flames envelop us, we're twirled round and round in space! I'm
carried off with a cart-load of prunes, the little fox terrier no longer
barking, a sewing machine and, I do believe, a cast iron tank trap
hooked with barbed wire... so far as I can see! We parted company
in mid air! . . . I could see higher than the clouds now... now *that*
was something special!... right up in the sky! up to the wild blue
yonder!... an enchanting vision... a severed hand I saw... a very pale
hand on flakes... on cushions of clouds with glints of gold... bleeding
drop by drop... a pale white hand and all around clouds of birds...
all red... flitting about after bursting forth from those very wounds...
the fingers shimmering with stars... scattered on the fringes of space...
in long tender veils... light colored veils of grace... (II, 526–27)

The real world is not ignored by any means. The situation sketched at
the beginning of *Guignol's band* would make that quite impossible.
There is plenty to horrify here. And yet naturalism is transcended progressively in this brief section which thus becomes a fitting prelude to
the story Ferdinand is about to relate.

Why, though, should Céline have elected to begin a book about
life in London during the First World War with a vivid and apparently
distracting glimpse of events taking place in France after war had
broken out again in 1939? Any open-minded reader who could not find
a direct answer to this question in the text published in 1944 had no
real cause to complain. The cover and title page of the book called
*Guignol's band* bore an asterisk—a sign to French readers that this was
the first part of a multivolume work. The list of the author's publications, inside, announced a second installment and a third one also.
Furthermore, the opening paragraph of the author's preface warned
everybody—"Readers, friends, less than friends, enemies, Critics!"—
against being in a hurry to judge *Guignol's band* as a whole on the
basis of this first episode alone. The second installment did appear, but
not for another two decades, almost three years after Céline's death.
As for the third volume, Céline either abandoned it or never even
began writing it.

Given these facts, we have no way of being sure how Céline
planned to finish *Guignol's band,* Possibly, he would have concluded
with a return to the recent past, so framing Ferdinand's period of
residence in the British capital between symmetrical opening and
closing episodes. Be that as it may, with the text available to us we
have to proceed cautiously.

Céline appears to have started work on the second part of *Guignol's band* in advance of surrendering the typescript of the first to his publisher. Then, before leaving France for exile, he entrusted the typescript of the second volume to his secretary, Marie Canavaggia. While in Denmark, he completed revision of Part Two by March 1947. Even so, he does not seem to have followed through to typescript stage the new manuscript material which he dared not send by mail. Moreover, returning to France in 1951, he neither turned over a corrected manuscript nor displayed any interest in seeing the unrevised 1944 version into print. Eventually, it was the 1944 typescript that formed the basis of the posthumous edition, prepared by Robert Poulet and published in Paris in 1964 under the title *Le Pont de Londres: Guignol's band II*.

Opening the book that Poulet called *Le Pont de Londres* (*London Bridge*), we face a tantalizing text. Céline's letters to Marie Canavaggia reveal that the original version was submitted to thorough revision later on. But the nature and purpose of the author's lost corrections remain hidden from us. We can assume Céline would have tried to eliminate the numerous typos surviving in the 1964 edition. One would hope, too, that he would have found it possible to grant his English characters a better command of their mother tongue than they display in the 1944 version. Still, it is not clear whether Céline engaged later in restructuring and reorienting the material intended for the continuation of *Guignol's band*. Pending fuller information, we can feel sure of one thing only, that going over his typescript Céline tried to polish the draft he had completed within a remarkably short time, no more than four months.

There is reason to believe the novelist refrained from recasting *Guignol's band II* from top to bottom, while in Copenhagen. The second volume as we know it follows so naturally upon the first that reading them in chronological order presents no surprises to anyone intent on following the plot. We have exactly the same impression of continuity, here, as if reading *Voyage au bout de la nuit* broken up into a two-volume edition. The opening pages of the second volume make no sense to anyone who has not read the end of the first volume. What is more, the narrative perspective adopted in the first installment is maintained throughout the second. It makes *Guignol's band* as a whole a work of fiction that stands out against Céline's earlier published novels as distinctively experimental in form.

As first-person novels, *Voyage* and *Mort à crédit*, and *Casse-pipe* too, all can be said to belong to the confessional tradition. In each case the omniscient author is replaced by someone who marshals his recollections in his own way. The narrator confides in his readers, ostensibly without artifice. Obviously, when doing so he arranges what he has to say in ways best suited to his purpose and (by extension) to his creator's purpose. Hence everything is conveyed in a manner that—even when apparently artless—is calculated to lead to certain results: creation of atmosphere and sympathetic or antipathetic response in the reader's sensibility. Nevertheless, while the writer has selected the confessional mode as the best means for letting his storyteller communicate with us on a certain level and to a certain effect, the person whose voice we hear generally speaks as if to himself, as though reviewing the past for himself alone. In marked contrast, Ferdinand addresses himself directly to the readers of *Guignol's band*. He habitually writes in a way that shows he regards the public as people to whom he can talk quite freely.

The striking thing is not that Ferdinand now openly confides in his readers, rather than maintaining the pretense of speaking to and for himself alone. The novelty of this approach to fiction was exhausted long ago. What merits notice in *Guignol's band* is the way Céline turns Ferdinand's awareness of his audience to special account, so coloring the impression the narrative as a whole will make on its readers.

At moments, Céline seems quite content to follow well-worn paths, for instance when he has his narrator try to whet the reader's curiosity: "It all turned out of necessity badly... I'll be telling how later on..." (II, 610). But the clumsiness with which they are employed suggests that Céline borrowed time-honored devices of authorial intervention in fiction with distinctly ironic intent, in *Guignol's band*. Reporting that a certain public house no longer exists, Ferdinand remarks, "There isn't much left of it, I can tell you straight off, it ended in a disaster, you'll learn reading what I got to say" (II, 541). Before long, his account reveals that Céline has no interest, really, in striking traditional poses. If he had wished to do this, surely he would not have laid the burden of narration on someone like Ferdinand.

For one thing, Ferdinand has a way of reacting to situations that underlines their ridiculous side. Thus, to give more force to her tale of how Sosthène used to come close to strangling her, his wife insists that Ferdinand re-enact the scene with her. This is how his account of the episode goes:

"Come on *you* do it to me too!..."
She had a soft neck full of creases... I squeezed a little bit.
"Squeeze little wolf!... Squeeze... Your tongue!... Your tongue!..."
I had to stick my tongue out too at the same time!... It was complicated.
I did the best I could. (II, 697)

Similarly, in his report on the circumstances under which he declared his love for Virginia, Ferdinand interjects exclamations that give the occasion more than a touch of the ludicrous: "The big scene..." (III, 77) and "Making my big play!" (III, 75).

Ferdinand has an excuse to offer for such inept intrusions, although he does not bring it forward until his story is almost over: "I didn't make up novels yet," he points out, looking back to the period about which he is writing, "I didn't know how to string out seven hundred pages just like that in lacework misunderstanding..." (III, 330). But such a confession can have only an ironic effect in a novel like this one. For there is another thing, also, to notice about the way Ferdinand tells his tale.

The narrator is given to flatly contradictory remarks in *Guignol's band* and makes no effort to reconcile these. At one moment he proclaims, "It's exact, all I'm telling you..." (II, 524). Later on, "I'm telling true" is his unequivocal claim (II, 622), even though he has stated in between, "Of course, I ain't going to tell you everything" (II, 531). And this confession will not stop him declaring again before long, during his account of Van Claben's death, "I'm telling everything precisely" (II, 642). Nor does it make him reluctant to harangue his readers whenever he sees fit: "And what I want to have you notice . . ." (II, 564), or again to parade his indifference. After launching into an extended description of the Jamaica Docks, he breaks off with the words; "Maybe this doesn't interest you... please excuse me" (III, 247).

Readers of good will may pass over such inconsistencies (occurring in the part of *Guignol's band* Céline saw no reason to revise before publication), were it not that the novelist permits his storyteller to intrude at every turn. The text is punctuated by phrases like, "Do you follow me?" (II, 540), "*That's* how he talks to me," "Like *that* he insults me" (III, 153), "Oh! What a scene that was! Shit!" (III, 59), "I'm going to knock Sosthène down! You hear?" (III, 35). It sounds very often as though Ferdinand cannot resign himself to letting events speak for themselves. On top of this, not satisfied with badgering his readers, he sometimes drops into a menacing posture: "A morose brute, anyone who contradicts me!... I've seen that! I can talk!..." (II, 605). He even loses patience with them: "A lot of good may it do you! ... Let's say no more about it!" (II, 539). Far from speaking quietly and beguilingly in our ear, Ferdinand has a marked inclination to bully us. It is fair to say that the reader (ignored most of the time in *Voyage* and *Mort à crédit*, even though privy to what is said) is cast in the role of protagonist in *Guignol's band*. He is someone the narrator is conscious of having to keep in mind at every step, because Ferdinand refuses to meet the public on any ground but his own. His cavalier approach allows him no time for subtleties. Hence he is far less concerned than we would expect with persuading his audience to his point of view.

Of course, however vague they may be, our expectations are conditioned by the assumption that Céline is using the first-person narrative quite conventionally in *Guignol's band*. So they confront us with an impression of inner contradiction, as we examine Ferdinand's manner of conducting his story. He actually stands guard over the "truth"— whatever that is—since he makes it very clear that he reports only what it suits him to tell, and in the way he prefers. The objective value of every incident evoked in his account is compromised, therefore, by the subjective element underlying the selective process governing the organization and presentation of the story. Meanwhile, we readers have the feeling that the more sharply he admonishes us to listen, the less convincing he sounds.

Can it be that Louis-Ferdinand Céline fell short of his goal, writing *Guignol's band*? Not at all; the effect produced cumulatively by Ferdinand's interpolative remarks, his various intrusions and asides, points to the originality of Céline's adaptation of the first-person fictional mode.

When a first-person novel offers so highly subjectivized a view of reality, everything hinges on the reliability of the witness whose impressions filter whatever reaches the reader's attention. Hence, as *Guignol's band* begins to take shape, we understand better why Céline treats the first-person approach with so much irony. Casting doubt on the fictional vehicle chosen is an essential feature of this book's technique. The interesting factor is that Céline does not rely on the intimacy Ferdinand strikes up with his public to encourage confidence in the veracity of his narrator's version of events. Instead, he works consistently in *Guignol's band* at undermining Ferdinand's credibility as a witness to life in a strange environment of which most readers have no first-hand experience. Not content with taking care to make us sensitive to the interposition of this man's viewpoint and feelings between us and events taking place here, Céline deliberately renders Ferdinand's version of what happens suspect and open to question.

As he intrudes between us and everything he has to tell, this witness-narrator-protagonist allows us to become very conscious of the degree to which incidents are modified in his report by his outlook upon them. As apparently was to have been the case with *Casse-pipe*, narrative truth in both parts of *Guignol's band* is a function of narrative perspective. Attention is diverted from what actually happened to the way the storyteller says it took place. Ferdinand's handling of the past easily convinces us that whatever he has to tell is only a *version* of actual events, naturally subject to the contingencies of memory. Moreover, when remarking that it is a pity he will never again see the places he is describing ("They'll not let me go back over there ...," he explains dolefully), Ferdinand frankly admits, "I'm obliged to imagine... I'm going to give you a little artistic effect... You'll forgive me... . . . Put yourselves in my place..." (II, 618). This is enough in itself to reduce the significance of narrative content in *Guignol's band* and give far more prominence to the impact incidents have had on the narrator's sensibility.

While the novelist does not require us, for this reason, to treat everything Ferdinand says as pure fabrication—necessarily false or falsified by intent—there is no cause for anyone to doubt how much the narrator's version of what goes on in *Guignol's band* is conditioned by subjective response to what he has witnessed and marked, too, by the vagaries of memory: "Ah! I'm losing my way! Ah! I deprave! Ah! I'm thrilling to memories!" (III, 251).

To a certain extent, the same might be said of any re-creation of past experience presented through the medium of first-person fiction, where the passage of time and the limitations of memory are influential mediating factors. What gives particular point to the latter, in this instance, is the special nature of the sensibility through which the past is filtered. Indeed, one cannot comprehend the nature of Céline's undertaking in this novel without first having asked what kind of a witness Ferdinand proves to be. And that question cannot be posed before we understand what sort of a man he is.

Some of the time, Ferdinand's function seems to be just the one customarily reserved in fiction for a first-person narrator. What he has to say carries the authority of his direct involvement in this incident or that. When Pépé tells him her husband, Sosthène, once tore her nipple off, she cries, "Well look! there!..." and Ferdinand confirms her story: "She shows me her breast... Indeed, the nipple's gone!" (II, 698). There appears little reason to impugn Ferdinand's veracity at such moments. For we have no difficulty believing that, given the opportunity to see the things he saw, we duly could make the very same report as he. But can we be equally submissive before his account of what goes on in other scenes?

Ferdinand insistently claims the role of responsible witness, as he takes it upon himself to tell of things seen and done long ago in London: "It's like another world now..." (II, 619), he says, not quite nostalgically. At the same time, he defends himself against anticipated recriminations by acknowledging that he feels obliged to imagine, here and there, to give us "a little artistic effect:" "Just put yourselves in my place...," he urges. "I don't want nobody to tell you things all screwed up... later on... when there won't be a single witness... no one alive... when it'll only be gossip... old wives' tales... scraps of half-ass garbage..." He recognizes, then, where his responsibilities lie, or so it seems: "If I don't take every precaution I'm quite dishonored in advance, if I don't tell this very day, now, all the details! not an hour from now!... everything very scrupulous, exact, meticulous!... . . . It was exactly like that... I'm not trying to touch your feelings... I'm not straining effect for you..."

These earnest and quite contradictory assurances have been culled from the lengthy passage giving a detailed account of Ferdinand's visit with Borokrom to Van Claben's pawnshop. While the two of them are there, the pawnbroker suffers an asthmatic attack. Delphine, his self-styled "governess," goes off to summon a doctor, meeting on the way someone who calls himself the sky physician. This strange little man, a veritable bag of bones, presents her with some cigarettes made from "magic leaves," guaranteed, so he says, to cure Van Claben.

Back in the shop, chewing the aromatic cigarettes gives everyone a raging thirst, making them drink copiously. The cigarettes act like a drug: Ferdinand becomes light-headed and Borokrom begins seeing double. Then smoking makes Ferdinand "see stars" (II, 625), prompting the anarchist to climb the stairs and jump down on the heaps of pawned articles littering the shop floor. He gets up covered in blood, with one ear torn off. As for Van Claben, apparently cured he falls into an erotic frenzy and throws himself on Delphine.

Now Borokrom attempts a sexual assault on Ferdinand while both Van Claben and his governess tear at the young man's pants—"they want to smoke my pipe!..." (II, 626). Ferdinand defends himself with a yataghan.

Ferdinand has a strange vision: "I see a great battle scene!... It's a vision!... a cinema!... Ah! it's not going to be ordinary!... in the dark over and above tragedy!... There's a dragon gobbling them all up!..." (II, 627). He helps himself to more cigarettes, smoking nine of them at once. Still, his reaction to Borokrom's persistence is as violent as before: "I'm going to cut that boor's nostrils off for him!... I don't like fags!... And what if I cut his equipment off!..."

Now Borokrom demands money owed him by Van Claben and the miserly pawnbroker pours a great heap of coins on the table. "It's a real hallucination!..." (II, 629). Borokrom takes it into his head to swallow a half-guinea piece, then ten more coins, then a mouthful of fifteen at one time. Incensed by Van Claben's protest, he decrees that the pawnbroker shall eat some money too and begins stuffing coins into the old man's mouth by the fistful. Laughing wildly, "the freak" swallows everything gluttonously, "all his gut making the sound of gold" (II, 630). His physical condition is sufficiently improved for him to want to make love to Ferdinand. To defend himself this time, the latter picks up a Winchester carbine, but "it melts in my hands! ... definite!... I'm telling true... it melts on me!... the butt stretches like putty, it trickles through my fingers!... marshmallow!... everything I touch melts!... and also everything revolves around the lamp-globe like on a merry-go-round..."

Borokrom is still in a wild rage, insisting on his money. "He's behaving like my father!...," observes Ferdinand, "his eyes are rolling about, starting out of their sockets, furious goggle eyes!... *that's* how he is" (II, 631). The anarchist seizes Van Claben by the throat, attempting to force him to spit out some coins. Then he climbs astride the old man's paunch, still garroting him. The pawnbroker soon changes color, "his tongue sticking out like that... He's not breathing no more that's for sure!... He ain't nothing more than an enormous fat yellow piece of wax... Ah! it's terrible to see! *I'm* not so keen to, no more!... I say so right off!... I don't want to see *that*!..."

To bring their victim some relief, Borokrom and Ferdinand pick him up by the feet. They drop him on his head on the stone floor.

When repeating this treatment has not produced the desired effect of making him regurgitate some of the ingested money, they drag him up to the landing and drop him from there. Van Claben dies of a fractured skull without having rendered up a single coin.

For a moment, Ferdinand wonders whether the pawnbroker is really dead. "I close my eyes to see if I'm not sleeping? I feel myself all over... To see if it isn't a dream... No, it ain't no dream!... *that's* very true!..." (II, 632). If Ferdinand "cannot get over the performance," nor can Borokrom. He vomits, then blames Van Claben's death on his young friend, who returns the compliment. Only fatigue now deters Ferdinand from killing both Borokrom and Delphine with his yataghan. Instead, he too vomits, "It's a relief!... but not too much of one..." (II, 637).

A comparable incident takes place in the second volume of *Guignol's band.* During a rainstorm a man comes up to Ferdinand and Virginia in Hyde Park. Ferdinand recognizes him as Mille-Pattes the midget, an associate of Cascade's whom he confessed earlier to having pushed to his death under a train in the Underground. "It's Mille-Pattes's face alright... but with a gleam under the skin... That's it... a gleam!... especially when he walks under the trees, in the shade... then he lights up like he's yellowish... his whole head... all of a yellowish gleam showing through... passing through him... under his skin... coming out of him..." (III, 114). Milles-Pattes now possesses a further peculiarity too, Ferdinand soon verifies: "I bend down on purpose... I sniff old Mille-Pattes... I sniff him again... He's got a smell. There's no denying it... a smell of something rotten. He stinks something sickening I must admit. I remark on it out loud... I make no bones about it... That makes him laugh, Mille-Pattes... that makes him laugh" (II, 115).

It would appear that Ferdinand is not imagining the smell of putrefaction. In the restaurant where the trio go for a meal other people notice it too—a smell of "old rat," of "meat a bit off," just as on the battlefield in Flanders (III, 117). As it turns out, Mille-Pattes is still capable of fascinating Virginia enough to be able to get away with making advances to her under cover of the tablecloth. Perhaps, then,

Ferdinand did not kill him after all? As he tells it, Ferdinand's narrative makes it hard to accept this reassuring explanation. He informs us that when the jacket worn by this "satyr ghost" gapes, scraps of green flesh are visible, hanging from his ribs (III, 126). Paying the check, Mille-Pattes seems to reach down into the pit of his stomach for the roll of wet bills he displays.

When Mille-Pattes raises his arm, he causes a terrifying explosion, with red smoke, an enormous cloud, and an immense flame—"just with his hands!" (III, 129). Is this simply fanciful exaggeration on Ferdinand's part, to which we need not pay serious attention? If it is no more than that, then why do the people at the other tables all rush out in panic, convinced a Zeppelin raid is in progress? And how are we to account for what Ferdinand says happens to Mille-Pattes next? Mille-Pattes flattens until he is as thin as a sheet of paper, then fills out again "all greenish and then all sticky repulsive!... there before my eyes!..." All this takes place before Virginia's eyes also. Yet she has never seemed aware of Mille-Pattes's putrid smell and is not the least alarmed even now. "The thunder clap, the panic that's all amusement to her!... Never has she had such a good time!... she's jumping up and down... She's in seventh heaven!... Before any explanation comes for the contradictory elements making this scene difficult to interpret, it is time to leave the restaurant. Under Mille-Pattes's guidance, Ferdinand and Virginia head for the Touit-Touit Club.

Joining in the dancing at the nightclub, Mille-Pattes seems resistant to the force of gravity. Bounding up to the ceiling, "a spider... hanging from nothing...," he "gambols over heads" (III, 133). The spectacle he offers is so hilarious that people leave puddles of urine on the floor where the black musicians roll about in convulsions of delight. "Never have I seen such a job! *that* I must say personally..." Hypnotized, wide-eyed and panting, Virginia is speechless with admiration.

Excited by Mille-Pattes's performance, the crowd separates Ferdinand and Virginia. Despite his resistance ("I'll only have a hard-on for Virginia" [III, 135]), Ferdinand soon finds himself in the hands of three women. They force him to watch everything happening to his beloved. Virginia has fallen prey to a whole group of men. "Ecstatic with pleasure," she is "yapping," uttering "supervoluptuous cries," and "squirming with happiness" (III, 136). Meanwhile, says Ferdinand, "All around me the mob is on the boil!... a wriggling mass of delirium!... jigging into one another! coming together in a jumble of asses!..."

During this orgiastic interlude, people are "beside themselves

with lewdness!" They jump on one another and pile up on the dance
floor, "heaps of society people in ecstasy." Carried away by the frenzied
atmosphere, Ferdinand too begins to howl. "I bray like a donkey," he
admits, as "angels run over my pants!... Their wings get caught in
my balls..." While he is raped—"They're going to destroy me!...,"
thinks this young man who, as an adolescent, learned to fear
sex—Virginia greedily embraces all comers, including a pair of bearded
men (both at the same time) and "an old woman in a little bonnet with
pince-nez" (III, 137). As the women "dreadfully abuse" his body, Ferdinand watches Virginia. "The further away she goes, the more I
adulate her... I see her again over there, hugged, sniffed at, licked,
licked all over, panting and caressing, she's writhing about, she's in
rapture on the carpet... over there at the end of the mirrors... Again all
the society men on top of her... They're grunting with joy... I'll kill
them all!..." (III, 139).

Up to this point the scene, as grotesquely exaggerated as any in
*Mort à crédit*, still seems to follow a realistic course, so long as we dis-
count Mille-Pattes's talent for aerial dancing. But now the episode is
closed by the arrival of a uniformed man, beating a drum. On his
cap is inscribed the one word *"Cimetry."* With the docility of a dog,
Mille-Pattes follows the cemetery employee up the stairs, through the
door (which opens all on its own to let them through), and out into
the darkness. With the "amazing succubus" gone, Ferdinand comments, "I hope the attendant was going to shove him under this time
once and for all..." (III, 140).

"Order established once again," Ferdinand finds his strength
has returned. He jumps for the stairs, dragging Virginia by the hair.
Encouraged by the crowd, who are in a delirium of excitement (*"Kill
her! Kill her!..."*), he tramples on Virginia's stomach. This action
sends everyone into a fit of violent rage, during which he makes his
escape with his girl friend, pausing only to give her time to vomit in
the street outside.

The dominant scenes in *Guignol's band* stand out as hallucinatory: the fight in the pub, ending when Borokrom throws one of his
bombs, Sosthène directing traffic in the middle of a busy street, and so

on. In each case, Ferdinand's version of events follows the same progression beyond the limits of realistic representation. True to pattern, the restaurant and nightclub episode begins in familiar reality—a famous London park—and it ends with vomiting, on a naturalistic note. Between whiles, it explores two situations, the second of which especially defies belief.

A partial explanation for the way Ferdinand narrates comes from his state of mind when, in the restaurant, he realizes Mille-Pattes has his hand up under Virginia's skirt and she is not inclined to object. His mental state is aggravated before long when he sees the girl he adores responding to other men in the nightclub. From the first, being in love developed acute impressionability in the narrator of *Guignol's band*. No sooner did he feel smitten with Virginia than he began seeing strange sights. "I've seen happiness in front of me in the colonel's garden!...," he confides (III, 78), happiness manifesting itself as a Biblical burning bush.

In a short while, Ferdinand has to grant that Virginia has been turning him into a "puppet," the *guignol* of the novel's title.[6] "I didn't know too well what I was looking at no more..." (III, 105). Talking with her causes him to lose all sense of time. "What evening?... Yesterday?... What morning?... I don't know no more!... I'm raving!... Everything's getting mixed up, going fuzzy before my eyes!..." (III, 92). More than once, in fact, Ferdinand realizes he is raving, just as he comprehends that he can do nothing to stop himself. "My mind is wandering... I've a presentiment of it... Are these too personal memories going to spoil my story?... I'm concerned... I offer them for what they are!... childishness... little narcissistic eccentricities, *self-complacency,* sweet moments... confessions!... anyway, shit! hard luck!... your health, for Christ's sake!..." (III, 110).

Ferdinand's point is well taken. All the same, while this last statement sharpens our understanding of his version of Virginia's conduct at the Touit-Touit, it hardly reconciles us to what he has to say about the cemetery caretaker, arriving like a Pied Piper to lead Mille-Pattes back to the grave.

It is not sufficient to note quite simply that Ferdinand is recapturing the acute emotion of past experience, just as he did when he raved in *Casse-Pipe* while recalling basic cavalry training. To appre-

6. Céline originally intended to call *Guignol's Band Pantin* (*Puppet*). The change of title permitted him to allude not only to the puppet Punch but also to the Grand Guignol theatre.

ciate what is going on here one needs to probe deeper than emotion, to search for the source of hallucination. Pausing over one brief incident enables us to begin doing this.

Spurred on by fear of the police, Ferdinand heads for the French Consulate. Once there, he absurdly mistakes the doorman for the consul general. " 'Duty calls me! Allons enfants de la Patrie!...,' I bray" (III, 663). Everything we know about Ferdinand suggests that he would have to be out of his mind to insist on being sent back to war. The hypothesis that he is temporarily demented while trying to re-enlist is confirmed soon enough by a vision he has at the Consulate. He sees the pimps he used to know, those who left London to do their patriotic duty in France, all lined up dead, displaying their wounds.

In the end, the consul general himself joins in forcibly ejecting the young man from the building. This war veteran is literally thrown out. "The big door opens!... The street!... I go off in trajectory!... A projectile! I rise up!... I hang above!... A rocket!... I soar over the side-walk, a new weapon, over the crowd!... and pzofff!... I fall right down into them!...," knocking over no less than five persons, one of them a man he will come to know as Sosthène de Rodiencourt (III, 669).

These narrative details present no novelty at all. They are typical of Ferdinand's story in *Guignol's band*. We begin to learn something new, however, in the official report made by the Consulate doctor who refuses to pass him fit for active duty because of an 80 percent disability rating.

When we first heard of Ferdinand's wounds, we took their effect to be purely physical—he had lost, as he keeps reminding us, the use of one arm. But in the second installment of his memoirs he points out, "It's written plain on my discharge: 'Trepanned, psyche has received a shock, but responsible for his actions...' " (III, 236). One of the prostitutes he knows expands on this laconic diagnosis of his mental condition, while in conversation with a policeman, Inspector Matthew, who suspects him of being a spy. She refers to Ferdinand as "a half-wit who's all screwed up in the head" and says he "falls on his mug on the sidewalk, they scrape him up with a spoon." He is "groggy," she asserts, a "wretch," a "dumb-bell," a "wretched loony" who is "weird" and "gets attacks" (III, 226). Ferdinand himself has admitted that, as a result of his wounds, he suffers from nightmares. It is obvious that these deeply affect his perspective on reality. He confesses that, seeing Mille-Pattes come back from the grave, he did not know what to believe, explaining, "I was subject to mirages!" (III, 234). Not feeling well one day, he sees things, as he puts it, "in a dream" (III, 321). On this occasion Sosthène tells him bluntly, "You're hallucinating" (III, 324).

A negro he sees embracing Delphine mistakes the young Frenchman for a policeman and is terror-stricken. "He's like me," Ferdinand remarks, "he's hallucinating... He sees police everywhere. He makes me crack up it's time I had my turn" (III, 326). In no time at all, " 'Kill me! Kill me!' He's howling. He cringes along the water's edge... He's possessed. A fine mess indeed" (III, 328). Ferdinand, of course, is fully aware of often having been similarly possessed. He shares his concerns with his readers:

> I didn't want to have no more hallucinations... I knew how they took me... I had experience by now... with a tiny drop of alcohol... just a little glass was enough... and then a bit of an argument... someone contradicting me... I'd blow my cool... it was all over!... Always because of my head, it said so in my discharge!...
>     "Cephalorized, memory disorders, comital hebephrenia, sequelae of shock and trauma..."

For those unable to cope with the language of medicine, Ferdinand has his own way of defining his condition: "This meant that for no reason at all I'd take off, my mind would wander, over any little annoyance" (III, 220).

On another page of his memoirs he sums up: "I was sick and bullshitting... I'd lost my bearings! A trance!..." (III, 184). His violent reaction to the Touit-Touit incident has made Virginia turn away from him. He complains now about the "fever" that has deprived him of her company, about the "attack of delirium." And he betrays the real source of his alarm: "I couldn't see the true from the false! And yet I was on the alert!... I'd certainly had some impulses... That was my first jolt!... but not ever as brutal as this one!... Since Hazebrouk I had jolts... since the hospital... my mind was rambling..." Not for the first time he feels a spasm of anguish, asking himself if the evening at the nightclub was not "just fever" or an "attack." Perhaps he has "imagined everything" (III, 157) and nothing really happened—not any of it, even the earlier fight in the pub. He concedes that this is very possible, in view of the operations he has had to his head.

Worrying about whether he has been unjust to Virginia, Ferdinand goes on to spotlight a difficulty his account of the visit to the Touit-Touit poses for readers of *Guignol's band*. Knowledge of his unstable mental condition leaves them wondering not merely whether the evening passed exactly as he described it, but whether they should believe he and his girlfriend even went to the nightclub at all. Uncertainty on this score casts doubt on the accuracy of Ferdinand's most memorable descriptions, including that of Van Claben's death which, we recall, he insisted was precise in every detail.

With its mixture of brutally realistic detail and disconcerting fantasy, the scene in the pawnshop could be bewildering, if Céline had not prepared it thoroughly by conditioning reader response to Ferdinand's version of past events. Well in advance, the novelist has accustomed us to be skeptical about the evidence brought forward by his prime witness, whether Ferdinand is engaged in telling what he himself saw and did, of whether he is reporting on things he says other people did. Certainly, no reader of *Guignol's band* need feel he must accept without demur everything he hears Ferdinand say. Specifically, no one need suppose Céline wants us to believe events in this novel took place exactly the way Ferdinand affirms that they occurred. Indeed, mentally checking off a list of now familiar devices by which the novelist casts doubt on the reliability of his narrator's testimony, we soon establish one thing. Like the scene in the restaurant and the one in the Touit-Touit, the murder scene in *Guignol's band* exemplifies the technique by which Louis-Ferdinand Céline tried to make this work of fiction very different from *Voyage au bout de la nuit*.

Borokrom forces Delphine to examine the wound on the back of Van Claben's head. She even "sucks the crack," we are told (II, 638). Does this mean the murder actually took place, and just as Ferdinand has related? We should feel it safer to make a positive deduction if Delphine were a more convincing witness than Ferdinand. The latter's veracity seems questionable of course when we hear him say, just after recounting Van Claben's death, that, before his eyes, the trees outside the pawnshop first grow to an enormous size and then shrink to tiny proportions. What of Delphine, though? She too hallucinates, it seems. Before the crime, she saw the sky physician roll into a tiny ball and disappear, no sooner had he handed her the intoxicating cigarettes. And after it, she takes herself for Lady Macbeth.

Perhaps, then, a police investigation will uncover the truth. After all, Inspector Matthew is especially interested in Ferdinand's activities. Once again, however, we are denied firm corroboration from a source other than Ferdinand. When Delphine has helped Borokrom and Ferdinand carry Van Claben's body down to the cellar, the anarchist explodes one of his homemade bombs in the shop above. Thus Céline sees to it that no objective inquiry will ever be able to reveal how Van Claben really died or what part his narrator played in his death. Could it be, then, that the old pawnbroker is not dead after all? This hypothesis would permit us to write off most of what Ferdinand claims to be true, treating it as no more than fantasy, born of alcohol-induced hallucination. It is an attractive hypothesis, scotched some time later. During the party that fills the closing pages of the novel, Borokrom and another man carry in Van Claben's rotting corpse, stolen from the morgue at the hospital where Borokrom's accomplice, Dr Clodovitz, is employed.

This time only Ferdinand seems to be aware of the stink emanating from the cadaver, which is in too advanced a state of decomposition (the head is "a bouillabaisse" [III, 302]) to give some clue as to the cause of death. Bigoudi, the prostitute who authoritatively explained Ferdinand's medical condition to Inspector Matthew earlier, now assures the young Frenchman that Van Claben died from falling under a train. Far more popular among those present is the assumption that the old man was struck by lightning. Only Delphine accuses Ferdinand of killing him. She does so while again thinking herself Lady Macbeth.

What now of Mille-Pattes? We are informed that the midget really did die under a train, pushed off the platform by Ferdinand. What is more, according to the narrator Mille-Pattes's death was witnessed by the police inspector, watching from the other side of the track. Are we to believe Mille-Pattes returned from the dead to eat dinner with Ferdinand and Virginia before taking them to a nightclub, where a cemetery attendant collected him to lead him back to the grave? Or, more exactly, are we to believe pure hallucination responsible for leaving Ferdinand with the conviction that this is what happened? This interpretation is hard to defend, since two men hurry ahead of Borokrom and Clodovitz to warn Cascade that Van Claben's corpse in on the way. And one of them is Mille-Pattes. As he appears before us now, he has neither the unearthly gleam that marked him as a ghostly figure nor the smell associating him with the tomb. Apparently he did not die after all.

Commentators of Céline's work generally share the opinion expressed by David Hayman when he spoke of *Guignol's band* as "the most gratuitous of Céline's works" (p. 37). In reality, however, this succession of supposedly "loosely connected adventures" is skillfully structured to definite purpose. The use of parallelism to bring out enlightening contradictions in Ferdinand's account of the scenes centered on Van Claben and Mille-Pattes demonstrates this beyond dispute. *Guignol's band* is not so much a chaotic novel as a carefully elaborated work of fiction, designed to appear chaotic on the surface.

It is evident that Céline refrained from disposing of inconsistencies that would undermine the reader's confidence in Ferdinand's version of events. As the narrative progresses, it becomes increasingly clear that the writer has no intention of helping his audience make up their minds about what really has happened. In short, *Guignol's band* was so put together that its narrative thread must break under the stresses and strains to which use of Ferdinand as storyteller subjects the novel's plot.

No matter how many times and how earnestly Ferdinand employs it, "telling true" is a meaningless phrase when it entails reporting, for instance, that a rifle has gone marshmallow soft. Now fidelity to subjective impression does far less to guarantee fictional truth than to open up an unpassable chasm between the storyteller and stable, everyday reality. The novelist's undertaking appears to lead him into gratuitousness because he allows his narrator to pause over incidents that do not lay down well placed steppingstones to plot comprehension. In *Guignol's band,* adoption of the perspective imposed by Ferdinand's obviously impaired mental condition places attainment of truth beyond the storyteller's competence. Hence, seeking to track down the truth is a frustrating experience for the reader. More important, it is a distracting one that draws attention away from the novelist's primary purpose.

In *Guignol's band* Louis-Ferdinand Céline appears to have taken a step that would look suicidal to any writer of fiction seeking to interest the public in the story his novel relays. He entrusted sole responsibility for telling the tale to a witness who openly admits that he cannot be sure, at any given moment, whether what he is recounting actually occurred or whether he imagines it happened. Together with the ever-present danger of incoherence and unmitigated dementia, distortion testifies to Ferdinand's mental condition at every turn and results inevitably in narrative *décalage*. This narrative shift causes reality to appear out of focus, very often. Therefore, even where *Guignol's band* seems to capture the real in true perspective and proportion, we cannot be sure the narrator's testimony is to be trusted. Ironically, the sustained effort Ferdinand makes to tell the truth brings everything he has to say under suspicion.

None of this would amount to anything but proof of Céline's distressing failure as a fiction writer, once *Mort à Crédit* was behind him, if examination of *Guignol's band* did not demonstrate one important fact. However distorted Ferdinand's account may appear, however garbled his version of some past events, the record he sets down achieves precisely the effect his creator demanded of it. Asking what this novel really serves to accomplish entails, before long, discovering how little value Céline attached to narrative content in his third published novel. And this, in turn, leads us to acknowledge that, when he was putting *Guignol's band* together, the story attributed to Ferdinand was of less consequence to Céline than something else altogether.

Plot is downgraded so that readers will not concentrate upon narrative incident so much as on the manner in which Ferdinand gives an account of events. Considered from this angle, *Guignol's band* is not weakened by the narrator's incapacity to tell true from false, or by his uncontrollable inclination to "bullshit," or again by his susceptibility to hallucination, or even his mental debility. Instead, it draws strength from the distorted perspective that these very limitations impose on the rendition of reality in this novel. Thus the circumstances of Van Claben's death matter less than Ferdinand's version of how the man died. The fact that Mille-Pattes is dead at one moment and alive at another is of less significance, ultimately, than the way Ferdinand describes the midget's appearance and conduct when he believes Mille-Pattes has returned from the grave.

Three years after the first volume of *Guignol's band* appeared, Louis-Ferdinand Céline wrote to Hindus, "The fact you find me a stylist gives me pleasure—I'm *that* above all—no thinker by God! nor gr. writer but a stylist I think I am."[7] Céline could hardly have persuaded himself that this fact had found general acceptance by 1947. For even Hindus, who saluted his style, apparently was not willing or able to appreciate how heavy were the demands made by the stylist in Céline upon the narrative content of *Guignol's band*. Only when we consider the distance separating this work of fiction from *Voyage au bout de la nuit* do we appreciate fully what impelled him to jeopardize in this novel—and some would say to sacrifice—his reputation as a major fiction writer.

7. *L'Herne*, No 5, p. 75.

# Féerie pour une autre fois

A PROSPECTIVE READER of Céline's fiction taking the trouble, first, to consult some of the critics who have written about his work as a novelist would be almost sure to set aside the two volumes of *Féerie pour une autre fois (Fairy-Play for Another Time)* unread, fully convinced that this novel, among commentators the least popular of those Louis-Ferdinand Céline saw into print, is a total failure.

Dutifully supplying notes on *Féerie pour une autre fois* for the Balland edition of Céline's writings, Jean A. Ducourneau is cautious and patently ill at ease. He sets down the basic facts of literary history: *Féerie pour une autre fois* was planned—under the title *La Bataille du Styx*—as an "interlude" between *Guignol's band II* and *Guignol's band III* during the summer of 1945, when Céline was still working on the second installment of *Guignol's band.* He points out, coincidentally, that the author's correspondence with his secretary reveals that the part of *Féerie* published second was really to have been Part One. His only evaluative comment, though, is that *Féerie I* and *Féerie II* are "unequal in interest" (III, 599). He conveniently omits to indicate which part he regards as the more interesting.

No serious protest has ever been raised against general condemnation of *Féerie pour une autre fois.*[1] The noteworthy measure of agreement reached over the years by those having occasion to pass judgment on this novel indicates, naturally, fundamental agreement all around regarding the defects said to betoken exhaustion of Céline's talent as a novelist. Everyone holds the same flaws accountable for making *Féerie pour une autre fois* an unqualified failure.

---

1. McCarthy does not give his favorable comments sufficient development to offset all that has been said against this novel. "The abundance of creative power," he writes, "makes the book really exciting. Facing up to himself, depicting the artist's destructive and constructive genius, Céline has written a novel which makes *Guignol's band* seem tame" (p. 262).

The weaknesses to which our attention is directed from all sides seem fated to bring this work down in ruin. They appear to undermine its content and to wreck its form. Viewed from one angle, in fact, this piece of fiction appears to exemplify the Célinian method, taken to its logically self-destructive extreme. It is as though the writer's obstinacy in persisting in treating the novel form the way he habitually did entailed, this time, inevitable collapse of his narrative technique, failing in the end to separate lived experience from its literary counterpart. According to David O'Connell, here "the now familiar older narrator" of the earlier works is "not chronicling the experiences of a mythical Ferdinand but rather of himself, Louis-Ferdinand Céline" (p. 127). Hanrez points more discreetly to the presence of no more than two "conducting threads" in the first volume: "a ready flow of language, often inopportune and as though asthmatic," and "a humor that has difficulty hiding still half-open wounds in the soul" (p. 171). He sees no reason to doubt that this book is to be read as a chronicle of "Céline's very destiny," with all the data corresponding to its author's "own odyssey." Hayman's argument is more subtle, referring to a "gradual sedimentary shifting and sinking" that permits us to share the writer's prison experience, not as it was lived, exactly, but "as it operates upon the consciousness of a pariah who sees himself as innocent and patriotic, maligned and persecuted" (p. 38). Going further, Knapp concludes that, while putting *Féerie I* together, Louis-Ferdinand Céline must have been experiencing "a series of 'dangerous' extremes" that could have led to insanity, or at least to "some functional disturbance" (p. 152).

All in all and with little variation, the litany of criticisms runs as follows. So long as Céline contrived to keep the experience of Louis Destouches at a safe distance, he continued to display some strength as a writer of fiction. However, once he allowed the barrier raised by literary adaptation to topple, he found himself defenseless against the effect of corrosive personal feelings. Running rampant in his work, these presumably brought about the disintegration of novelistic structure.

In short, the unpopularity of *Féerie pour une autre fois,* and especially of its first volume, shows what a high price its author paid for being associated, in the minds of his public, with a repellent persona. Hayman, for example, writes, "The voice of Dr. Destouches is dark, venomous, an underground voice hurling confused echoes of his hatred, disgust, pain, and despair up through the tiny window" as he lay in "a dismal cell in the death-house of a Danish prison" (p. 38).

Thus even a commentator whose reaction to Céline's work is untouched by moral indignation or antagonism of any kind does not manage to evade the temptation to express less disapproval of the novel itself than of the man he sees not only behind it but everywhere present in it. It sounds an exaggeration to say that critics generally castigate Destouches-Céline more than *Féerie pour une autre fois*, until the following questions have been raised. What if they knew nothing about its author before opening *Féerie pour une autre fois*? How would it look to them, if read simply as a work of imagination?

In itself, close identification of the sources of fictional material with a writer's personal experience of life does not lead straight to the breakdown of fiction, or even to its crude distortion. But if we endorse Bettina Knapp's reservations, it makes *Féerie I* nothing more or less than a manifestation of "the physical and psychological distortions" its author underwent "in his twisted and tormented world" (p. 148). Instead of being credited with having relived the past in a manner appropriate to endowing its fictionalized version with esthetic form, Céline is found guilty of having been quite incapable, this time, of taking up past events competently. Far from dominating and imposing meaning upon his own life, his writing now appears to have fallen prey to it. In consequence, he is represented as having succumbed to bitterness and blind rage in *Féerie I*, which recreates his life in France, at the time when the Allied invasion of Europe threatened him with retribution, and goes on to describe his subsequent existence while incarcerated in Denmark.

The narrator of *Féerie I* does not situate himself in time with respect to the incidents he places on record. As a result, the story he tells appears in shifting perspective, with no stable vantage point provided from which readers can judge its content. The underpinning of the conventional novel in memoir form is absent. Every event clamors for attention on an equal footing with every other. So we are given no sense of temporal sequence, beyond that necessarily imposed by the act of reading itself. Nor does the narrator establish any perceptible order upon the scenes evoked in his text. As a result, this work of fiction appears loosely structured, not to say quite without form. As the storyteller's mind wanders, mental drift or thought association dredges up images from both the past and the present. All in all, time is subjected to permutations that do away with chronological arrangement. For instance, at one point the narrator sees someone appear before him in his prison cell, carrying several copies of *Féerie I* that he wants inscribed.

The physical and psychological strain to which circumstances subjected Céline for several years is deemed the cause of his inability to see either part of *Féerie pour une autre fois* through to the satisfaction of practitioners of literary criticism. O'Connell speaks plainly for these people when, finding it "difficult" to talk of a plot in either of the two volumes, he asserts that "in *Féerie I* at least, it is even somewhat risky to even [sic] talk of a novel" (p. 126).

Underlying this fundamental objection is the widespread notion that Céline's novels are to be graded according to the degree of narrative unity they attain. Measurement of his fictional writings by this scale naturally leads the majority of readers to look upon *Voyage au bout de la nuit* as the pinnacle of Céline's achievement and to place *Féerie* well down the list of his publications, if not at the very bottom of it. Yet, examined in succession, all the novels Céline published before *Féerie I* show beyond question that his conception of fiction writing was evolving consistently away from concern for coherent narrative content. This may not be enough to induce us to accept the idea that *Féerie I* is his greatest accomplishment, merely because here the shifting currents of memory mingle scenes in prison with earlier ones, evoking life in Paris during the German occupation. All the same, when considering the novelist's aims in this work and asking how well he reached them, we need to bear in mind that the publication of *Féerie I* in 1952 marked the most advanced stage reached by Céline up to then, once dissatisfaction with *Voyage* had launched him into experimentation with fictional form, drawing his attention further and further away from the demands of narrative consistency.

Taken together, the objections raised to *Féerie I* cast grave doubt on Céline's control over the subject matter it assembles and over the way this material is brought before the reader. Extremes of unfavorable critical response are complementary in this respect. The conclusion is the same, whether one acquiesces in the view that, working on this book, Louis-Ferdinand Céline was still too sensitive to recent historical events to draw upon them for elements that would lend themselves usefully to novelistic re-creation, or whether one follows the lead given by Bettina Knapp, who feels the storyteller "has lost all contact with reality" and now "has regressed into his own subliminal world" (p. 150). Those who condemn *Féerie pour une autre fois* take it for granted that the novelist and his narrator are one and the same. Their assumption is that Céline—who once confessed, as they know, to understanding "only the subjective"—found it impossible, this time, to do anything but write as a helpless victim of painfully subjective impression.

Even commentators not motivated by measurable hostility consider themselves free to pass over Céline's statements about his work, when these conflict with their own interpretation of it. No one seems inclined to deny, for instance, that in *Féerie I* he wanted to plead his cause and settle scores if he could, even though this hypothesis flatly contradicts the prefatory announcement following its dedication:

> Horror of realities!
> All the places, names, characters, situations presented in this novel are imaginary! Absolutely imaginary. No relation to any reality! It's only a "Fair-Play"... and not only that!... for another time!
> (III, 421)

Can it be that his critics know more about what Céline the novelist was doing in *Féerie pour une autre fois* than he himself did? Where he persisted in stressing that we need to acknowledge transposition to be no less fundamental than before in his creative effort, are they right in recognizing only random historical reminiscences, gaudily colored by ungovernable emotion?

At first, it looks as though the claims set forth in the preface to *Féerie I* are spurious and fully deserve to be ignored. We know the events recounted therein to be substantially those through which its author had to pass from the mid-forties onward. Writing this book, he apparently made no attempt to elaborate upon his own experience, as he had done in *Guignol's band* and even in *Mort à crédit*. Instead, he seems to have been content with bringing fiction so close to historical fact that readers would have every right to treat his new novel as openly autobiographical. The person speaking throughout *Féerie I* paints himself as a social outcast, demented with rage much of the time. So the process of distilling past experience that constituted the art of fiction for Marcel Proust (here called Prout Prout) seems fundamentally at variance with Céline's handling of his material. So long as we regard him as simply speaking in his own name, it will be permissible to infer that the author of *Féerie I* could not help saying anything and everything we read in it. Seen this way, the whole of this part of *Féerie pour une autre fois* looks to be damning evidence of its author's unresisting, artless surrender to pettiness and spite. In other words, Céline appears now to have depicted himself exactly as his enemies believe him to have been. His account supposedly can be taken at face value, because it looks like documentary evidence confirming the Céline legend.

In fact, *Féerie I* does not make its claim on our attention as a true picture of reality, faithfully recorded by a first-hand witness, earnestly though ineffectually striving for some degree of objectivity. This fictional episode filters events gone by in a manner that detaches them from normality, even the horrible normality of life on Death Row. Often the narrator's subjective reaction to what has happened or what he sees happening blurs its outline, instead of sharpening it realistically. His presence at the very centre of this chronicle creates an atmosphere of hysteria, bordering at times on madness. Even the most violently antagonistic critic of the novel would admit as much, confident that it supports their assessment of *Féerie I* as a badly flawed work. But if we feel tempted to accept their conclusion that Céline's art went into decline with *Féerie pour une autre fois,* it is advisable, first of all, to set this novel in perspective against the background of his previous publications.

From the very start of his career as a writer of fiction, it was Céline's custom to show life from the standpoint of the individual, isolated in society and at odds with it. His approach to human existence, therefore, did not take on its fullest implications until he wrote *Féerie I.* Here, like his creator, the narrator is ostracized for what he has done, literally imprisoned for his anticonformity. He declares, "My reason indeed is shaken but not the sense of the order of things..." (III, 496). As reflected in his outlook on reality past and present, this man's mental state indicts the society that hounded Ignaz Semmelweis and—as Céline had discovered from harsh experience—neglects no opportunity to treat others it has rejected in fully comparable ways.

Protesting that Semmelweis' work to benefit mankind does not deserve to be categorized with Céline's irresponsible political and racist outpourings, one loses sight of essentials. The moral implications of the writer's conduct are not at issue, when we are reviewing his subjective interpretation of the enraged response it elicited from so many segments of society. The important thing is this. Louis-Ferdinand

Céline lived to see people begin conducting themselves toward him the way he always knew, deep down, they surely would if given the chance. He saw in his own life indisputable confirmation of his earlier judgment that "the crowd" is "sadistic and cowardly and envious and destructive." Thus his own suffering became just another example proving the rule, so far as he was concerned. This is why the tone of *Féerie I* is set from its fourth page: "It's the fashion... Fashionable hate... There's always hate, the same hate, but fashionable!... There are four million of them in Paris boiling with the same hate, fashionable hate!..." ( III, 426).

What complicates matters in *Féerie I* is the following. The incidents recalled obviously parallel Céline's recent experiences, well publicized in France before the novel came out. What reason is there, then, to doubt that he can be heard speaking through his storyteller when the latter remarks, "I've reached the point of confiding in you. I got some little secrets believe me!..." ( III, 453)? Surely there seems no cause to do so, as we read, "Doctor Destouches, *he*'s the sensitive one!" while Céline, we learn, "don't give a damn" ( III, 436). Evidence of the author's wish to transpose the past is hardly likely to impress any reader of this novel who takes its early stress on hatred for a sure sign of the novelist's compulsive preoccupation with private misery. Céline's handling of fiction on this occasion incites his readers to look upon *Féerie I* as confessional reminiscence, presumably set down the way it was because the writer found himself powerless to express himself any differently.

Are we back where we started, then? Must we side after all with those who grant *Féerie pour une autre fois* value as proof of its author's deteriorating psychological condition, but who firmly deny it any abiding interest as a work of fiction? Did Céline expand in *Féerie I* upon themes from his earlier fiction, merely because he now was writing obsessively and so could not help repeating himself? Or does the presentation of material used here reveal the influence of a controlling sense of purpose? And if this is indeed the case, did the writer's sense of purpose precipitate the sad collapse of fictional form, or culminate in further noteworthy and profitable exploration of novelistic technique? Sweeping comments about the mental condition of the man who began composing *Féerie pour une autre fois* in 1947, after his release from prison, at once suggest affirmative answers to the first three of these questions. However, only examination of the text of one of Céline's longest novels can lead to reliable answers to the last two.

In its own way, *Féerie I* expands upon the sequence in *Voyage au bout de la nuit* where Bardamu recounts his voyage on the *Amiral Bragueton*. The surface resemblances are easy to detect. In each case the weaker sex are thrilled at the prospect of seeing a man brutally sacrificed to public opinion. "The women," we read in *Féerie I*, "have a hard-on, they do! to put it bluntly!... the young ones worse! They already see me on the hook, spreadeagled, emasculated! Quick! quick! they say to one another! His tongue! His eyes!" (III, 427). An important difference is no less apparent. Bardamu provoked the other passengers into confirming his estimate of them, then executed a tactical withdrawal over the ship's side before being obliged to pay a heavy penalty for his effrontery. In *Féerie I* no such escape is possible, since the narrator has become, in his own words, "the Judas in chief" (III, 548).

With no illusions left, and no possibility of evading punishment, the storyteller speaks out frankly: "I selected the agony 'frequency,'" he informs us (III, 492). Tuned in to the agony frequency, he communicates the horror of existence as best he can, even when doing so makes his narrative overspill the limits of his creator's life to record, in addition, a succession of hallucinated visions. This is to say that, writing *Féerie I*, Louis-Ferdinand Céline followed his customary practice of "working from within." A disconcerting feature, this time, is that he did not work outward but confined the story, such as it is, to boundaries set by his narrator's dominant obsessions. Hence the impression his writing leaves with many a reader of being so faithful a reflection of mental imbalance that he must actually be permitting the public to contemplate his own disturbed state of mind.

The idea that Céline remains a prisoner of his past in *Féerie I*, incapable of objectifying his life history enough to succeed in bringing sufficient professional skill to the task of recreating it fictionally, leads to a very narrow view of what he set out to do and in fact accomplished in this novel. The long-standing problem facing his audience is as challenging here as ever it was. Readers find themselves wondering once again how much of what they are being told is really true. An added difficulty with this piece of fiction is that they tend very often to relate content to lived experience. In consequence, they are far more alert to signs of transcription than inclined to look for evidence of creative transposition.

What is more, such evidence as they might be able to notice, as the novel begins, is too ambiguous to look immediately convincing. From the opening page onward, the tone of *Féerie I* is frenzied. Its narrator does not simply admit to being detested by a few malevolent persons. He contends that everybody wants to kill him, and he anticipates being torn to pieces by the vengeful mob. "It will happen before an immense crowd, the whole city on holiday," he predicts with masochistic pleasure (III, 429). The tone adopted throughout suggests that a major criticism leveled at Céline regarding the content and mood of *Féerie I* is well founded: that we really *are* dealing with a writer who has lost control of his medium. And yet Céline puts the following words into his storyteller's mouth: "I'm getting carried away, that's my nature." In addition, demonstrating the very detachment he has been accused so often of lacking in this novel, Céline even puts some of his readers' thoughts into words: "*There's* a man who's going off the rails!" And on the next page he transcribes this brief but pertinent exchange between such a reader and his narrator:

"Oh, you're sailing right out into dreams!"
"Me? I'm not dreaming."

In *Féerie I* the mixture of reality and dream—what the storyteller assures us is reality and what he confesses is dream material—is worth a moment's attention. When one of his tormentors has trouble pulling down an undergarment so as to be able to urinate on him as he lies helpless in liquid manure, people come to her assistance, ten, twenty, thirty of them at once, all straining to tear away the crotch of her drawers. This is said to happen just after the narrator has been trundled for miles in a wheel-barrow ("the road from Gonesse to Paris!... the barrow's smoking!" [III, 494]). He now insists, "I wasn't dreaming! I wasn't dreaming" (III, 495). When Céline does let him dream, or at least admit to having dreamed, the storyteller reports on things no more grotesque than what passes for factual in *Féerie I*; for instance the sight of one of the people wanting to kill him, said to be lying in wait in a public urinal, with a carnival mask of pink silk over his face. If anything, this man's dreams and nightmares strike us as less horrible than the things he experiences when awake.

In fine, *Féerie I* treats reality on three levels at once. First, it alludes directly to Céline's own lived experience, and on a recognizably factual plane. Then it embroiders on this material by way of the fictional narrator's account of things he says occurred. Finally, it intersperses "dream" passages, sentences and whole paragraphs where imaginative flights take us no farther in the direction of monstrosity and pain than reality already has done. Meanwhile, as the novel proceeds, Céline maintains a distance between himself and his storyteller precisely where a casual glance detects none at all. Restraint is absent from *Féerie I*, as true-to-life detail goes by the board and readers are drawn into a world of wildly exaggerated proportions.

Reporting that his enemies have been discussing how they will go about assassinating him, the narrator declares they have spent months, already, wrangling over the matter: "just on putting out my eyes, quartering me, or burying me they can't manage to agree" (III, 424). Louis-Ferdinand Céline certainly was branded a traitor in France, but never on this humorously grandiose scale: "What I've been able to betray in the way of cities! fleets! generals! battalions!... Toulon harbor!... the Pas de Calais!... the Puy de Dôme a bit!..." (III, 485). Anyone who complains that artistry has been swallowed up in self-pity must be insensitive to the gusto with which catastrophes are described in both parts of *Féerie pour une autre fois*. The verve displayed makes this anything but a dreary novel of decline and fatigue. We soon notice in *Féerie I* how well Céline is served by his ill-fated narrator, who confides, "Nothing intoxicates me like big disasters, I get drunk on calamities, I don't look for them exactly, but they come to me like dinner guests who have rights of sorts..." (III, 430). And so a mood of intoxication sustains his tale, at the expense, very often, of narrative unity.

No greater error could be made than that of taking this work of fiction, structured to give an air of incoherence, for the regrettable product of an undisciplined mind, floundering about at the whim of uncontrollable emotions. *Féerie I* possesses a cohesiveness not so much formal as thematic. It plays endless variations on one or more of its major themes: violence, menace, victimization. What leads us astray at first is that Céline, who prided himself on being lucid, appears to have lost the gift of lucidity because his narrator gives little or no sign of it. The confusion resulting from identification of the character saying "I" with his creator has disastrous consequences for readers' appreciation of what this novel is meant to accomplish and by what means. The first step back in the right direction, then, is acknowledging surrender of lucidity in *Féerie I* for what it really is: not the dismal loss of professional competence but the intentional effect of a conscious esthetic decision. Much remains hidden from anyone who does not realize that sacrifice of coherence is deliberate in *Féerie pour une autre fois*, a price Céline gladly paid so that he could go on expanding the limits of inherited novelistic form.

Any novelist who successfully practices the first-person mode must have very clear and precise ideas about why he is writing as he does. At the same time, his storyteller too must be imbued with definite motives for telling his tale, since these govern the manner in which he addresses his audience. We have only to think of certain self-incriminating stories told in the first person, that have achieved wide success during the twentieth century, to remind ourselves that the writer and his character do not necessarily have to view storytelling from the very same angle. The difficulty with *Féerie pour une autre fois* is this. Even if we separate Céline in our minds from his fictional narrator, neither of them states his position at very great length and in such a way as to explain fully why this book develops quite as it does. None the less, each implies his viewpoint in a text that the storyteller repeatedly urges readers to buy.

It is important to begin by noticing one thing. The narrator of *Féerie pour une autre fois* does not throw himself blindly into a wholly disorganized tale, too confused to know what he is doing. He is quite aware that, in both parts of his account, chronology is disrupted enough to make many readers consider his story formless or even chaotic. He gives his audience to understand that a writer cannot aim at creating a conventional literary work of art when producing under the threat of death. Moreover, since every individual lives out his existence under sentence of death, this estimate of the writer's role does not apply only to passages in *Féerie I* alluding to life in a death cell. *Féerie pour une autre fois* marks an advance over both *Voyage au bout de la nuit* and *Mort à crédit* in posing a spirited challenge to literary conventions. Through the storyteller's treatment of his past, it represents an effort to broaden the scope of realistic representation. Céline aims to attain greater authenticity by relying on the services of a spokesman artless by design, not through inexperience or incompetence. "The critics will tear my work to shreds?" the narrator speculates in *Féerie I*, "No importance at all!... They will ignore it?... Even less!..." (III, 483).

When we look over the first installment of *Féerie pour une autre fois* in its entirety, there seems good reason to suppose the following. Coming together, incomprehension of *Guignol's band* among the critics commenting on its appearance and his pariah status after 1945 encouraged Céline to bolder narrative innovations, when writing *Féerie pour une autre fois*. Certainly, a hint in this direction may be inferred from remarks he has his storyteller make, here and there:

> I've ridden out other storms! . . . the whole world barking at me, waiting outside to tear me to pieces...
> Oh, I'll bark ten times worse!
> Not only the guards not only the walls I got it in for! for the Classics, for the Thinkers first! . . . Petrarch, Dantus! Prout Prout! (III, 483–84)

Elsewhere we find this comment: "You've the rights of the strongest, vengeful reader! You say: 'This show-off is putting us on!' I'm going to show you my backside" (III, 443). And so, when he appears to have wandered off into a digression, the narrator stoutly defends himself, "Oh but I'm not digressing at all!" Then he lets almost forty closely printed pages go by before giving some intimation of his approach to past events: "Life is filigree, what's written clear don't amount to much, it's seeing through that counts... the lacework of Time like they say" (III, 480). For Céline, in other words, "truth" in *Féerie pour une autre fois* does not mean respect for historical fact. Rather, it is fidelity to his fictional character's recollections, impressions, and thoughts, all set down in the order in which they rise to the surface of consciousness. The criterion is neither truth to lived experience nor careful arrangement of past events into meaningful patterns. This is why the storyteller exclaims, "I told you that already?... I ain't going to read over what I've done!..." Revision, excision, and recasting are identified with traditional narrative concerns that this narrator hold in contempt. With *Féerie pour une autre fois*, then, Céline moved further along the path he had begun to travel in *Mort à crédit*, *Casse-pipe*, and the first volume of *Guignol's band*, unequivocally demonstrating his continued indifference to plot line by releasing his novel from the restrictive limitations of lucid storytelling. He centered attention, now, less on what happens (or on what we, as readers, can be persuaded to pretend occurs) than on how his first-person narrator has grasped events and responds to them.[2]

2. Addressing Jean-Paul Sartre in *A l'agité du bocal* (1948), Céline recommended, "Think it over, horror is nothing without Dream and without Music" (III, 416).

The method applied in *Féerie pour une autre fois* places special importance on the way the storyteller communicates with his public. Most of the time, this novel gives the impression of being a long monolog, uttered by someone who never for an instant doubts that he has a captive audience. As in *Guignol's band,* the narrator addresses himself directly to his readers, ostensibly speaking just for their benefit: "I'm writing it for you from everywhere in actual fact! from Montmartre where I live! from down in my Baltavian prison! and at the same time from the seaside, from our hut! Confusion of place, of time! Shit! It's a fairy-play you understand... That's what a fairy-play is... the future! Past! False! True! Fatigue!" (III, 431).

Still, the storyteller has a clear concept of his role in talking to his readers: "I got to situate everything just right for you... to recapitulate!..." (III, 561). Like his predecessor in *Guignol's band,* he takes his duties seriously, just as sensitive to the fact that, without his testimony, something from the past will be lost forever. His primary concern, he insists repeatedly, is therefore to meet the supreme obligation to be honest and accurate: "and no lies... I'm not making up no story... facts are everything!" (III, 497–98). This obligation sweeps all else before it, disrupting the ordered presentation of events that can come only with due reflection on the significance of the past.

As he engages familiarly in a conversation during which the reader only occasionally has the chance to interject a remark of his own, the narrator's manner is sometimes easy, confiding, almost engaging. At other times it is aggressive, becoming alternately defensive and offensive. This is especially the case when we hear him treat the reader as one of the many people he feels sure are determined to see him dead: "In short, you're stinking, dangerous, chicken..." (III, 462). However he goes about holding his reader's attention, though, his approach has one consistent aim—to attain and sustain a high degree of intimacy with his public.

There is a good reason why intimacy is important to the narrator of *Féerie I.* He wants to break down the barrier separating him from people whose lives have never subjected them to experiences as cruel as his own. When first speaking of his prison term, he observes, "Let's be serious, let's admit the facts, twenty months in a cell, thirty months, thirty years, for you that ain't nothing!... You're on the outside! being outside is divine alcohol!... . . . I don't got your ambitions, I'd be happy to see things a bit more clearly, to suffer a bit less from giddiness... and even to have a bit less pellagra..." (III, 451). The

whole problem of communication by the written word lies here.[3]
It interposes the obstacle of literary convention between readers and
whatever they are being told. In consequence, the account provided
in *Féerie I* testifies to the narrator's unremitting struggle to cast that
obstacle down, to eliminate the distance between his public and a situation they can know only through the medium of words. "Ah! oh!
reader, I bow to you! forgive this moment of high Art, these hung men,
the weighty sadness! this little libertinage too!... I wasn't leading you
astray at all!... you are there with me, upstairs, on the seventh floor,
overlooking the gardens..." (III, 437).

Anything tainted with literary contrivance is in conflict with the
storyteller's avowed purpose. "Look here," he asserts, "I ain't speaking gratuitous, this is the modern regimen top grade... Ten minutes
of pure air a day, twenty-three hours fifty minutes, locked up..."
(III, 458). Suspicion of literary effect goes with haughty contempt for
sentimentality, as he announces, "Oh, I ain't trying to move you!..."
(III, 500). Here, then, lies the central difficulty he has to confront. All
he knows for certain about those reading his chronicle is the distance
his experience of life has put between them and himself. "Inevitably,
there, in the chain of events, I become a little bit personal... so to
speak almost intimate... Forgive me! I'm going maybe to give offense,
I don't know your profession, your taste, your little trifles, your station
in life..." (III, 433).

The underlying urgency of the storyteller's enterprise in *Féerie I*
and his sense of responsibility as a witness to the past leave him no
time for the unenticing luxury of reading over what he has done ("I'm
telling you everything here a little there a little. I ought to read it all
over! You kidding?..." [III, 551]). They spare him the illusion that
rereading will further his aims. "I told you already?... I ain't going
to read over!" (III, 481). When the reader protests even so ("You've
already told!" [III, 493]), the narrator is quite unabashed: "That adds
up to a lot of pages! What's more I bullshit, that's natural... after
the torments I been through! I don't hide! They rough me up I defend myself!" Indeed, he insists at this stage, "What's more, from one
first reading you ain't going to retain nothing! Just think, I know what
I'm talking about!" Any way, we gather, he feels sure readers would
gain nothing if he did go over everything he has written: "If I reread

3. "There are two kinds of Humanity," Céline wrote in a letter to Albert
Paraz dated November 21, 1948, "—the one that has been in prison and the
other—we don't speak the same language." See Paraz, *Valsez, saucisses* (Paris:
Amiot-Dumont, 1950), p. 328.

all the pages, like they ask me to I'd find secret thoughts... Oh, you wouldn't make much of them!..." (III, 552).

The point is not lost on anyone who avoids the mistake of interpreting this anticonventional narrative as proof that, in *Féerie pour une autre fois*, Louis-Ferdinand Céline fell victim to an undisciplined rambling delivery having a therapeutic effect, possibly, but still displaying no real professional competence. All too easily, the posture of gaucherie makes those reading with insufficient attention believe they have before them a text that runs out of control, stampeded by rage and hatred. In actual fact, the storyteller's posture brings repudiation of literary artifice through an act of voluntary rejection. This disposes of the erroneous supposition that *Féerie I* is a book that, so to speak, wrote itself. The self-conscious attitude habitual with the narrator ("Oh, but I was forgetting my story!...") sheds light directly on Céline's persistent effort to break the traditional narrative mold and to replace it with another of his own design. The storyteller gives fair warning when he writes, "That's life, an orange juice when you weigh sixty-six pounds!... I'm telling you all this without thinking it over! I'm not sure it's not earlier on page 510!... Here's a kiss, you'll manage!... I got so many things to tell that I'd have to live a hundred-twenty years and not stop writing, to get you to know just the beginning... two hundred years to really get going and you wouldn't understand nothing!..." (III, 552). Just two pages later, we read, "I got others to tell you, very much more pathetic ones still, with words and music... very carefully thought over... when you've bought *Féerie*!... not all at once! not before! greedyguts! your heads are too narrow... little foreheads too low... first there's your unspeakable way of reading... you don't retain one word in twenty...   . . . My style gives you a jolt? and my peeling sphecelating pellagra and scrotum? You think you're eternal? Ah I can see you admiring your asshole!... I disgust you? I'm too beastly?..." (III, 554).

In *Féerie II* (1954), subtitled *Normance* in honor of one of its characters, again we are taken back to the forties, when France was occupied by German troops. Now Céline offers a chronicle centered on one incident only, exhaustively recounted in a volume comparable in length with *Féerie I*. A letter the author wrote to Hindus on June 11,

1947 explains, "It has to do with the bombing of Montmartre in 1945 by the R.A.F. with various incidents—all of it done fantastic."[4]

The narrator handles his material in *Féerie II* much as in the first installment of *Féerie pour une autre fois*. As before, he addresses his public familiarly, as though he and they were face to face: "Are you with me? you follow my story? I ain't leaving you at all!" (IV, 66). Familiarity is apparently to be taken as a sign of honest forthrightness, unstudied simplicity, and directness, as one of the leitmotifs of *Féerie I* returns: "I'm telling you things without thinking... nature..." (IV, 33). "I'm telling you everything as the hours passed by... the way things happened... in an ugly zigzag!..." (IV, 98). This means the reader must show some good will and play his part. "If you'd seen the hallway!..." cries the storyteller, "the accordion the walls made... shaking! and re-shaking! end to end! it's something to have seen!" (IV, 126). Blast from falling bombs opens up "a moving chasm" the whole length of the hallway, "I ain't lying to you... a chasm!" (IV, 122). "If you was where I am, on the very edge of the chasm... you'd lose your hard-on..." (IV, 160). "If you make an effort with me I'll go on... if you don't, you don't help me? heck? I give up! . . . you won't know nothing and that's that!..." (III, 98).

The narrator of *Normance* demands the reader's confidence be-cause, as he says, "I'm telling you things like they were... I ain't very modest?... so what?... the modest don't win!" (IV, 229). This narrator's self-confidence does not waver, even when lapses of memory impair his account and need to be remedied, so far as possible: "I'm forgetting the Avenue Gaveneau for you! I'm talking to you about Jules more than I need to..." (IV, 20). "Heck! I'm forgetting the very thing that's going on!" (IV, 173). "I'm talking to you about Jules, I'm cursing him, about Bébert, I'm talking to you about the Avenue Gaveneau that's in torrents of flame, I'm mixing everything up for you! what a story! can you keep track of it? There's a thread running through it I swear!... It's 'tutti-frutti'? O. K.! but since it's direct experience this is the honesty of a chronicler!" (IV, 47).

In *Féerie II* the storyteller makes his position even clearer than in his first volume. Speaking early on about Normance's son, he reports, "André ain't at the market no more! I told you the market! my mistake! excuse me! no longer at the market! the conscientious chronicler cor-rects himself!" His tone is still aggressive, now and again, however. Questioned by the reader about something left out of his account,

4. *L'Herne*, No 5, p. 79.

he retorts testily, "Oh, if I went into every little detail for you!... ain't I already told you too much?" (IV, 160). Most of the time, though, he is apologetic about omissions: "My fault that you don't know! . . . What was I thinking of? I wanted to set myself up as a chronicler... and I forget whole characters!" (IV, 134). When his reader is angered by one digression, he replies blandly, "You're right, dear reader, purchaser! I'll take everything up for you at that very point! precise!" (IV, 100).

Corrections along the way take the place of a general revision of the narrator's text, which thus is more faithful in the end to oral narrative practice than to literary tradition. And so at times incoherence threatens, both a persuasive sign of authenticity and a measure of credibility. Hence the narrator will tolerate no criticism of the way his story comes out. "I'm repeating myself you'll say... I'm telling you things just like they are..." (IV, 45). " 'Oh! Oh!' you'll cry, ' . . . he's wasting our time!' . . . not at all!... I'm right in the middle of the story!..." (IV, 228).

> "Your story is disjointed!..."
> "I know what you mean... I'm listening to you... I've spoken to you about Rodolphe... about Mimi... [in fact, this is the first mention of their names] I'll be speaking to you again about these two tenants: Rodolphe, Mimi... it's terrible what I've forgotten!... I ain't told you a 'hundredth part' a 'thousandth' of the air raid! but you won't lose nothing by waiting! I'll get back to you a bit later!..." (IV, 130)

In short, the treatment of narrative content in *Normance* bears out something revealed by Céline in his correspondence: that *Féerie pour une autre fois* was conceived as a unified work, which circumstances forced the novelist to publish in two stages. All the same, a significant change of focus marks the transition from *Féerie I* to *Féerie II*, concealed at first beneath their common characteristics.

In *Féerie I* the storyteller reports events based on Céline's own experiences. In *Normance*, though, the central incident is one the novelist could not have known at first-hand. He was still in Denmark when the 1939–45 War ended. Yet neither this nor the fact that the R.A.F. is said to be using Flying Fortresses to bomb, of all places, the French capital deters the storyteller of *Féerie II* from assuring his readers time after time that he is telling something that is true, because he saw it happen.

We are in the presence of the same narrator, now reporting on something we *know* to be untrue, after telling us earlier things that sounded true enough:

> "A *miracle!*" you'll cry, "a *miracle!*"
> A *miracle!* but right before your eyes!... I could have doubted but for the mines... but the mines weren't no dream!... (IV, 16)

The chronicler is willing enough to grant that people down in the subway (why are they down there, we wonder, if not taking shelter during the air raid?) will have the nerve to deny what he is saying, and to claim that "nothing at all blew up! . . . that the firmament was serene, that I've imagined everything." Yet he stands by what he has said: "Ah, but I reiterate and I affirm! shrapnel and a lacework of fire from one end of the horizon to the other!" (IV, 101).

Acknowledging *Féerie I* to be fiction more than fact leads to a conclusion of greater importance than the simple admission that we should be gravely mistaken in judging Céline by our estimate of his storyteller. We have to recognize the latter to be a truly fictional character and must view the incidents he relates accordingly. Unless this is done, we face a serious problem when going on to read the second installment of *Féerie pour une autre fois*, where historical fact lends no weight at all to the narrator's version of the past. Looking upon *Féerie I* as factual and *Féerie II* as fanciful conceals from sight the underlying unity of the novel, so impeding understanding of Céline's goal in writing it.

It is essential to begin by noticing that the narrator draws no distinction between his recollections in the first installment of his memoirs and what he tells us in the second. The very last words he writes down in *Normance* are "these are the facts, exactly..." (IV, 258). They clearly echo an earlier affirmation, "I know what I'm saying ... . . . I was brought up in the truth I was... in my grandmother's day, the false had a smell, today it don't smell no more! if it still had a smell we'd have to close all the Museums" (IV, 132). Elsewhere too we find the same insistence upon the truth of what Céline patently has invented: "That's the way Norbert was!... this ain't no muddle... I'm fair equitable, that's all!... I observe!... I don't embroider!..." (IV, 244). He returns to harp on the same theme: "the way I'm telling you! I observe... meticulous always! I look... being scrupulous, my strength!... I'm reporting everything to you!... I don't want to leave out one detail for you... I'm a stickler for honesty! it's a mania with me, my enemies will say..." (IV, 247).

All this sounds so routinely familiar that initially it does no more than encourage us to classify *Normance* as fiction masquerading as truth, after the tradition of first-person novels. Before long, however, we see that Céline is not content in *Féerie II* to tread a well-worn path leading only to a destination others have reached before. For one thing, he stresses that recollection is complicated, in *Normance*, by the very process and mechanism of recall. "I'm telling you the story as memories string together," comments his narrator (IV, 31), whose very first statement runs, "To tell all *that* after... this is easy to say!...  . . . time ain't nothing but memories!...  . . . You'll see... I'll capture them all . . . I won't deny you nothing!..." (IV, 5). From its opening page, *Féerie II* develops out of an inner contradiction. Its narrator promises to omit nothing, while yet confiding that capricious memory plays an essential role in his recreation of events. Moreover, memory takes a part over which he cannot exercise enough control to convince his readers—or even himself, as it turns out—that his true account of what Céline has invented is really quite as true as his version is supposed to be.

The storyteller's determination not to beguile his public with literary commonplace remains as firm as ever. "Look," he points out, "I'm precise... I irritate you with small details? ah, that's tough! that's tough!... I ain't playing the artist, the more-or-less-ist! 'I was there, such and such a thing happened to me' *that's* my law!" (IV, 69). To what aggravatingly precise detail is he alluding on this occasion? To the incredible sight of ten or twelve fishermen blown by an exploding bomb onto each factory chimney stack in Montmartre.

At one moment during the air raid, the narrator remarks, "Sure there ain't no mistake it's much quieter... Still a bit of an echo... just some *boom boom* far away... the window's open, the nightingale is singing... I ain't giving you no literary effect... it's a nightingale..."

(IV, 9). Yet this assurance of honest-to-goodness fact does very little to make us believe our ears shortly after, when he reports the following scrap of conversation with his wife:

> "Look, Arlette, look at the wardrobe! the wardrobe's bumping its way toward the the door... it's going off!...  . . . I ain't dreaming Lili, huh?... it's leaving?..."
> The furniture's changing into people, waddling along, flying... and the walls!... the walls too!...
> "No... no... Louis..."
> "Oh yes!... Oh yes!... Oh yes!..."
> I'm certain.

It is all very well for this man to eschew embroidery of fact and to place his trust in observation ("you'll notice... observation above all!... I'm an observer, first" [IV, 244]). He nevertheless still tells about someone called Norbert while he himself is being carried downstairs, slung over another man's shoulder: "I'm beginning to feel the effect of being broken in two, folded, head down!... you think yourself lucid and it's all over!... you think your eyes are facing the holes... you're in fact mixed up... in any case, for sure, Ottave didn't stumble! he didn't miss a single step!... I think... I think..." (IV, 244).

Even though he feels certain at times, he still is compelled to doubt the evidence of his own eyes, where dream and reality, fact and hallucination mingle inextricably. When this happens, he makes no secret of his inability to establish where the one ends and the other begins.

Sometimes he defends himself, as when the reader comments that he is frightened: "yes indeed!... but who wouldn't have been? ... in my state?..." (IV, 233). And let us not forget by the way that, like other narrators in Céline's fiction, he cannot refer to his mental and physical condition without alluding pointedly to "those wounds in the temples, that buzzing of the whole head" (IV, 233). The storyteller's cry of anguish has a familiar ring in Normance:

> "Don't you hear the sirens howling?"
> I could hear them filling the stairway... and through the windows... and through the leaded glass windows!... was it an illusion on my part?... I ask Lili...

"Do you hear them?"
"Yes indeed!... Yes indeed!"
Ah, that's good! I ain't batty! Lili hears them! (IV, 242)

When Ottave has carried him all the way down the stairs of the apartment building where he lives, the narrator thinks again about a dead woman he saw lying in a bathtub on one of the upper floors, about the maid under a heap of crockery, and about Norbert too: "I'm recapitulating... proof I ain't woolly-headed!... . . . I ain't so hare-brained!... the proof: I'm still thinking things over!..." (IV, 246).

If all this is proof of anything at all, though, it can only be of the narrator's demonstrable unreliability as a witness. His unsteady grip on events serves Céline's purpose of presenting everything in *Féerie II* "dans le fantastique." Enough evidence is forthcoming during the early stages of *Normance* to dispose of any doubt readers may entertain about the kind of first-person testimony being marshalled here. "I'm hallucinated," the storyteller confesses (IV, 12). At one moment he sees a great crevasse appear in the roof of the building where he lives. The whole place is now toppling over: "there was enough to make you dream just a bit... I dream and I see everything in a haze" (IV, 254). He now sees "tornadoes and tornadoes" of sheets of paper—manuscript pages from his unpublished novels. The avenue and the sky itself are white with paper. And he hears a new kind of siren, not an air raid warning but a signal that paper is falling "in a double, triple avalanche!" He confides, "I couldn't see very clear myself no more... . . . opaque retinas?... maybe?... maybe?..." (IV, 254). As a result, our appreciation of the novelist's aims in the second part of *Féerie pour une autre fois* rests upon the answer furnished by the text, when we ask how much credence Céline wishes us to grant his narrator.

At first, the answer seems straightforward. It looks as though Céline's intention is, quite simply, to explore further the dementia possessing his storyteller in *Féerie I*, to examine more closely a mind unhinged by suffering, even at the risk of having readers take it for the writer's own. Only after reading *Normance* do we comprehend fully what the narrator meant when asserting earlier, in *Féerie I*, that his public would not understand his story. Throughout *Féerie pour une autre fois* the incidents providing the raw material of narration are not the novelist's primary concern at all. When we consider how his storyteller regards his own experiences in *Normance,* his allusion in *Féerie I* to life as filigree to be looked *through* rather than *at* begins to take on fuller meaning.

Awareness that the experiences related in the first volume of *Féerie pour une autre fois* parallel Céline's own tends to limit appreciation of the significance of the events described. Autobiographical elements here actually reduce the book's impact; particularly upon readers who imagine that Céline used *Féerie I* just to tell his side of things, while recreating a painful phase of his own life. As he entrusts his fictional narrator in *Normance* with the task of describing an air raid through which he himself has not lived, we realize that narrative content based on historical fact is less important to Céline the novelist than we might have considered it fair to assume.

Once willing to separate *Féerie pour une autre fois* from confessional fiction steeped in autobiography, we are on the way to giving due attention to the following significant feature of *Normance.* It is dedicated to Céline's publisher and also to Pliny the Elder. Thus the novelist raises in *Féerie II* the crucial question of fiction's relationship to history, and proposes a very personal answer.

In *Normance,* Céline occasionally allows his narrator to betray signs of stress. "You'll pardon these digressions... I'm a bit wound up... but I'm getting back quick to my state of mind which is on the benevolent side... so I was telling you about the mill..." (IV, 39). As before, the storyteller's excuse is intended to lend authority to the account he gives: "You'll tell me," he remarks, "not in much of an order, your chronicle!... What's in order in a Flood?... moments like that?... and he'll be a liar, you can be sure of that, the guy who tells you calmly that he's seen thunder, in what order!" (IV, 121). Even his wife, to whom he turns for reassurance when the spectacle before him becomes so alarming as to convince him he is undergoing some form of hallucination, momentarily succumbs to emotion. He reports, "she was on the roof throughout the Flood... so what?... that's how catastrophes are... all true on one side, all false on the other!..." (IV, 214). Foreseeing objections, he tries to forestall them: "'That's incredible!' you'll shout... but all delirium is incredible! and what about the Flood do you find that credible?..." (IV, 78). This is a teller of tales who sees it as his duty to face the demands of history, not literature. "But history commands! I owe you History! I'm in the porter's lodge that's swelling and pitching... no place else! I don't want to take you in or lie to you... tragedy!" ( IV, 115).

At one moment of stress during the air raid, he sees his neighborhood as Bluebeard's garden, "there's optical effects, I grant you! ... but ain't it retinian, yes or no? ah?... and what about the floor... ain't this a physical phenomenon, a seismic one? I got to note everything down for you! I do so! they'll buy my books later on, much later on, when I'm dead, to study about the first seisms of the end" (IV, 15). For "a Flood badly observed in a whole Era for nothing..." And when humanity has been good "only for the maggots," he believes, "That's blasphemy of the worst kind! Glory to Pliny!" In short, this is a man with a clear understanding of his obligations: "You got to observe phenomena with more than serious attention, especially when they're 'catalytic'! just so no one can challenge you no more ten... twelve centuries later!... nobody don't challenge Pliny the Elder! he's still an authority...  . . . he paid for his 'phenomena' did Pliny the Elder!... me too I've paid a bit..." (IV, 244).

"Don't tell me to get stuffed!" the narrator warns roughly in *Normance*, "the best part's still to come!... don't fire the honest chronicler!... just have a look at Pliny the Elder, it took him years to work himself up to his big moment, to go sniff Vesuvius! to make certain it really was sulphur... I'm not asking you to make a sacrifice like that!... I ain't out to see you dead!..." To Céline's storyteller, Pliny the Elder is a hero, never forgiven for being enough of a man of science to take his fleet close to Vesuvius during a volcanic eruption to be able to smell the lava: "he came to a bad end, but a sublime one! It's him I want to glorify!... my dedication above proves it!" ( IV, 142).

Now, despite the obvious parallel between Pliny's pursuit of truth—at the cost of universal condemnation—and the dedication to truth of which Céline's narrator boasts, there is a profound difference between the spectacle witnessed by the former and the sights to which the storyteller of *Normance* is determined to testify. It is the difference between a phenomenon time has consigned to history and one that exists, so far as it exists at all, only as testimony to a novelist's fertile imagination. One wonders, therefore, why Louis-Ferdinand Céline should have chosen, firstly, to transpose a brief moment of history— his own recent suffering—and then to compete with history by inventing a pseudohistorical event, witnessed by a fictional historian whose mental state brings his veracity into question.

As a tribute to Pliny, *Normance* is a strange-looking work indeed. It opens with a sequence that sets this installment of *Féerie pour une autre fois* beyond the scope of verifiable history and consequently invalidates the narrator's claim to scientific accuracy in reporting what he says he has observed. It has to do with a character introduced in a fairly long closing section of *Féerie I*. This is Jules, an erotomaniac artist who invites school girls to pose nude in his studio, so that he can seduce them. As *Normance* begins, Jules is perched on one of the vanes of a windmill, guiding in the British planes to make sure they drop their bombs right on Montmartre.

There is proof here that *Féerie I* and *II* were meant to be read without interruption, as one novel. Anyone taking up *Normance* without having read *Féerie I* does not learn for quite a while that Jules has no legs. When the discovery does come, it can only have the effect of making the opening scene of *Féerie II* even more incredible than it looks at first.

From his apartment in Montmartre, the narrator watches Jules. He does not trouble himself to explain how the crippled artist has managed to climb up one of the windmill's vanes without falling from the little trolley in which he pulls himself along by his arms. He concentrates instead on the antics of this "navigable torso." Jules is phenomenal, endowed as he is with the ability to maintain his balance and to signal to the planes overhead even while the mill, uprooted by a bomb, is flying through the air.

How does the storyteller meet the objections common sense inevitably raises to much of what he has to tell? First, by resorting to his customary assurance, "I'm not inventing nothing... what a night!... there's fantastic  forces on the move!" (IV, 20). Then with a frank admission to having no acceptable explanation to offer: "the mill stands up again? it's not believable but that's the way it is" (IV, 25), "and then things pitching... let's admit it... the whole building pitching there, under us... the truth! nothing but! and me looking across the street all the same! I want to see if the windmill's flying away with Jules on it...  . . . Yes, Ma'am, he's rolling backward Jules is and rolling forward! . . . he's almost out of the box!..." (IV, 19).

No concessions to plausibility can be detected in this part of *Féerie pour une autre fois*, where the narrator comments all the same, " 'But this is a world!' you'll shout! Sure! I'm in full agreement! . . . I told you: I won't lie nothing... supernatural phenomena go beyond you, that's all! chroniclers without a conscience reduce, explain facts,

make them shabby! Oh, your servant... not at all! respect for sumptuousness!..." The storyteller has his answer all ready for those who will
accuse him of lack of restraint: "this will be historical one day! they'll
teach it in school!" He even imagines a final oral examination running
as follows:

> "Who got Paris capital of the working-girls destroyed?"
> "Jules!"
> "Well done," the Jury will exclaim! "passed straight off! Most
distinguished Candidate!"

Louis-Ferdinand Céline lived to see the grim predictions made
in his homage to Emile Zola borne out by contemporary history. *Féerie
pour une autre fois* reveals plainly that he came to believe a novelist
really attuned to our time could no longer be expected to react to a
major catastrophe the way Zola had done with *La Débâcle*, his fictional
reaction of the Franco-Prussian War, or even after the fashion of
Jules Romains's *Verdun*. "But the music of Time changes," he wrote to
Albert Paraz on August 4, 1952, "and is never the same from one
century to the next—only it's death that gives this music and death
only—*you have to pay*—it's dreadful and sad."[5]

This is the irony of the narrator's refrain throughout *Normance*
("What I'm telling you is accurate stuff, it ain't jazzed up!" [IV, 41]).
Factual detail faithfully drawn from observed reality does not convey
the enormity of modern-day catastrophe adequately. Hence the only
way to be true to the spirit of the times is to inflate the real to fantastic
proportions that command attention by challenging the imagination.
"Brroom! Brroom! it would be only 'brrooms' my story would if I let
myself be stupefied... but no! oh no!... details! exactitude! I ain't leading you astray with 'brrooms'!..." ( IV, 60).

> *Vrrom! vrromb!*
> You're going to find me monotonous... I'm imitating the
bacchanal for you... what can I do? that's the way it is, that's all...
(IV, 22)

Still, we can sense in the account given in *Féerie pour une
autre fois* an impatience with the clumsiness of words for which the
closest parallel comes in some of the writings of Samuel Beckett. How-

5. *L'Herne*, No 3, p. 152.

ever, whereas Beckett turns his characters' frustration with language to comic account, Céline concentrates instead on the inadequacy with which the effort to use words satisfactorily leaves his storyteller. The latter contrasts himself unfavorably with a friend who has had more success as a writer: "Luis now his malady makes him work... me, mine overwhelms me... I'm left there all dopey... going over the same old stuff... Look at this page!..." He goes on to grumble, "Look here, for example, this book rarely don't come out all wrong!... disastrous!" (IV, 436).

*Féerie pour une autre fois* communicates a paradoxical impression. Words, the medium of exchange in fiction, seem to swamp everything, to submerge the story. The result, in Bettina Knapp's estimation, is that *Féerie I* represents "a turning point for Céline the writer." His prose in this volume "resembles a scatter of pebbles, globs of dirt, and fistfuls of sand being catapulted out of some abyss" (p. 154). The comparison is apt. Knapp goes on to relate the way Céline uses language here to his "living in the dim, fearsome, mysterious world of the autistic, oscillating as it were between the undifferentiated inner world and an equally foggy conscious realm" (p. 156). Such an interpretation, however, limits Louis-Ferdinand Céline's achievement, representing him as hypnotized by his woes and as bereft of critical or esthetic sense. It takes no account of the self-consciousness evidenced in the version of events he has his narrator provide: "The amusing mingles with the tragic... I'm reading my stuff over here, I ain't proud of it... I'm afraid people will get mad as hell!" the storyteller exclaims, bemoaning the fate he foresees for *Normance* (IV, 72).

Offered at the close of the volume, the narrator's own summary of *Féerie I* calls it "a little words, a little music" (III, 556). He talks at this stage of "the 'Digest' style," a form of condensation that he needs to use, so he says, because people have time to read at most thirty pages at a sitting. How could they find time to read a hundred pages, he asks. "But I'm going to put a new value on Art for you. I warned you earlier!" (III, 555).

In a 1947 letter to Hindus, Louis-Ferdinand Céline claimed the transposition of spoken language practiced in his novels to be a spellbinding form of poetry. At the same time he insisted, "you have to choose your subject."[6] Thus a fundamental misapprehension has led many readers of *Féerie I* astray. The subject matter of this volume seems so myopically private and personal as to engender reluctance to

6. *L'Herne*, No 5, p. 73.

acknowledge Céline's esthetic motives in drawing upon his own experience. In all fairness, though, one cannot point accusingly to the shapeless plot of this part of *Féerie pour une autre fois* and of the installment following it without at the same time weighing a statement made by the narrator in *Normance*:

> and so the novels one writes, they begin more or less well, and then they end any way they want to... down to the core.
> Just so long as they find their tone! who cares about what comes after! (IV, 94)

We can only misjudge *Féerie pour une autre fois* if unwilling to evaluate this novel in the light of Céline's statement of esthetic principle in *Bagatelles pour un massacre*, where style is said to be emotion first and last. The narrator's pretension in *Féerie II* to give new value to art deserves to be taken seriously, because it bears out what Céline says in *L'Ecole des cadavres*: "We are in the century of self-complacency. It is appropriate to express our opinions self-complacently" (p. 299). The result, in *Féerie pour une autre fois*, is that history is transformed into apocalypse.

# D'un Château l'autre

AFTER THEIR RETURN from Denmark, Louis-Ferdinand Céline and his wife settled in the small community of Bellevue-Meudon, on the outskirts of Paris. Having survived experiences that would have left another man of his age exhausted, or at all events glad to relapse into the routine of professional practice, Céline, already in his sixties, began work on an avowedly autobiographical book called *D'un Château l'autre* (*Castle to Castle* [1957]).

Reflecting on the mistrust he sensed all around him, the narrator of this new book shares with us his conviction that, so far as his neighbors and patients are concerned, his custom of wearing a suit dating back to the thirties and having neither domestic servant nor automobile, and even carrying out his own garbage do him less harm as a physician than one damning fact: he writes books—"they don't read them, but they know..." (IV, 274). Meanwhile, those who do read his writings seem no less hostile: "If only, look, I could count on the Critics... a mention now and then... even insulting... not of course the whole Mauriac circus!... . . . or Trissotin Tartre... all the survivors of twenty years of bullshit!... no!... a murmur now and again would be enough for me" (IV, 295).

In a 1948 letter to Ernst Bendz, Céline had remarked, "In truth I don't like to write. That game gives me the horrors. I'm a doctor—I have no literary vocation! Writer seems to me a vain title, verbal and ridiculous."[1] Making this statement, he flatly contradicted another, in a letter to Milton Hindus dating from 1947: "no, nothing interferes with my work, no tragedy... even in my cell, I'd tinker with rough drafts—I'll not go so far as immortal lines under the guillotine like Chénier! But everyone does what he can doesn't he?"[2] What was it,

1. *L'Herne*, No 3, p. 120.
2. *L'Herne*, No 5, p. 93. In one of his letters, Céline warned Mahé, "As

though, that kept Louis-Ferdinand Céline writing when so painfully conscious of his unpopularity as a novelist, his reputation overshadowed now by that of men like Jean-Paul Sartre, called Tartre (Tartar) in *D'un Château l'autre?* The text of his novel does offer an explanation for his persistence. However, it is not a totally satisfying explanation, and causes us to wonder about things it leaves unstated.

We are given to understand that, but for financial need, *D'un Château l'autre* would never have come into existence. This is a statement we have heard before—from Céline, if not from his fictional narrators. At the same time we are assured once again, as in *Guignol's band*, that the storyteller is motivated by his sense of obligation to place on record certain things that would be lost forever if he did not speak out. What is new is that in *D'un Château l'autre* Céline apparently intended to discontinue transposing lived experience through fiction, dedicated for now to filling the role of faithful witness to past events in which he had been directly involved: "I can say that I've lots of memories for the life of a seedy guy like me... and not picturesque freebies... memories I've paid for! even paid a horrible high price for..." (IV, 332).

Céline's new book takes up a familiar refrain. "I know what I'm talking about," its narrator affirms more than once (IV, 275; IV, 382). "I'm telling you how things happened, historical!..." (IV, 323), he asserts, stressing later, "I'm telling you exactly" (IV, 427). In part, the importance of these declarations lies in helping bring out the writer's awareness of being engaged in an uphill struggle: "I repeat... I'll never repeat it enough... they pretend not to hear me... just the things that ought to be heard!... and yet I'm dotting the i's... everything!..." (IV, 262). Noting that "there's nobody more deaf than those who don't want to hear," he advises, "don't be afraid to go over things time and time again."

Why, then, write such a book as *D'un Château l'autre?* This question is harder to answer than Céline at first leads us to think, because the true nature of his undertaking in this text is not immediately apparent.

The storyteller in *D'un Château l'autre* announces that he wishes, quite simply, to explain about Sigmaringen, "before the lies get into it... lies and the pox and bed bugs!... gossip by people who never set foot there!... what do you think of that! it's a promise!..." (IV, 324).

---

you grow old you'll see what's left. Nothing at all. Except for the violent passion to perfect, cousin of death." See Mahé, *La Brinquebale avec Céline,* p. 117.

At the same time, he makes quite clear that he regards his goal as possibly unattainable. "All in all and without pretension it's best I tell you just like it was... the public's spitefulness will manage of course to turn everything rotten! subject it to sacrilege!... stuff it with horrible lies!... so that I myself, in everything, in the end, will have the impression of being a funny sort of a show-off!... a kind of ectoplasmic tattle-tale... a ghost who don't know no longer... . . . the words he must say?..." (IV, 388). And so Louis-Ferdinand Céline deliberately introduces an element of doubt into this account of life in and around the Hohenzollern castle of Sigmaringen (ironically called Siegmaringen throughout *D'un Château l'autre*), where for a short time in the forties he and his wife found themselves, among refugee members of Pétain's collaborationist government. The shadow of doubt lengthens. The narrator scrupulously notes that memory is precise, then all of a sudden—because of his age, perhaps ("senility don't excuse everything..." [IV, 277])—has gone. The best one can hope to do in the circumstances is hold to this thought: "One is a memorialist or one ain't!..." (IV, 329).

What kind of a memorialist does Louis-Ferdinand Céline become in his new novel, where he does not bother to put on a disguise, seemingly quite willing to speak to his public without prevarication or subterfuge? Tackling this question, we begin to grasp how difficult it is to identify his real motive in embarking upon the writing of *D'un Château l'autre*.

At first everything looks perfectly straightforward. The novelist of *Casse-pipe* appears to have discarded the convention of the first-person fictional narrator, entrusted with responsibility for offering his viewpoint on life. Céline brings Céline on stage, "slobbering, a has-been, for sure!...," yet at the same time as passionately aggressive as ever: "I hope they die before me! all of them!" (IV, 271). Soon he has painted a portrait the public will recognize without difficulty, taking it without hesitation for his own. He seems, now, firmly committed to speaking in his own name. Quite early on, he even proffers the following apology: "I apologize for speaking so much about myself... I dwell on myself... disappointments?... you have your own! these men of letters are terrible! so afflicted with me-me-ism!..." (IV, 272). All the same, the irony underlying this remark invites caution before the ostentatious display of honesty to which we are treated in *D'un Château l'autre*. As we read on, we are well advised to bear in mind that *Féerie pour une autre fois* has shown one important thing above

all. Louis-Ferdinand Céline did not draw directly upon personal experience in his novels until he had mastered a technique for transposing
reality, even while apparently devoting himself quite simply to recording it with utmost fidelity.

When we open *D'un Château l'autre,* one of the first things we
notice is this. Speaking now with the declared purpose of reliving moments from the past in the interest of historical truth, as a narrator
Céline begins to function just like the fictional storytellers of his
previous novels. This self-styled memorialist handles his material
exactly as Ferdinand did in *Guignol's band* when reporting strange
incidents set against the background of London during the Great War,
or when chronicling in *Normance* an imaginary air raid on Paris, occurring some thirty years later. In his own words, once he has begun
talking about Sigmaringen, "I'm telling you everything here a little
there a little" (IV, 344). As before, in *D'un Château l'autre* the narrative thread is severed time and again, then clumsily knotted once more.
"I'm digressing again... taking you for a walk, I'm going to lose you!...
I want to show you too much at the same time!... I got the excuse of
this... that!... of a certain precipitation!..." (IV, 362). The narrator expresses regret over his "mania for always slipping away... leaving
you stranded!... what am I thinking of?..." (IV, 366). All the same,
he knows he is incorrigible and even seems to derive some satisfaction
from confessing to the fact: "Hey! there! gee-gee! my mare's getting
away!... where am I making you galop to this time?" (IV, 377). Indeed,
he punctiliously brings to our attention certain of his weaknesses as a
teller of tales: "All those little stories... mishaps... had kept me from
going out, from going where I ought to... did you notice?..." (IV, 418).
"I'm late... I'm irritating you maybe?..." (IV, 303). "Oh, you don't ask
so many details of me!... sure!... just let me get back to my story!..."
(IV, 390).

Among the digressions this obviously inept storyteller expects his
readers to find distracting are numerous asides in which he cannot
refrain from complaining about the way he has been treated in the past.
Now and again, the injustice by which he feels victimized causes him
to explode, even though he realizes only too well that "my curses don't
advance my fine book much! the snags I face and my miseries!" (IV,

389). Thus the man speaking to us in *D'un Château l'autre* is no more philosophical about his fate than the one we met earlier in *Féerie I*. On the contrary, confessing openly to feelings of resentment, the former now seems bent on convincing us of his sincerity. From his very first sentence he evidently aims to earn our trust through plain dealing. "To speak frankly, there between us, I'm ending up even worse off than I started..." (IV, 261). On the same page he writes, "I was forgetting you!... I'm a doctor... a medical clientele, between you and me, confidentially, ain't only a matter of knowledge and conscience." Later he remarks, "I tell you so in complete confidence" (IV, 270).

Céline affects a familiar colloquial style in *D'un Château l'autre*. His storyteller uses ungrammatical phrases to leave the impression we are hearing unvarnished truths from the lips of someone talking with so little concern for literary artifice that he does not hesitate to go back over his story to fill in details left out along the way. These stylistic and narrative features present no novelty to readers acquainted with Céline's earlier work. Their function, now, is to help predispose his audience to listen to a man who knows full well that the odds are against his meeting sympathetic response: "Oh whether I answer this! that! it's all the same... I'm not the one they'll believe! . . . total mistrust! . . ." (IV, 274).

*D'un Château l'autre* presents a selfconsciously ill-structured account. The pretense of unstudied narrative flow is maintained throughout. Its narrator often promises along the way to return to tell his readers things that, at the end, he still has not related. Upon the slightest provocation his attention wanders. When this happens, he appears more concerned to highlight the fact than to try remedying matters. "I was supposed to go to Laval's and I brought you to Abetz's... to that dinner... forgive me!... Another little digression... I'm full of digressions... the effect of age?... or the over-flowing wealth of memories?... I hesitate... I'll know later on... the others will know!... oneself, it's difficult to realize!... anyway I'll pick up for you where we left off..." (IV, 436). The book rambles without discernible plan, giving little evidence of being controlled by the narrator's devotion to his declared purpose. As he has done in all his novels from *Mort à crédit* onward, in *D'un Château l'autre* Céline often allows the story to fade from sight, using it simply as the occasion for piling reminiscence upon reminiscence, apparently haphazardly and without predetermined order. Toward the end, his storyteller feels obligated to concede, "I'm taking you away from Siegmaringen... a puzzle, my head is!..." (IV, 429).

Viewed in its entirety, then, *D'un Château l'autre* can scarcely be regarded as the work of a competent memorialist, seriously and persistently dedicated to chronicling a moment of time in the interest of history. Should we infer that its author fell prey to a grandiose delusion and, as a result, failed to achieve his goal? Did he produce, finally, a book quite different from the one he had tried to write? Before being tempted to make deductions of this sort, we must weigh an important piece of evidence. This comes before us in an early section of the book, situated in time at a point in the narrator's life when, practicing medicine in Bellevue, he is about to look back over the years and review the months he spent in Sigmaringen. It is in connection with the incident reported in this section that he makes his assertion, "One is a memorialist or one ain't..."

Taking the storyteller strictly at his word and treating *D'un Château l'autre* as a document of historical value about life in Sigmaringen, we shall be tempted to single out the episode in question as by far the longest digression in these memoirs, and apparently one of the least relevant to the novel's main theme. The narrator offers less an acceptable excuse for this sequence than an open challenge: "don't take offense at me jumping here!... there!... zigzaging and turning back on myself!... that funny story about *La Publique*... would you have gone into it in my place?" (IV, 333).

After administering an injection to a patient, Madame Niçois, the doctor stands at the window of her room looking down at the Seine. His attention is attracted immediately by an old wooden *bateau-mouche,* one of those pleasure boats that run tourists up and down the river. Seeing passengers come and go, he finds he can watch their activity despite the darkness outside. "Not a street lamp!... not a store window!... I've explained... was it me?... a dream?... I've been grossly mistreated!... sure!... I admit... I feel certain shocks deeply... I got an emotive, inner style!... yes!... my privilege!... but hallucinations like these? auditive, alright... maybe?... but visually? literature!... visual ones!" (IV, 320). Admitting he has suffered considerably ("all Europe up my ass"), he confesses to "certain disorders" as proof that he "ain't very certain of really seeing this to-ing and fro-ing on the embankment" (IV, 308).

Going out into the street, he relies on his dog—which never fails to bark at strangers—to let him know whether or not, a "victim of illusion," he is seeing ghosts (IV, 309). The animal does not even growl, although it does sniff at the passers-by. A touch on his arm, and the narrator is face to face with someone he has not seen since he was in Sigmaringen. This is Céline's old companion, the actor Le Vigan. He explains that the *bateau-mouche*, named *La Publique*, is Charon's ferryboat. Why then can the doctor see its passengers? "Oh that's because you're up to seeing us!...," Le Vigan remarks, "special, you know! special!... you wouldn't understand." The storyteller comments dryly, "That's a pretty convenient sort of explanation" (IV, 314). Still, it is one he cannot ignore because of the smell of death on the people he sees going by. The odor he notices, just as his dog does, brings convincing proof of the intrusion of the impossible into everyday reality, in exactly the way it did for Ferdinand in *Guignol's band*. And anyway, we read in *D'un Château l'autre*, "I'm too old and tired to find anything impossible" (IV, 319).

When the narrator tells his wife of his encounter, she is incredulous, being sure Le Vigan is still in Argentina, where he found refuge at the end of the war. Her commonsensical dismissal of the whole incident leaves the doctor confessing to his readers that his trying experiences in Denmark make him "talk bullshit" sometimes (IV, 326). Doing so, he uses the very same verb that Ferdinand used when explaining, in *Guignol's band*, how head wounds sustained during the First World War affected his outlook on the world, so compromising the truth of his account of events witnessed. Moreover, the chill night air along the Seine occasions an attack of malaria and the storyteller comments, "I understand straight off... the attack! it's an attack!... no doubt about it... at the beginning of the attack you know what's happening to you, after, you're delirious..." (IV, 326). When your temperature has risen to a certain level, he points out, "you see everything!..." (IV, 335). The slightest touch of fever interrupts the smooth operation of the head, likened now to a factory. Stressing the inescapable effects of malaria ("you've got it for life")—first the shivers, then "talking bullshit"—Céline's narrator remarks that he was about due for another bout, having had none in twenty years.

Like *Mort à crédit*, written roughly twenty years earlier, *D'un Château l'autre* draws momentum from fever-induced memories. Its narrator observes that his memory is not "moderate" but "agitated." It "moves about" (IV, 334) like the bed on which he lies sweating, yet "writing hard... somehow or other..." (IV, 368). And so *D'un Château l'autre* opens with the same kind of hallucinated, hallucinating prelude as *Mort à crédit,* which similarly purported to re-create past history. Now the storyteller's insistence that he is speaking the truth and his assertion, "I'm not exaggerating anything" have to be weighed against the undeniable effect of "disorders" for which he has this alarming proof: "I'm not very certain of seeing, very clearly, the coming and going on the embankment" (IV, 308). Everything he says thereafter must be evaluated against the background sketched at the beginning of the volume. Here his strange vision presents him with a reminder of Sigmaringen in the person of Le Vigan, and an attack of fever creates the atmosphere in which he will relive the past.

After reading over what he has written so far, at one point the narrator predicts that the public will bear him no grudge, once they know everything. However malaria affects him and colors his account, "I don't want to lead you astray no how..." (IV, 339), he assures us. Now this sounds like a poor excuse for what becomes of history in *D'un Château l'autre,* where the voice we hear admits to trying to attain the goal of speaking true by transcribing the delirium released by fever. In reality, it is no excuse at all, for none is needed in this novel.

The Céline speaking to us from one end of *D'un Château l'autre* to the other is more like a Bardamu or a Ferdinand than he resembles the writer who fled France in 1944. The first-person narrator of this book is a persona, an image Louis-Ferdinand Céline projected of himself to bear witness to events transposed by his alter ego's testimony. Hence Céline, as we meet him here, is as much a fictional character as Ferdinand was in *Mort à crédit.* We seriously underestimate the novelist's intention and accomplishment in failing to recognize *D'un Château l'autre* as fiction more than history. This is no less a work of imagination than *Casse-pipe* or *Féerie pour une autre fois*—a story told by a witness whose recollections at the same time filter events and mask them. The base matter of lived experience has not been simply refined, but actually transmuted: "I'm a little bit of an alchemist, you've no doubt perceived this..." (IV, 342).

One has only to read E. E. Cummings' *The Enormous Room* or

David Rousset's *Les Jours de notre mort* to appreciate that *D'un Château l'autre* does not compare, as a record of the day-to-day miseries of confined existence. Céline makes no attempt to compete with these writers in sobriety and restraint. Rather, his customary use of three dots, liberally sprinkled over each page, suggests that the past was gulped down but not digested before involuntary regurgitation occurred.

Occasionally there are indications in *D'un Château l'autre* that, had he wished to do so, Céline was quite capable of offering a perspective on the past illuminating enough to give his novel real value as an historical document. For instance, he speaks of the Third Reich as having found, for the French refugees in Sigmaringen, "a certain kind of existence, neither absolutely fictitious, nor absolutely real, that without pledging the future, still related to the past... a fictitious status, 'half-quarantine, half-operetta' " (IV, 428). There are enough of these insights to demonstrate that sharing them with his audience was not one of Louis-Ferdinand Céline's major preoccupations when he wrote his book. At no time does his review of past history in this work of fiction probe the psychology of notable figures with whom he had occasion to come into contact or presumably met, as physician attending the French colony in Sigmaringen.[3] And nowhere does it shed light on their conduct or motivation, apparently, except once.

Céline describes Marshal Pétain as setting an example of unruffled bravery that prevented his entourage from panicking. The Marshall was out walking, so *D'un Château l'autre* tells, leading a veritable procession of ministers (following behind, naturally, at a respectful distance) when an R.A.F. bombing raid took place. "I insist," we read, "because on the subject of Pétain people have said he'd become so senile he couldn't hear bombs and sirens no more, that he took the Kraut soldiers for his own Vichy guards... that he took Brinon for the Nuncio... I can restore the truth, I who he detested can say with perfect independence that if he'd not taken command at the bridge, set the procession moving again, no one wouldn't have got away!" (IV, 360). This tribute to the courage of a disgraced old man is in fact no tribute at all, the whole incident being apocryphal. Someone who knew Céline in Sigmaringen (where, of course, the novelist did not neglect to grumble about the effects of trepanation on his physical well-being) has reported, "The town was never bombed,

3. According to Simone Mittre, Dr Louis Destouches volunteered to minister to the sick in Sigmaringen (see her untitled note in *L'Herne*, No 5, p. 283). Mittre paints a picture of pure devotion when reporting on his work as a physician.

but night alerts were frequent."[4] Thus the picture drawn in *D'un Château l'autre* of the whole party, including Pétain himself, urinating as they huddle for safety under a bridge ("I knew all their prostates") has no basis in truth, despite the narrator's earnest assurance, "I remember exactly" (IV, 358).

It is not especially noteworthy that Céline should have invented an air raid, just as he had done before in *Normance*. What is significant is this. In *D'un Château l'autre* he used the invented incident as the occasion for saying something historians and biographers of Pétain must surely find of interest. The hoax is quite elaborate, one of several indications in this novel of the author's comic intent.

It seems inappropriate to look for comic elements in a book such as Céline's fictional storyteller has announced his intention of writing. Their presence in *D'un Château l'autre* would appear unlikely indeed. Early on, though, acknowledging that "nobody won't advance a red cent for a story like *Normance!*" admittedly "a ghastly flop," the narrator draws the conclusion that "the reader wants to laugh and that's all!..." (IV, 292). The stand taken by a publisher inclined to handle his work encourages him in this belief: "Get your drollery back again, Céline!... just write as you speak! what a masterpiece!" (IV, 284). Both this man and a rich friend keep repeating, "How droll you used to be once!" (IV, 271). The publisher urges, "Make us laugh! you used to know how, don't you know any more?" (IV, 269). Presumably acting on this advice, before long the storyteller is speaking to his audience of "working at making you laugh" (IV, 327).

To begin with, emphasis falls on the comic opera aspect of Sigmaringen, with its great Hohenzollern castle: "What a picturesque stay!... you expect the sopranos, the high tenors... for the echoes, the whole forest!... . . . the Black Forest... your floor, the stage, the town, touched up so pretty, pink, green, a bit chocolate box, semi-pistachio, taverns, hotels, shops, ill-proportioned for a 'pro-

4. Abel Bonnard, "A Sigmaringen" (*L'Herne*, No 5, p. 67). In a letter to Hindus, Céline wrote on March 5, 1948, "I never treated Pétain, I never saw him in Sigmaringen—(or anywhere else!)... at Sigmaringen Pétain had no contact with the other French émigrés.... he lived in Sigmaringen Castle—a *recluse—unseen*." *L'Herne*, No 5, p. 106.

ducer'... all in 'Kraut baroque' or 'White Horse Inn' style... You can hear the orchestra already!..." (IV, 336). And what about the castle, rising above the town in "stucco papier mâché"? All this, we are told, would be quite a tourist attraction, transported to the Place Pigalle.

True, we learn that Sigmaringen (a famous spa and tourist haunt, with its place in history) offered no comic opera existence to the eleven hundred forty-two persons said to be dying of hunger on "a stage for the condemned to death" (IV, 337). And it cannot be argued that the novelist declines to take the situation seriously, or is incapable of doing so. All the same, when roughly halfway through his story, the narrator is entitled to say, "and you ain't finished laughing!..." (IV, 343). Attempting to keep the promise implied in these words and confessing, "I ain't yet had no occasion to make you laugh much" (IV, 358), he soon is sharing "a good laugh" with us: the story of Pétain's bravery.

Comedy enters also into what *D'un Château l'autre* has to tell about Pierre Laval. On one occasion Laval has invited the doctor to his suite, where he hopes to obtain from him a supply of cyanide, now that Leclerc's army is dangerously close. In exchange, the narrator asks to be appointed governor of the Saint-Pierre and Miquelon Islands.[5] The only trouble is that Laval " 'embodied' France too much to have time to hear you" (IV, 437). The doctor can count himself fortunate, therefore, that Laval asks the only other person present to make a note of his promise to see the appointment confirmed. Unfortunately, this man, Bichelonne, later dies while undergoing surgery, leaving the storyteller without a witness.

An act of bravery that never took place, a promise to which no one can testify: Céline's contact with the famous yields very little indeed, in *D'un Château l'autre*, on which future historians can lean confidently, especially when they view this novel in the light cast by an observation its narrator makes toward the end: "Instead of working up a fever, of imagining myself Governor of Mont-Valérien... or down there, of Saint-Pierre-Langlade... it would be a bit more serious to ask the mailman really if Madame Niçois had really got back home?..." (IV, 481).

---

5. In 1937 Destouches had served as ship's doctor aboard a vessel bound for Newfoundland. During the voyage he spent time examining old maps, attracted to the tiny French islands of Saint Pierre and Miquelon. See Mahé, *La Brinquebale avec Céline*, p. 172. These same islands will be mentioned again, in *Nord*.

The man so busy assembling his "historical memories" admits to doing so while "wandering in his mind" (IV, 347). Thus in *D'un Château l'autre* Céline denies history its gravity. Generally speaking, the episodes he places on record ridicule historical truth, as passages of the I-know-because-I-was-there variety take from the dignity of history because the witness is patently unreliable. Irony and a sense of amusement, meanwhile, give a distinctly petty cast to events. Céline's detachment and skill at provoking people into displaying foolish vanity and pretentiousness endow this novel with some of the characteristic qualities of farce. "The sense of History slips between your buttocks!...," his storyteller declares (IV, 262).

Amusing effects are sometimes brief glimpses of comedy. For instance, *D'un Château l'autre* evokes the ludicrous spectacle of the official delegation to Bichelonne's funeral, trying to bring back to Sigmaringen the French flag, flying from its long staff in a high wind luckily blowing from east to west. When Céline's aims are to achieve more elaborate results, his technique is equally characteristic.

"I speak to you an enormous amount of the w. c.," the narrator remarks, the very first time he mentions it (IV, 361). Against reason, he assures us gravely that everyone in Sigmaringen necessarily passes through the toilets across the hall from his room, so that the staircase is jammed day and night.

In one way, these toilets resemble the New York public conveniences described in *Voyage au bout de la nuit*. In another, this "shit-house" that "overflowed in waves, cascading right down the stairs!..." (IV, 449) reminds us of the urine-drenched stables in *Casse-pipe*. And the exaggeration the novelist brings to his descriptions in *D'un Château l'autre* put us in mind of Ferdinand's experience of seasickness in *Mort à crédit*. Militiamen were forbidden to enter the bathroom, we learn. "Why?... they used to defecate right in the bathtubs!... and they'd write all over the walls! and in shit! 'all for Adolph'..." (IV, 455).

The laxative effect of the monotonous daily diet was only too evident, it seems: "people went in three... four at a time... men, women... children... any way they could!... they had to be dragged out by the feet, removed by brute force!..." (IV, 361). And so "the most magical moment of the day" came at about eight in the evening when the toilets could take no more and "blew up," a veritable "shit bomb" producing "a geyser right out in the hallway... and our room," a "waterfall down the stairs!... talk about every man for himself!..." Now it was time for Herr Frucht to come ("Herr Frucht died insane later on... later

on..." [IV, 364] ). Threatening to cement the toilets over, he would un-
plug them and replace broken door locks. Two minutes later, the water
closets were blocked again and people once more were fighting in the
hallway.

Whether or not they find the narrator's description of inadequate
toilet facilities as amusing as he anticipates, readers of *D'un Château
l'autre* are sure to be aware of a frenzied note here that affects their
impression of how daily life was for the French exiles in Sigmaringen.
There is no need to dwell on the symbolic value of the plugged toilet
to sense what Céline wished to do. His novel creates a delirious atmosphere as crazily remote from the normal as that of the Touit-Touit
nightclub in *Guignol's band.* The people it brings before us inhabit a
world apart, reduced to the level of perpetual and irresistible preoccupation with bodily functions, and become grotesque caricatures
of the human race.

However much or however little we like the picture of mankind
painted in *D'un Château l'autre* through the microcosmic world of
Sigmaringen, there is no denying one thing. We shall remember this
novel more for its over-burdened water closets than for what it tells
about the lives of Vichy government officials in Germany. This fact is
all the more noticeable because Céline's spokesman makes no secret
of the advantages he enjoyed as a physician: "did *I* know this Hohenzollern town, in all its alleyways, deadends, attics!" (IV, 425). Instead
of turning this advantage to account and trying to share with readers
a faithful impression of how Pétain and his associates spent their time
in Sigmaringen, he lets his attention fasten on oddities no less strange,
sometimes, than those to which *Casse-pipe* introduces its readers. In
*D'un Château l'autre,* Céline appears less interested in the historically
enlightening anecdote than in the curious. He shows us Alphonse de
Chateaubriant dressed up like a character from the film adaptation of
his own novel *Monsieur de Lourdines,* complete with piolet. And when
his storyteller narrates a fight between Chateaubriant and a German
official, Abetz, it is worthy of the scenes of parental rage in *Mort
à crédit.*

Bichelonne is described as "the monster spermatozoon, all head!"
He and another man of similar physique are "monstrous tadpoles" (IV,

441–42). The German guards are "enormous wardrobes with muscles" and have "gorilla foreheads" (IV, 384). In *D'un Château l'autre* caricature distorts people beyond the level of fancy, transporting them to the realm of the grotesque. Yet Céline continues to work within the narrative frame of the chronicle, letting his spokesman report as an eye-witness. "It takes a lot to surprise me but all the same there I have a second look!... on my own palliasse, the one to the right, a man is stretched out, clothes in disarray, unbuttoned, spewing and gasping ... and on top, astride him, a surgeon!... at any rate a man in a white coat getting ready to operate on him forcibly! three, four lancets in his hand!..." (IV, 362). The surgeon turns out to be a madman. Soon after, the narrator records another equally vivid sight. The police bring a large package up the stairs and drop it outside the lavatory. Looking just the way the storyteller remembers seeing Houdini as a child, it is a man wrapped from neck to toe in rope and chains. This is Papillon—special commissioner for the Castle Honor Guard and special attaché to Pétain. He has been captured while trying to escape to Switzerland.

And now another strange figure arrives, "yes, a bishop... I'm not making this up!..." (IV, 401), blessing everyone as he climbs the staircase. The cleric introduces himself as the Cathar bishop of Albi, on his way to request a pass that will enable him to attend a synod at which he will meet two other Cathar bishops, from Albania. His arrival is opportune. It distracts the crowd savagely stripping a young girl outside the doctor's door. She is Clotilde, unmarried daughter of a government employee who has got herself pregnant ("it's difficult in a zoo to get small animals to reproduce, but the lowest of the low, condemned to death, even hunted by Leclerc's Army, even with the woods full of the F.F.I., and the whole R.A.F. over their heads, thundering day and night, don't lose the urge to couple! oh no!..." [IV, 448]). Clotilde has asked the doctor for an abortion, but without success. Now her condition is described as one of "the funny side-effects of great upheavals of History." As such, it is of more interest to Céline, in *D'un Château l'autre*, than the historical upheaval in which he found himself caught, during the mid-forties.

Historians will see less to admire in this book than readers who enjoyed the thumbnail sketches in the opening pages of *Casse-pipe*. Surely, everyone is going to remember Commissaire Papillon's fate as much as the conduct attributed to Pétain in *D'un Château l'autre*. In fact, if we did not know in advance of reading Céline's novel about Sigmaringen the historical importance of one or two persons in it, they would be overshadowed in our memory by others, more peculiar characters caught up in strange situations. Although these people have no place reserved for them in history, they hold the novelist's attention and stimulate him to demonstrate his artistry.

*D'un Château l'autre* does not claim to provide a day-by-day account of existence in the French colony in Sigmaringen. It offers instead a series of vignettes, arranged without perceptible order of appearance or progression. It assembles a succession of unrelated events that its narrator happens to have witnessed. In the main, these come back to him as he lies sick with malaria because, despite the ravages of forgetfulness, their picturesque nature makes them stand out in his memory, highlighted by fever. "Picturesque" is the word this fictional Céline uses to describe one shop in the town of Sigmaringen. It was, he says, the headquarters of a political organization, the P.P.F. In its two windows could be seen people really sick "with hunger, old age and tuberculosis, and with cold... and with cancer too..." (IV, 446). One window has folding chairs, the other deck-chairs. The narrator reports, "I've seen an old P.P.F. grandfather dying for two whole months, with his grandson on his knee... just like that without moving, in a deck-chair, coughing up his lungs..." As we read these lines, we cease to care whether the P.P.F. really existed or whether it was simply a product of Céline's imagination.[6] For as a chronicler, the author of *D'un Château l'autre* is not so much intent on distorting history as he is inclined to let himself be distracted by eye-catching, memorable accessory details.

The individual attempting to perform an operation on a man who does not need one is evidently insane. Although, as a maniac, he is a person who holds our attention only momentarily before slipping out of sight, he is not an entirely exceptional figure. The mob always seen fighting their way up the stairs toward the toilet facilities are transformed by circumstance, becoming no less demented than the jostling crowd to be seen at the railroad station. Like the other Célinian novels since *Mort à crédit*, *D'un Château l'autre* focuses upon moments of crisis that bring men and women to extremes of behavior, to a point where their conduct expresses a common denominator of selfishness and cruelty.

6. The P.P.F. was the Parti Populaire Français founded by Jacques Doriot, one of the people the narrator of *D'un Château l'autre* speaks of meeting in Sigmaringen.

The narrator of *D'un Château l'autre* insists throughout that his account is factual. It is futile, however, to ask whether events recounted in this novel occurred the way they are reported, to wonder whether the storyteller has his facts right.[7] Louis-Ferdinand Céline was not a newspaper man, proud of having a scoop that only an inside witness could present. He was a writer creating fiction out of the raw materials furnished by observation. Hence in *D'un Château l'autre*, as before, his primary concern remained to use fiction as an instrument for casting light on the horror and comedy of life, not just on the details of lived experience. This is not because his own experience failed to yield anything noteworthy. Far from it. The narrator mentions an imaginary writer and says, "I do this on purpose, it pisses him off, I talk to him on purpose about prison cells... he ain't never been in one, by God!... him!... nor Achille!... nor Malraux neither!... nor Mauriac... and the foetus Tartre!..." (IV, 332). How, though, to communicate with others the impression of experiences they never have had? "Months in a hole for you that ain't nothing of course... obviously...  . . . Till you've seen the prison's civilian driver appear framed in the doorway you ain't seen nothing..."

In *D'un Château l'autre* the spatial limits imposed by the confining life led by the French colony in Sigmaringen coincide productively with the temporal limitations set by historical circumstance. What is more, Céline did not have to elaborate upon plot, upon what happened to his characters before their arrival in Sigmaringen or know what will happen to them after their departure from the town. He was free to concentrate on a significant moment of hiatus in their lives. But at the same time, he interspersed passages in which he allowed his storyteller to return to the point in time from which he looked back from Bellevue-Meudon over the past in Germany, or again was reminded of his stay in Denmark.

Thinking of Madame Niçois at one moment distracts Céline's

7. Simone Mittre reports that Dr Destouches and his wife lived in uncomfortable conditions in Sigmaringen, their living quarters being used as his consulting room. Abel Bonnard confirms that at first Destouches's hotel room did serve for consultations, "but I intervened and was able to obtain for him the consulting room of a German doctor who was absent" (*L'Herne*, No 5, p. 67). Lucien Rebatet's version of events runs counter to both Mittre's and Bonnard's: "At the end, in his room at the Löwen Hotel, transformed into an overheated hovel . . . he dealt with a series of specifically Célinesque maladies, an epidemic of scabies, another of militiamen's clap" ("D'un Céline l'autre," *L'Herne*, No 3, p. 51). Like the narrator of *D'un Château l'autre*, each of these witnesses is "telling true" from personal recollection.

narrator. "I lost you...," he notes afterward, "you and the thread!...
let's see! let's see!... we was in Siegmaringen... right across another
memory... there!... another one rises inside me!... another memory!...
of Le Havre this one!..." (IV, 369). Memories compete with one
another for this storyteller's attention, in a way that obviously denies
his involvement in notable historical events the importance a conscientious chronicler would have acknowledged. And so history loses
some of the prestige he claims to grant it.

The haphazard quality of the reminiscences brought together
in *D'un Château l'autre* is in perfect accord, however, with the novelist's disinterest in sustained plot and with his disinclination to impose
an overt interpretive pattern on experience. The shapelessness of this
narrative, repeatedly emphasized in the text itself, is ideally suited to
its author's talent for presenting brief sketches, deftly executed and
unhampered by the obligation to meet requirements set by a broad
narrative design. To the extent that *D'un Château l'autre* communicates
a sense of the meaning of life in our time, it does so by underscoring
the inconsequential, transient features of human existence, subject to
the irresistible ebb and flow of external circumstance, and stripped of
nobility by man's innate tendency to insensitivity, egotism, and cruelty,
upon which as much stress is placed, here, as in Céline's previous works
of fiction.

All in all, though, Louis-Ferdinand Céline demonstrated command of no new skills as a novelist, when composing *D'un Château
l'autre*. This piece of fictionalized experience has nothing to teach
readers about its author's novelistic art that they have not had the opportunity to learn from his earlier writings. *D'un Château l'autre* affords
us the opportunity to watch a craftsman using his techniques confidently and competently within a narrative framework developed in
previous novels. In concept and execution, it is a work of consolidation,
a recapitulative piece of fiction in which the writer reaps the harvest of
earlier experimentation with form and substance. Céline displays too
much energy, too much sensitivity to atmosphere and to the quirks
of human character for us to have reason to accuse him of fatigue. And
yet, considered exclusively on the level of technique, *D'un Château
l'autre* is disappointing. It offers nothing unprecedented in Célinian
fiction. Reading it brings the inescapable impression that, by the time
he came to write this novel, Céline had passed his peak as an innovative novelist. In this sense, *D'un Château l'autre* closes the second
phase in his career as a novelist, terminating the period during which

he boldly challenged the conventions of fiction, disregarding the cost to the reputation *Voyage au bout de la nuit* had earned him.

*D'un Château l'autre* is by no means traditional in form. It certainly has never seemed conventional enough to placate readers puzzled or aggravated by Céline's methods. Still, implementing no exploratory techniques, it suggests that the bold adventurousness of *Guignol's band* and *Féerie pour autre fois* is a thing of the past in his fiction. While, along the curve that plots Céline's evolution as a novelist, *Mort à crédit* marks the transition between the first two phases of his creative activity, *D'un Château l'autre* intervenes between the second and the third.

We can only conjecture about Louis-Ferdinand Céline's motives in drawing back from further experiments with fictional form. Had he lost confidence in himself? The fact that he made no effort to publish the most innovative of all his books—the second volume of *Guignol's band*—lends this question some pertinence, Ducourneau's explanation not being entirely convincing.[8] Céline's unexplained indifference to the publication of *Guignol's band II* looks more like diffidence when we remember how he drove himself to finish *Rigodon,* completed the very day he died.

One thing only is clear. *D'un Château l'autre* was relatively successful when it first appeared. Céline commented soon after, in a letter to Raoul Nordling, consul general of Sweden, "I was counting on seeing myself awarded the two Nobel prizes: the one for peace and the one for literature... the two in one go! think of my mortification!"[9] Are we to take this seriously? Are we to read behind the irony touching this statement a hint of genuine disappointment in a writer who felt victimized by society? Céline's writing methods had not changed by the late fifties. Nor had his ambiguous attitude toward his work, his public, and himself.

8. Ducourneau implies that when Céline abandoned *Guignol's band* without seeking to have it published, he was running true to form. "Céline never went back to writing a book. *Casse-pipe* is a convincing example" (III, 567). McCarthy comments, "In 1945 he began to revise *Le Pont de Londres* and he finished a second draft while he was in solitary confinement. But he lost interest in the escapades of Boro and Cascade [sic] and turned to *Féerie pour une autre fois*" (p. 211).

9. *L'Herne,* No 3, p. 140. Letter dated August 2, 1957.

# PHASE THREE

PHASE THREE

# Nord

T HE RELATIVE POPULARITY of the fictional work Louis-Ferdinand Céline published after *D'un Château l'autre,* called *Nord* (*North* [1960]), is striking and really quite perplexing.

David Hayman takes pleasure in noting *Nord's* "uncluttered plot" and "well-paced narrative" (p. 43). Bettina Knapp remarks, evidently with some sense of relief, that it "has taken on the stature of a structured work, with an outline, organization, and recounting of events along relatively fixed lines, an assertion one can certainly not make when referring to either *Guignol's Band* or *Fairy-Play for Another Time*" (p. 202). This familiar identification of observable structure with fictional stature has done too much to harm Céline's reputation as a novelist to call for further comment at this stage. What matters now is that, toward the end of his career as a fiction writer, Céline appears to some commentators to have reformed sufficiently to earn the praise they consistently denied him during his most productive years. It seems that he was less interested, then, in experimenting with formal incoherence, or—to put it another way—he must have been less subject than previously to a weakness for writing incoherent novels. At best, in fact, he even encouraged some observers to find in *Nord* signs of belated concern for narrative cohesiveness. Thus, Marc Hanrez for one salutes the novel with positive enthusiasm: "Rarely has a storyteller been served by a more effective technique," he asserts. "As for the very texture of the work, one has to go back to *Mort à crédit* to touch a plot as rich in exciting events" (p. 178). Others too interpret *Nord* the same way, as signifying its author's welcome return to the inspirational sources that had nourished his first and second novels. One such observer is Ducourneau, who writes, "Of the three works of his return, *Nord* is undoubtedly the first that links up with the Céline of the thirties. . . . There is continuity once again with the Céline of *Mort à crédit*" (V, 503).

177

Certainly it is true that, from the first page of *Nord*, we hear clear echoes of one of the themes that gave *Mort à crédit* its impetus: "Oh, yes, I say to myself, soon everything'll be over..." (V, 13). One finds here, too, a whole episode in which sex is treated much as it was in Céline's second novel. Moreover, *Nord* may be viewed without distortion as a full-scale development of the scene aboard the *Amiral Bragueton* in *Voyage au bout de la nuit*: "everything," comments the storyteller with unequivocal emphasis, "is farce and hypocrisy as soon as you are like we was, closely watched, gallows-birds, suspect every which way, traitors to France and Germany..." (V, 187).

While Céline never states his reasons for giving his narrators the central position in his later novels, he allows us to infer that their version of his own catastrophic existence represents human fate in our time—the tragic hero having been replaced by the hapless scapegoat. The latter's obligation is plain, he intimates: "Fatigue is a big luxury, very justly punishable, the galley slave who falls asleep, his oar sticks in his belly, knocks all his guts out... serves him right!... once you're hated, eagerly chased after by millions millions of disembowelers, you got only one thing left to do: never sleep again!" (V, 98). And so in *Nord* we hear very distinctly the kind of self-pitying lament that a large section of the reading public found unpalatable in *Féerie pour une autre fois*. At the same time, the narrator harps too on the theme of unjust rejection that underlay the opening pages of *D'un Château l'autre*: "Exact! I was telling you in the last book, once you stand out, it's your neck, the rope!... you only aggravate your case by being picked out as not quite convinced, balking at the knot..." (V, 132). In fact, *Nord* is offered as a continuation of the chronicle begun in *D'un Château l'autre*. "I told you," its narrator points out, "the last book about Sigmaringen, at a given moment, provided all the 'information' re-applies, meshes well, holds together... everything's O. K.!..." (V, 16–17). When an imaginary reader interrupts, just as his counterpart did in *Féerie pour une autre fois* ("You call yourself a chronicler in short?"), the laconic response is predictable: "No more no less!..." This reply fits in perfectly with an aside—its vulgarity characteristic of Céline's writing ("To each his quick-shits epic poem" [V, 19])—delivered by the novelist's irascible alter ego, "the old man tramp in shit" (V, 20).

Not until he wrote *Nord* did Céline really bother to try to explain his ambitions as a writer, stating through his fictional spokesman, "I grant you, everybody can recognize a fever, a cough, a bellyache, big symptoms for the public at large... but only the small signs interest the clinician... I'm getting to the age when without being at all a moralist recalling little dirty tricks, thousands of them, analogous or contradictory, can make me think things over again... in this connection I'm often blamed for dwelling too much on my misfortunes, for making too much of them... . . . sure, I ain't the only one with 'certain troubles'! but what have the others done with their 'certain troubles'? they've used them to blacken me, at least as much as those on the other side!" (V, 84–85).

Even so, "Life's got to go on, even when it ain't no laugh... Oh, to pretend to believe in the future!... True it's a touchy moment, but you know that with confidence, grace, and good humor, you'll see the end to your problems... if you've chosen a course of action, a perilous one for sure, but well in line with the tight thread of History, you'll evidently be pampered..." These words would sound more natural from the lips of a Camus or a Sartre than from Céline's. They are rejected soon enough: "The thread of History?... you're balanced on it now, in the dark all around... you're committed... what if the thread snaps!" (V, 186). This pessimistic outburst brings into sharp focus the essential question Céline had to face in his last years. Why go on writing?

The question was a pressing one for an aging man who had found that legal exoneration had not dispelled doubts and suspicion all around him and that he still attracted hate as much as he had ever done. Why not seek refuge in silence, letting people forget? Apart from vanity, which surely would have made such a course of action abhorrent to Céline, in his case we must take into account the urgent need to testify. Louis-Ferdinand Céline clearly felt he must bear witness to a period of history which circumstances had compelled him to view from an angle he regarded as particularly if painfully enlightening. His continued devotion to his craft shows us that, for this novelist, writing was not the relaxing avocation to which he turned gratefully from his professional responsibilities, but an obligation he felt to be inescapable.

The confidential tone, the horse's mouth authenticity of the narrator's account, in *Nord* as in all the Célinian novels coming before, grant the reader a sense of privilege, even while often eliciting feelings of revulsion. He is dependent on the narrator for all that he grasps of the past. Céline's claustrophobic tales—*Féerie pour une autre fois* marks the logical culmination of his narrative method—let in light upon events from no other source than the storyteller's recollections. This is why Céline's chronicle-novels place more stress on the tone and character of the narrator's testimony than on the incidents related. The novelist selects episodes that most of the time draw attention away from major historical events, so as to depict a microcosmic world of horror, suffering, cruelty, and death.

All in all, the inference critics like Hanrez and Ducourneau invite us to draw from their praise of *Nord* is misleading. Their admiration obviously originates in pleasure at seeing Céline demonstrate some ability to sustain interest in this novel with narrative material they find relatively cohesive, and to offer the sort of fiction they recognize as having been illustrated years before in *Voyage au bout de la nuit* and *Mort à crédit*. Yet one cannot comprehend *Nord*'s themes or come to terms with the techniques employed in their development and still isolate this book from the works of fiction Louis-Ferdinand Céline wrote immediately before it.

None of those who react so positively to *Nord* appear to have noticed that Céline could not have written the book the way he did without taking full advantage of the experiments with narrative form he had conducted since publishing *Mort à crédit*. The fact is, his 1960 novel implemented once again an innovative method that had been greeted, in the past, with comments like André Rousseau's, assessing *Nord*'s immediate predecessor, *D'un Château l'autre*, in *Le Figaro littéraire* on July 6, 1957: "There are literary banquets at which vomit is passed around. Our table is laid." On the technical plane, therefore, Ducourneau's praise of *Nord* actually is distracting: "Comedy and pathos mingle in it; the power of language has never been so strong; situations and men are painted and analyzed with such truth that they find themselves stripped, stylized, rendered in their implacable human naturalness" (V, 503). Such admiration suggests that Céline merits respect for displaying traditional skills in a novel that is far from traditionalist in form.

Lauding the comic and grotesque effects achieved in *Nord* does nothing to alter one important fact. By the time this piece of fiction appeared, Céline had educated his public somewhat; they already knew what to expect of him. Perhaps, then, the best way to explain the success of this work, over *D'un Château l'autre* or *Guignol's band*, might be to say that, writing it, Céline seemed, at first anyway, content to meet his audience at least halfway, to tell his tale, in other words, in a manner he had conditioned many of them to accept, or at all events to tolerate. Although this hypothesis is not altogether convincing, one thing is clear. Most of the time, on the technical level *Nord* presents no greater challenge to experienced readers of Célinian fiction than that of identifying features already made familiar by his previous publications.

This is not to say by any means that *Nord* is a pedestrian work, contrasting unaccountably with the Célinian novels it follows. On the contrary, the really surprising thing is that *Nord* has fared so well with commentators and readers having little sympathy for the experiments with narrative form observable in Céline's earlier publications. The contrast is quite remarkable between Bettina Knapp's approval of *Nord* and her condemnation of the "chaos" of *Guignol's Band I* (p. 133). How different, really, is *Nord* from *Féerie I*, which Knapp sees as "neither a novel, a novelette, an essay, nor a pamphlet," and even more irrational, she argues, than *Guignol's band*: "an outpouring . . . of raw material from the unconscious in the form of fantasies, visions, dreams, obsessions, and revelations, all set down helter-skelter" (p. 147)? The answer is not provided in Knapp's complaint that *Féerie I* is "dull and repetitious" and that *Féerie II* is "painfully dull and routine" (p. 157). Nor does it emerge with any clarity from Hanrez's remarks, bemoaning the absence of temporal and spatial unity in *Féerie I*. For Hanrez is categorical ("no continuity maintained"), as he grumbles that it is hard for the reader to remain interested in *Féerie I* (p. 171). He is even more critical of *Féerie II*, where he finds the narration "especially diarrheal, jerky, hallucinating" (p. 172).

Perhaps, then, it is simply a matter of degree? Yet whatever critics imply, the redeeming features with which *Nord* may be credited have nothing, really, to do with its plot, no less cluttered than *D'un Château l'autre*'s. Nor do they relate to basic narrative structure. As its narrator openly grants, *Nord* is no better constructed than *Guignol's band*, shall we say:

> Yes, I admit it, no order at all!... you'll find your bearings, I hope! I've shown you Sigmaringen, Pétain, de Brinon, Restif... oversights!... heck! Baden-Baden first!... it was only later, much later, that we met the Marshal and the Militia again . . .
> Let me get back to my story... (V, 33).

As is his custom in later years, Céline permits his narrator to offer a running commentary on his story, conducted intermittently yet with the effect of stressing the obvious: that he is telling his tale in a manner less than coherent. Throughout *Nord* authorial interjections have a familiar ring. "But I don't want to lose you again!..." (V, 85); "Oh, pardon me!... let me find you again!" (V, 107). The narrator sounds as though he is muttering to himself and taking the reader into his confidence at the same time: "I got to watch out, not to wander from the point too much, I musn't go lose you, you reader, on the road to Moorsburg" (V, 207). At one moment he wanders off into recollections of wartime Flanders. Too late, he warns himself, "But where am I going to lose you again; enough!... enough!... I won't talk to you about the war" (V, 249). After another digression, he realizes, "I told about that in another book, you'll say... you're getting old, you're going over the same old stuff, so what?... you can't do nothing about it!... . . . I see, I'm leading you on, . . . tough luck!... I'm getting up in years" (V, 206–7). The same excuse returns as a veritable leitmotif running through his text: "Me by the way, I'm going to lose you... my age it goes without saying" (V, 250). Nevertheless, the storyteller acknowledges quite frankly that his excuse does not hold up: "I'm losing you again!... some excuses sure enough, but anyway... losing you is serious!... my last reader maybe?... come!... come!... where was we" (V, 289).

The truth of the matter is that Céline's narrator makes too much of his concern over losing his readers for us to take his fear seriously. He tells us, in fact, "But let me get back to the point! I'm taking you to this party! and I lose myself in philosophies!... you're going to say; he's making fun of the reader!... not at all!" (V, 277). His true motive in putting his story together the way he does becomes clearer when one reads, "There, I'm distracting you, I'm having fun, but we was in Zornhof, late for supper... let me tell you!... we hadn't finished at all!..." (V, 180). Evidently, this is a storyteller who counts on his readers' sharing his fun. "All this to amuse you, little asides... the mere account of our ups and downs may seem monotonous to you... when you've so many things to do or just have to sit down, drink..." (V, 131).

If the digressive interruptions are essential to giving *Nord* the kind of texture we associate with Célinian fiction, the disordered nature of the tale told in this novel is no less characteristic of Céline's work in general. Persistently emphasizing his desire not to lose his reader, its narrator performs his task in a manner that reveals him to be a story-teller basically unrepentant about his incorrigible inability to keep to the point. In this respect, he has not changed from the time when he was recounting his experiences in Sigmaringen.

In disregard of historical sequence, *Nord* relates events that took place before those recorded in *D'un Château l'autre*. On one of its pages we read, "don't be angry with me if I tell you everything in a dis-orderly way... the end before the beginning!... a fine story! the truth alone matters!... you'll find your bearings! I find mine alright! a bit of good will, that's all!..." (V, 18). Not for the first time in Céline's fiction we are dealing with a storyteller who identifies truth with the free flow of reminiscence, unrestrained by the demands of literary artifice: "to draw attention to themselves people invent any-thing at all... you'll say: and what about you, dirty dog? with me it's what's true, exact, nothing gratuitous... and don't forget it!... I minimize rather... the amiable chronicler..." (V, 281). The refrain returns: "me, you know: truth first!... truth is thinking things over... you'll wait a while..." (V, 169). As before, though, the pursuit of truth is complicated by the passage of time. Now, however, stress falls less on the fallibility of memory as such and goes more to the insidious side effects of old age: "present, past! I allow myself everything!... so old, I say to myself: heck! tough luck! I won't always be able to write, what if I do leave something out?..." (V, 230). Rarely, he re-minds us, can people suffering from mental illness say exactly when they became senile. But "me 'Berlin-Anhalt,'" he observes, when de-scribing how, after the attempted assassination of Hitler, he and his wife and cat moved on from Baden-Baden to Berlin.

Anyway, temporal sequence has no meaning in *Nord*. Neither has its concomitant effect in fiction, suspense.[1] Instead, Céline seems bent on achieving results that any reader acquainted with his work knows well. Narrative unity is disrupted to such a point that, like the novels he published before it, *Nord* may be described as orchestrated chaos.

Like his predecessors, the narrator of *Nord* tends to look upon

1. Telling of a train ride taken in the company of two policemen, one French, the other German, the narrator of *Rigodon* writes, "But what awaits us? where are those men taking us? are they real cops?... where will we settle upon arrival... maybe... what are we going to find?... maybe we won't find nobody no more... stop! *suspense* they'd say today... basic-Franco-gibberish..." (V, 404).

a meandering presentation, and even near-incoherence, as a measure of credibility. Speaking of the attempt on Hitler's life, he remarks, "You got no reason to be surprised, reader... at the time of the attempt facts, incidents, mistaken identity was all mixed up, so that even now you find yourself in parallel misunderstandings... contradictory plots... the best thing I believe, imagine a tapestry, top, bottom, across, all subjects at the same time and all sorts of colors... all sorts of patterns!... all topsy turvy!... to claim to present them flat, upright or laid down would be lying... the truth: no order no more in nothing at all from that attempt onward..." (V, 24).

Just as in *Entretiens avec le Professeur Y* (1955) Céline cites contemporary painting, when contending that his innovative fiction is appropriate to our time, so he goes on in *Nord* to remind the reader, through his fictional spokesman, "You look at a modern painting you take a bit more trouble!..." The reader is advised to consider the difficulty of deciphering the narrative text unquestionable proof of its authenticity: "so find it pretty natural that I'm telling you about the Simplon Hotel, Baden-Baden, after the 'Stern,' Sigmaringen... where we went only much later though!... do your best to find your bearings!... time! space! Chronicle, as best I can!... I say!... painters and musicians do what they like!...  . . . me here, historical, I'd not be allowed to sew everything together in a mishmash?" (V, 24).

The rhetorical question at the end of his aggressive statement gives the right cast to references in *Nord* to the work of fiction with which Louis-Ferdinand Céline had most success among critics and the general public alike. An imaginary representative of that audience voices objections only too familiar to Céline in the years since 1932: "If he didn't have his three dots, his style as he says, oh well now people would read him maybe a bit more!... since 'Voyage' he's unreadable!... 'Voyage' and even that! now he's a dummy, he has a look of being, even on television, unwatchable, the proof, Mr Petzareff has just cut, in the nick of time, 'an hour's interview' with him..." (V, 217). Toward the end of the novel, the narrator tells of pausing to take stock:

> There I could see where I stood, almost at page 2,500... at the spot where I had three people dead, three murdered, I must say who can that interest?
> Just then Miss Marie comes to see me, my secretary... I ask her what she thinks...

"Oh you know... your books since *Voyage*..."
"What about *Voyage?*"
"You can't expect much any more..." (V, 285)

If the writer would be well advised to expect but little of his public, it is evident that among the latter are many readers who share Patrick McCarthy's dissatisfaction with the final trilogy of Célinian novels, completed when *Rigodon* followed *Nord*: "To write three long novels about a writer who has less and less to say and a Europe that is going under is a tremendous gamble. It does not entirely work" (p. 313). But their reservations and objections would make little impression on Céline, who in *Rigodon* counters sharp criticism ("He has no syntax, no style! he's not writing anything any more! he no longer dares!") with unflagging asperity: "full of style I am! oh yes!" *Rigodon* takes up one of the noteworthy themes of *Entretiens avec le Professeur Y*, as its narrator declares, "much more, I'll make them all unreadable!... all the others! . . . the epoch is mine! . . . anyone don't imitate me don't exist!... simple!" (V, 447). It is surely naive to interpret Céline's allusion (in other novels, as well as in *Nord*) to the popularity of *Voyage* as sadly nostalgic. It was not regret that prompted him to mention his best-liked work of fiction but the determination to stress that he was no longer interested in approaching life the way he had done when writing his first novel.

In *Nord*, recapitulation of an argument first set forth in *Entretiens avec le Professeur Y* serves to emphasize that disordered presentation reflects authorial intention, not technical inadequacy or an embarrassing decline in mental powers. Here Céline takes care to let his narrator pass judgment on weaknesses in his own version of what has happened. On the plane of realistic fiction, it would have been more convincing to show the storyteller either doing the best he can to conceal such faults or—in some respects, anyway—unaware of their deleterious effect on his tale. Instead, throughout *Nord* we face a flagrant discrepancy, present too in each of Céline's other experimental novels. While the fictional narrator insists that he is speaking the truth, the disjointed character of his account of past events helps readers see the whole story as a fabrication, its purpose and anticipated effect to be measured by standards other than that of fidelity to factual truth.

When telling of his brief stay in Baden-Baden during a journey through Germany that brought him to Sigmaringen eventually and thence to Copenhagen, the narrator of *Nord* forgets at first to mention the town's casino. The reader's attention is held at this point less by the storyteller's forgetfulness than by his reaction, once he realizes he has left out a detail he considers important: "And I don't tell you about the Casino!... an unpardonable omission!..." (V, 17). The exaggeration of the adjective, standing out in a phrase that sounds quaintly literary, functions ironically. For the oversight is soon corrected, and with less interruption of narrative flow than the storyteller's self-condemning exclamation has caused.

The narrator of *Nord* confesses forthrightly to having passed over a detail he judges to be of some importance and he blames himself for his mistake. The air of authenticity with which such signs of honest intent invest his tale is offset by the consequent impression of fragility that his jumbled account of past experiences inevitably communicates. Readers may well regard his version of events as less than satisfactory or even as irritatingly unacceptable. All the same, they have ample opportunity to appreciate how precariously the narrative balances on the storyteller's impaired capacity to recall what he has seen, his willingness to try to remember being weakened by inability to muster his recollections as he would have liked to do. And so when *Nord* is examined after the other novels Céline brought out before it, we notice this important fact. The characteristics that entitle us to treat this sequel to *D'un Château l'autre* as a fabrication—neither unambiguously and impeccably true nor yet willfully falsified—are just as visible in *Féerie pour une autre fois* or *Guignol's band*. It is hard to see how they could help win approval for *Nord* after contributing to the unpopularity of those other novels.

The question of the witness' reliability comes into clear focus once again, as *Nord* opens. Since the start of Céline's career as a writer of fiction, the first-person narrative mode has served one purpose above all in his fictional universe. It conducts the reader into a world that, over the years, has closed in tighter and tighter, viewed increasingly from the narrowing perspective of personal impression culminating before long in private vision. From *Casse-pipe* onward—that is to say, from the moment when Céline began placing his spokesmen in environments more and more remote from the one where he can expect to find his audience—it has been his custom to introduce his storyteller as the public's only guide through a labyrinthine world that sometimes distorts their own quite beyond recognition. The Baden-Baden Casino becomes "an opera, the comic kind...," as the narrator of *Nord* asserts, "you're there... I'm telling you" (V, 18). He describes Baden-Baden the way he remembers it from July of 1944. "You'll tell me I'm inventing... not at all!... a faithful chronicler!... one had to be there of course... the circumstances!" (V, 16).

From the time when Céline first began granting his storytellers a chronicler's rights and privileges, he did so without, for all that, rigorously imposing upon them the full obligations of their role. He made a practice of letting the public hear a man—more speaker than writer, it turned out every time—who suspects very often that no one is listening and who is convinced no one listens to him gladly. Therefore the Célinian chronicler is at once aggressive and defensive in his relations with his audience. And so quite early on an indispensable element underlying the exchange between the teller of tales and those listening to him—trust—becomes an elusive ingredient in the relationship of chronicler and public in Céline's fiction. At moments, *Nord*'s narrator obviously fears trust may have gone for good and all, leaving him with nothing better than faint hope: "just so long as you don't get lost, with my way of going forward too soon... of not knowing no more..." (V, 33). At other times, though, he seems full of confidence, perhaps more sure of himself in fact than he has good reason to be: "no order to my story?... you'll find your bearings alright!... no head nor tail?... man alive!... I left you at the Stern hotel, without giving you the key... I didn't have time..." (V, 20). Now the pendulum swings to the opposite extreme from self-doubt and suspicion of the public at large: "You ain't got no cause to be surprised, reader...," the storyteller assures (V, 24). "I bring you back quick to Baden-Baden! forget the above! beside-the-point commentary! . . . here we are back at the 'Simplon'... remember?" (V, 32).

The pendulum swing between trust and mistrust, between apology and aggressiveness, causes the narrative to oscillate disturbingly, its stability vertiginously threatened. In this regard, *Nord* gives an impression that presents no novelty to anyone picking it up after reading *Normance* or *Le Pont de Londres*. As before, this impression gathers strength from the novelist's customary use of a principal witness (the only witness, in fact) whose testimony does not carry equal weight at all times, because his credibility is indisputably open to question. In *Nord*, as in the past, the significant factor is the same. The narrator's unreliability is not something readers are permitted merely to sense, or to glimpse faintly as an unfortunate and annoying flaw in the novel they have before them. Céline brings it to everyone's attention, without prevarication, as a potent feature of the story, not to be ignored in any balanced assessment of what the narrator has to say and of his way of expressing himself.

Set in perspective by the novels coming before it, *Nord* can be seen to have a title of particular significance. In one sense, of course, it alludes quite simply to the direction in which the storyteller's wanderings took him, on his way north to the sanctuary of Denmark. In another, however, it may be interpreted as meant to bring to mind once again a phrase used in *Guignol's band*—"J'avais perdu le nord!" ("I was out of my head!")—in a passage where one cannot overlook, incidentally, key words like *malade, déconneur, trance, fièvre,* and *délire* (III, 184). The latter interpretation ceases to seem prejudicial when one gives some attention to the tone of the novel as a whole. Without delay, it reaches a pitch of intensity hard to explain, unless taken as a sign that the narrator functions in a state very close to dementia:

> The class of 1912 dates you, that goes without saying... but I'm going to tell you a good thing, from a hundred years B.C. we ought to be!... everything we tell is boring! stage plays, the same yawns! and the movies and T.V.... calamity! what the rabble and the elite want: Circus!... dripping executions, guts all over the arena!... no more silk knee-high stockings, falsies, sights and moustaches, Romeos, Camelias, Cuckolds... no!... some Stalingrad!... tumbrels of severed heads! heroes, penis in mouth! let's have back the guy from the big festivals with his barrow-load of eyes... no more little gilt-edged programs! something serious, blood-red... no more "rehearsed" St Pancras make-believe, no!... the Circus will close all the theatres down... forgotten fashion will be all the rage... three hundred years B.C.! "at last! at last!" the novel, are you kidding! I'm getting a move on!... dress formal? oh no! oh no! "vivisection of the wounded"!... there! so much art, from the so-called masterpiece centuries for nothing! swindles! crimes! (V, 14)

Cruelty, the essential inhumanity of the Roman Circus, is a central theme in *Nord,* where the S.S. doctor, Harras, refers pointedly to those in the stands of the amphitheatre as "voyeurs, all!... depraved" (V, 87), while the fictional Céline responds with a mention of Monluc, whose *Commentaires* were modeled after Julius Caesar's. So as not to bore his public, we are informed, the writer must be a gladiator, "and a gladiator with his belly ripped open!..." (V, 90). And "of course the Roman gladiators detested Rome!..." (V, 104).

Remarks like these do not merely define the subject matter of *Nord*; they clearly establish the narrator's attitude toward his public. *Nord* soon returns to the theme of the *guignol*, we notice: "the moment you are driven out of your four walls you become a plaything... everyone has fun making you afraid, seeing you hoe... everything turns enigma..." (V, 79). The storyteller reports that at one moment he thought everything was a plot and he himself was "the puppet" (I, 181). Looking back to the experiences he, his wife, and their friend Le Vigan had in Germany, he comments, "we became real horrible... three monsters... there's no denying! how did we change into monsters?... . . . in one go... it's since Baden-Baden that I stagger about... it must also be since the 'Simplon' our scared criminal puppet mugs?" (V, 47–48). Before long he is writing, "later with so many others I had a very clear certainty that we was puppets... and I think for life..." (V, 107).

Now the theme of the *guignol* is linked with that of the Roman Circus and its variant, the bullfight, to which readers of Céline were introduced for the first time in *Mort à crédit*: "by the way the worst kind of trick, the one to be feared most: benefactors, the worst sadists... really have a laugh at your contortions... what a sect!... the public at corridas and all the circuses... once you can't 'lodge a complaint' no more you become a 'plaything,' it's only a matter now of making you howl more or less..."

As one would expect of the narrator in a Célinian novel, the storyteller in *Nord* is forever intruding upon the tale he is telling. When, for example, he points out, while speaking of the bombing of Berlin, "I'm sparing you *braooms!* and *vrangs!* I've done enough of those for you" (V, 263), we are reminded of a similar consideration granted readers of *Normance*, though none too soon. Céline continues to imply, as he has done before, that financial need alone has motivated the writing of the fictional chronicle in the reader's hands. For our enlightenment, the narrator of *Nord* daydreams. "I'll go where I'll have to talk, tell, explain least!... terrible, explanations are!... look there now,

I'm explaining to you... I got to!... and a thousand pages more! if I was rich, I wouldn't explain nothing at all to you!... I wouldn't have no contract, no Achille [ = Gallimard, his publisher]... I'd go to the beach, I'd take a vacation... tired, panting... everybody'd be sorry for me..." (V, 259).

This time, though, the storyteller's frequent interruptions stress one thing even more than before: it is to him alone that his audience are indebted for the tale they are hearing, entirely dependent as they are not only on his memory but also on his good will. No one is ever allowed to forget for an instant that "me there telling you the story I could shut up too..." (V, 259).

"Well, now! well now! I'm getting carried away! I'm going to lose you!..." This familiar cry ushers in the following: "as incoherent a prick as so-and-so... or so-and-so!... drunk with words!... where was I, now? You tell me with *Professor* Harras in that big *Reichskammer* park... I'd never have believed it!..." (V, 66). The intimacy Célinian narrators have always made a habit of striking up with their audience has been advanced, in *Nord*, to the stage where the teller of tales is no longer simply taking listeners into his confidence. He goes a step farther when interjecting remarks like, "Evidently even abridging as much as possible, I've asked a lot of you... a reader patient indeed, almost attentive, friend or foe, you're getting close to the thousandth page, you can't take it no more..." (V, 260). In Céline's company we have gone beyond the whimsy of Laurence Sterne, warmly apostrophizing his readers as "good folk." For it is clear that the narrator of *Nord* has estimated many a reader's reaction accurately enough: "you'll say: God is *he* tiring!... he'll never get out of it!..." (V, 216). Yet *Nord* still offers no compromise. Its storyteller does nothing to placate or accommodate the skeptical reader, let alone the hostile one.

Céline's alter ego falls naturally into his customary role of witness–participant, speaking directly to a public whose interest he expects to hold even while he ironically questions the attentiveness with which they listen. However paradoxical this may seem to some people, he remains serenely confident—the adverb is oddly appropriate, even though *Nord* is such a frenzied, disjointed exercise in fiction—that readers will not dispute his right to tell his tale the way he chooses to tell it. Narrative flow is interrupted, for instance, by an interjection beginning, "I'm giving you these details because later on . . . ." Then comes a promise, never to be kept: "I'll tell you about it..." (V, 161). This is not the first time that one of Céline's spokesmen has promised to supply details still not furnished when his story is over. Mostly, though, one can rely on the storyteller in *Nord* to function like Céline's other narrators, as a kind of overseer of the past, playing scenes off one against another, treating the past as a gateway to the present, or to illustrate truths that seem to him immutable and eternal because they sum up his own dreadful experience.

Generally speaking, then, the mode of presentation adopted for *Nord* presents readers who know Céline's earlier fiction with no surprises of any consequence. As before, this novel fosters an impression of immediacy and intimacy. Its central figure assumes and maintains the posture of chronicler who, as a first-hand witness, speaks authoritatively of a past he has known from bitter experience. Thus we are made to feel we are present with the storyteller, as he watches Frau Kretzer's bizarre dance of grief over the death of her two soldier sons, just as we were present during Sosthène de Rodiencourt's tantric dances and watched him direct London traffic, in *Guignol's band*.

All the same, there are curious departures from the narrator's custom of reliving the past so as to give it vitality and added impact. When reporting the insults heaped upon himself and his companions by a raging mob of German prostitutes—"traitors! spies! assholes! thieves"—at the risk of endangering the mood he is working to create, he takes care to point out, "I'm translating approximate for you, but that's the gist of it..." (V, 253). At any moment in his account of what has happened, the present may intrude in this manner, to give a special cast to the past, appearing at times to defeat the purpose we suppose the narrator has set himself.

Actually, Céline makes use of two forms of the present tense in *Nord*. He intersperses here statements set in the narrative present, that is, situated at the point in time from which his narrator (now living at the end of his life, like Céline himself, in Meudon) looks back on past events, which he very frequently records in the historic present. Now a temporal shift produces an overlapping effect, mingling past and present. Recalling having dinner at the Kretzers' home, the storyteller moves without transition from the narrative present to the historic present. And when he employs the latter, he both describes what took place and notes thoughts passing through his mind at the time the scene was being played out: "I tell you: he's getting ready again [to toast Hitler's portrait with the slogan "Strength through joy"]... let's not stay here, people'd say we're responsible!" (V, 269).

There are moments when, reading *Nord*, we are unable to place this or that statement with any assurance as belonging to past time rather than to the narrative present. "It's best I shut up... we'd never be finished with it..." (V, 276), is typical of these. Considered in isolation, the ambiguous notes struck at such times do not seem to call for special attention. Only cumulatively do they bring to our notice a feature of Céline's narrative method that merits examination.

One example will suffice to illustrate the technique under consideration:

> They couldn't understand... I explain to them, the very big drawing room, the one with the store-cupboard, they'll be comfortable!... they won't be alone, *we*'ll sleep in the armchairs, Lili, me, La Vigue... I'll have everything I need to hand... cotton wool, phials, gauze... the fractures, I'll see about them... I couldn't deal with them there... first, so long as they stop shivering!...   . . . we rummage about, don't find nothing... nothing that can be pinched at once, pillows, sheets, blankets!... I've seen at my place Rue Girardon (4), in Saint-Malo, in Sartrouville... you're scarcely out, *psst!* ain't nothing left! disappeared like a rocket!... first clean sweep!... all great national recoveries begin with the theft of bed linen... that very instant!... you'll never find a sheet after!... not after the Convention, nor the White Terror neither, nor after the one in 44... a régime, another one! head on! but the sheets! someone!... I say to Lili...
> "Don't waste your time, . . ." (V, 258)

The opening phrase indicates unequivocally that the function of this paragraph is to recreate a situation summoned up from the past. The first set of three dots brings liveliness to the story, Henceforth, it seems, events are to be reported in the historic present. Marked off by three dots before and after, "I couldn't deal with them there" may be read as either a return to the narrative past tense (faithfully recording an evaluation made at the time) or alternatively as a statement belonging to the narrative present, and hence as an explanation offered retrospectively. Immediately after, the imperious demands of the historic present make themselves felt quite unambiguously. Next, the narrative past tense again dominates for a moment, only to give way once more to the historic present.

Since narrative past and historic present both deal with action confined to past time, there is nothing noteworthy, so far, in the organization of the paragraph—nothing that cannot be explained quite satisfactorily by the colloquial tone that, according to his custom, Céline uses throughout *Nord*. Now, though, comes a sudden and unannounced break with the narrator's recollections of Germany during the mid-forties. Thought association occurring in his mind—that is to say, in the narrative present—leads to mention of three other earlier periods in his life. These are linked in his memory with the names Saint-Malo and Sartrouville (from where, in 1940, Céline had set out with an ambulance along roads blocked with refugees[2]) and with the address where Céline lived in Paris just before his flight from France in 1944 (on a street whose name, reported accurately here, was changed to Gaveneau in *Normance*).

This unbidden interruption, this break in narrative continuity, shatters the framework to which, as an account of events taking place in Germany, *Nord* as a whole belongs. It opens the text to an observation about life deduced from the novelist's own experience, a generalization about human behavior that, extending beyond the chronicle begun with *D'un Château l'autre,* evades even the limits of modern French history represented by the most memorable of the French Revolutionary Assemblies, the Terreur blanche (either the one centered on the year 1795 or the period after the second Restoration [1815]), and Céline's climacteric, the year 1944. It is impossible thereafter to place with any degree of accuracy the disconnected notation "someone," showing where it fits into the jumbled time scheme of the paragraph. Only when the latter finally resumes in the historic present are we sure that the narrator has a firm grasp once again on the thread of his story.

No solid barrier separates past from present in *Nord*. Offered in historical perspective, fictional events based on the novelist's own experiences are not kept apart from present time, the time at which the storyteller assembles his data and places his tale before the reader. Moreover, the past does not break down neatly into segments that can be examined each on its own, independently of the others. For while

2. Recalling in *Rigodon* his trip from Sartrouville by ambulance, the storyteller interjects, "You'll tell me: inventions! not at all!... proof: the kid, the smallest one, I still remember her name: Stéfani!..." (V, 344).

telling what he remembers, Céline's narrator has to bear the full burden of the past. At any moment, therefore, his attempt to focus on one incident, drawn from one period of his life, may be thwarted by another episode, pressing itself associatively upon his attention, by way of memory. And this intrusive episode may present itself from the recollected past or from the present, from the point in time at which he is setting down his chronicle.

Considered by the standard of narrative cohesiveness, the result must seem to be an inexcusably rambling discursive account. In other words, we can speak of the unity of *Nord*, no less than when we examine the Célinian novels coming before it, as resting not so much upon narrative content as upon interrelated emotions, communicating the anguish of the storyteller's experience of living. Thus past and present invade and occupy his thoughts at the same time, on an equal footing, and with equal claim to his attention and to the reader's. And so *Nord* helps complete the portrait of the Célinian narrator sketched in the preceding novels. It shows us a storyteller haunted no less by the present than by the past and hence never able to report either recollected or current experience in a confidently organized manner. In *Nord*, as before, it is a measure of Céline's craftsmanship, not of his failure as a novelist, that this is the case.

# Rigodon

$\mathbf{P}$ UBLISHED POSTHUMOUSLY in 1969, *Rigodon* closes a trilogy begun with *D'un Château l'autre*. It advances Louis-Ferdinand Céline's fictionalized version of his wartime experiences to the point at which *Féerie pour une autre fois* takes over without hiatus. Hence the novelistic transposition of his months of wandering and exile was completed when, a few hours before his death on July 1, 1961, Céline wrote a note to Gaston Gallimard announcing that *Rigodon* was finished.

Possibly because this novel fits so neatly into the pattern imposed on his fiction by Céline's biography, it is not uncommon to hear commentators suggest, as Ducourneau does, that, with his last completed novel behind him, Céline had finished his life's work as a writer.[1] The inference is that, had he survived writing the book he called *Rigodon*, he would have had nothing to offer, any more, through the medium of fiction. There is no firm evidence to substantiate this hypothesis, though. In fact, the thought of Céline in graceful retirement, having run out of material, is not at all persuasive, when we bear in mind that *Rigodon* shows his energy as a writer undiminished at the very end of his life. As for suitable material for novelistic treatment after *Rigodon*, could he not have felt tempted to write a fictional version of a strange incident from his own past? Vacationing on the Isle of Jersey, in 1937, he was suspected of being implicated in a plot to assassinate King George VI. Significantly perhaps, this episode is mentioned in none of his novels. Elaborating upon it would have been consistent with Céline's view of himself as victimized by a stupidly

1. "After *Rigodon*, it is certain that Céline had nothing more to say to humanity. The chronicle comes to an end with the death of the chronicler" (V, 508).

hostile society.[2] Certainly, doing so would have provided him with an ideal opportunity for displaying his special gifts. As he once confided in Robert Poulet, "Here's what one mustn't forget: my *danse macabre* amuses me as an enormous farce, the world is comical, death is comical."[3]

It is quite clear, however, that *Rigodon* does not mark a new departure in technique. In the final analysis, it stands as a summation of its author's experiments with fiction. In content and structure, it suggests that, if Céline had lived to write another novel, he would not have deviated, in doing so, from the path he was still exploring at the time of his death.

All the same, next to the titles of his other fictional works, the title of Céline's final novel does appear recherché, on first contact. The word *rigodon*, we are told, entered French literature under the pen of Mme de Sévigné in 1673. Pedantically retracing its origin and the history of its usage is of little importance, here. What is noteworthy is that, prior to writing his last piece of fiction, Céline had used *rigodon* and its derivatives no less than forty-five times in his novels.[4] More significant still is the fact that the *rigodon*, the rigadoon, is a gay, brisk dance in duple time, for one couple only. We may guess that Céline, who prided himself on the musical quality of his language, named his last completed novel, which bears no dedication, as a tribute to a professional dancer: his wife Lucette (Lili, in his fictional universe), his faithful companion before, during, and after his years of exile, imprisonment and disgrace.[5]

Plainly, Céline chose a title of multiple significance, when bringing his trilogy to a close. *Rigodon* is the name given in French to

2. In *Rigodon* the narrator warns, "notice, I ain't moralizing, it's always the trouble you take that turns against you... you think you've done the right thing, you've damned yourself!... just have a look around, the lowest vulgar charlatans treacherous felons don't have no difficulty at all getting themselves weighed down with gold and honor..." (V, 468).

3. See Poulet, *Entretiens familiers avec L.-F. Céline*, p. 99.

4. Alain Hardy, "Rigodon," *L'Herne*, No 5, p. 209.

5. In connection with the musical quality of Céline's writing, we may note that the storyteller in *Rigodon* announces that, in his chronicle, he wants to sing three or four "soothing notes after the tornado..." (V, 427).

the bull's eye at which soldiers aim during target practice.[6] In the French Army it used to be the custom to signal the number of bull's eyes scored by sounding a bugle or beating a drum. A drum was used similarly as an accompaniment, called *rigodon*, to the ritual of parading offenders before the ranks, prior to their punishment. In the final installment of Céline's trilogy, the narrator will continue to paint himself as a scapegoat, marked for punishment, and drawing fire like the center of a target on a firing range.

Far from being an uncharacteristic token of taste for the esoteric, *Rigodon*'s title signifies that it was its author's intention to continue the story broken off with characteristic abruptness at the end of *Nord*, where we read, "As limited and dense as we are, we could be almost sure to see our executioners pop up from one moment to the next, from the air or from the plain, with really everything needed, baskets, guillotines, bagpipes and a thousand tambourins, to make us dance the rigadoons" (V, 146).

The focus and framework of the story begun back in *D'un Château l'autre* undergo no modification at all in *Rigodon*. The point of view is that of a narrator who now identifies himself openly as "chroniqueur des grands guignols"—still a puppet–chronicler, but one who has been caught up in events that have made existence seem analogous to the kind of spectacle put on at the Parisian theatre of horror and violence, the Grand Guignol.

*D'un Château l'autre* proves it, and both *Nord* and *Rigodon* go on to confirm it: any reader who turns to Céline, hoping for an historically accurate picture of the kind of life led by French political refugees in the nineteen forties, will be profoundly disappointed and even quite confused. From the start of his trilogy Céline laid stress on minor incidents, not on major events. Even so, in *Rigodon* his narrator contends that "a day will come, a communist historian, yellow no doubt, will write a book: the martyrdom of the 'collabos' let's say in a century... I'll have my hour... my 'memoirs' will be on the school curriculum... you have here an unparalleled chance you who are so very fond of the very first thrills with me letting you live through a moment they'll know in a century... you appreciate, I'm sure, born as we was you and me, right in the middle of 'relativity'!" (V, 496). This is a storyteller who stands ready to defend himself against possible criticism: "it's traveling here and there a bit that you're forced to really

6. Cf. *Nord*, where the narrator speaks of Russian markswomen, shooting German officers from high in the trees: "they don't miss! *ptaf!* with one bullet, bull's eye [*rigodon*]!" (V, 118).

watch out, that you let the whole world disappear for a yes or a no, that it's a miracle even to remember, the proof is the trouble I myself have, giving you a little bit of proof, . . . pity the poor chronicler!..." (V, 371).

In the circumstances, it is odd to hear Ducourneau apologizing for *Rigodon*: "Even if the narrator invents or arranges the facts, all through the story runs an Ariadne's thread that lets us sense in a certain manner the real suffering behind the appearance of romance" (V, 508). Why single out *Rigodon* by such excuses, when it is obvious that Céline never failed to make one thing clear in each of his novels— the truth of his spokesman's account of the past is bounded on all sides by the framework of fiction? The narrator of *Rigodon* duly places stress where he believes it should fall: "I know what I'm talking about," he declares twice (V, 488; V, 491); "don't think I don't know what I'm talking about... oh yes I do!... oh yes!..." (V, 490). After telling of a dead shopkeeper found sitting at his till, his intestines spilling out into his lap from a large wound in the abdomen, this man emphasizes, "I'm telling you how it happened" (V, 457). And he remains no less firmly insistent than before: "only I wouldn't want nobody to think this chronicle a tissue of nonsense..." (V, 470).[7]

When the narrator pauses in *Rigodon* to supply details, it is "so you won't think I'm inventing..." (V, 473). It definitely is not, he assures us, "to make you feel sorry for me, I'm just pointing out..." (V, 469).[8] Playing upon his reader's feelings is quite contrary to his purpose. This purpose is to be exact ("I'm telling you exact..." [V, 398]), despite the speed with which he must write: "I'm writing fast for you, like it happened..." (V, 399); "I'm telling you everything quick quick!... for thinking over later on!... . . . I don't know for sure!... you're going to laugh... . . . later on people will know... maybe..." (V, 401). Meanwhile, "I look like I'm repeating myself... but you know I got to... I want to give you an exact idea..." (V, 452). "I'm going to repeat myself a bit, tough luck" (V, 446).

7. This statement reaffirms a declaration made earlier in the novel: "many that boast of having seen German anarchy, they're lying, they wasn't there, *we* was, and not for fun... I seen lots of things but Germany in a nihilist fury you don't never forget..." (V, 372).
8. Cf. "you can imagine, I ain't got no desire at all to make you feel sorry for me... four books already about my misfortunes!" (V, 436).

Because Louis-Ferdinand Céline did not live long enough to review *Rigodon* from end to end, at leisure, some literary critics have made a point of referring to the published version of this novel as no more than a first draft. There can be no doubt that their mistrust of the text brought out by Gallimard some eight years after its author's death owes much to the circumstances of its preparation. The novelist's widow saw fit to entrust the task of deciphering the manuscript to his lawyer, not to someone who had studied her husband's previous fiction thoroughly. Pique has clouded the issue. As a result, many readers who otherwise would have taken the novel at face value have been led to believe that they have before them a text unfaithful, somehow, to its author's intentions.

We can feel certain that, had Céline survived completion of *Rigodon,* he would have made some revisions: his mania for effecting stylistic changes is well documented.[9] We have no proof, however, that the textual revisions he made routinely, once he had come to the end of a novel, ever entailed considerable substantive changes like modification of character or reorientation of plot or editorial cuts. There is nothing to suggest that, when he wrote to tell his publisher *Rigodon* was finished, he meant to report anything other than the completion of his latest novel.

Even supposing, then, that reconsidering its language would have prompted Céline to trim the text of *Rigodon* here and there, we have no grounds for assuming that repetition would have been suppressed everywhere it occurred in his manuscript. Even a cursory examination of the text indicates one thing for sure. Repetition is an essential feature of this work of fiction, one the storyteller neither chooses nor wishes to eliminate. The novelist counted on his public to notice the presence of repetitions in *Rigodon* and had its narrator stress these accordingly. Hence it is perfectly clear that the storyteller does not merely repeat himself in this tale; he repeatedly directs the reader's

9. Speaking of how *Nord* was written, Lucien Rebatet reports, " 'Sick as he was,' Lucette told me, 'and in so much of a hurry to finish his book, he still would struggle for a whole day to find a word, the word he wanted' " ("D'un Céline l'autre," *L'Herne,* No 3, p. 55). Prefacing the Gallimard edition of *Rigodon,* François Gibault mentions two successive versions of the novel, with corrections on almost every line. He comments, "Céline had so much concern for style that he would not leave his sentence alone until he had assured himself that from then on his reader could believe it had not been written, but said... and just once" (p. iii). The text of Céline's last novel warns against "solid 'good sense' " of the kind one can expect from proof readers: "solid 'good sense,' the death of rhythm!..."

attention to the fact that he is repeating himself. Time after time, he
underlines what he is doing with interjections we cannot ignore like,
"at least twenty times I've told you..." (V, 444). And on each occasion he exaggerates the number of times he has repeated the information supplied.[10]

Among the effects Céline evidently had in view when writing his
last novel is one to which he attached comparable importance in his
other fictional writings also. Repetition helps inculcate the impression
that the storyteller is pouring out his memories spontaneously before
us, in an outburst over which literary pretension and narrative art
exercise no control at all. Meant by the narrator of *Rigodon* to impress
us as a sure sign he has not trimmed his account to influence the
reader's interpretation of the facts assembled in his account, repetition
is a technique by which the storyteller tries to set the seal of authenticity on his fictional version of his creator's lived experiences. Talking,
for instance, of abandoned ships left high and dry in a seaport, their
propellers pointing to the sky ("at least twenty times I've told you
this"), the narrator breaks off to say, "I'm going on seventy [Louis-
Ferdinand Céline was just sixty-seven years old when he died], that
I don't run off at the mouth as much as those young dummies is very
extraordinary... especially working, my strenuous way, I can say so,
going over things ten times, twenty times...  . . . if I was absolutely
senile, that'd only be natural..." (V, 444–45).[11]

The chronicler seems to flounder about in *Rigodon*, often losing
his way, apparently, among the ramifications of his own tale, in as-
sociative and digressive asides that impede its clear presentation. His
recurrent cry is, quite understandably, "Well, say where we have got
to?... just let me find you again!..." (V, 497). This is a teller of tales
who seems to lose the thread of his story time after time. All the
same, we notice, he never fails to pick it up again without difficulty,
just as soon as he needs to do so: "I find you where I left you...

10. "At least ten... twenty times I've told you... ," he notes at the
second mention of the platform in a certain railroad station (V, 463).
11. One hypothetical reader's interjection runs, "Sure, he's senile we saw it
in *Paris-Match*! a back number, a back number! he used to wet his pants!" (V,
427). After a digression that disrupts chronology with an allusion to his later
years of imprisonment in Denmark, the narrator avows, "I'm wandering from the
point, I'm going to lose you, but it's instinct because I don't know if I'll ever
finish this book, a very fine one, a chronicle of feats and actions that had some
importance twenty years ago... thirty years ago... but what about the feats
of today then?...  . . . we know a life don't amount to much, especially me my
case when I feel the Fates scratching at my thread."

facing Hamburg... the ruins of it anyway... me too you know I absent myself... just long enough for a little summary, reminder of shadows, aspects . . . an inventory, in short I don't ask you where *you* was... I pick up for you just as it is... I've told you the sea was right close by..." (V, 445).[12] Although punctuated by digressive material, his story retains quite strict narrative unity. The only serious omission in his version of Céline's travels through war-torn Germany into neutral Denmark is the interlude in Sigmaringen, for which readers have only to turn back to *D'un Château l'autre*.

Not until his account of the past has come almost to an end does the narrator of *Rigodon* make it clear that, like his creator, he looks upon digression less as a breach of the storyteller's code than as a productive narrative technique. "I'm getting carried away," he confesses. "I'm forgetting you...," he apparently is quite ready to admit. But no, "not at all!... I'm taking you with me..." (V, 493). We miss something important if we do not realize what lies behind his apparently nervous self-admonition, "come! come! to my duty!... let me tell you the story!... let me not wander from the point..." (V, 496). In meandering, his tale does not lose its point at all; it simply does what he and Céline intend it to do. Along the way, the narrator makes an illuminating reference to his publisher: "my contract with Achille is drawn up different! that I tell you the story and that's all!" (V, 483).[13] Boasting on one occasion of how he displayed presence of mind, he remarks, "you'll say to me: I'd have done as much!... maybe... I'm not judging you! I'm here to tell the story..." (V, 475). Yet this apparently undisciplined, self-indulgent aside reveals plainly that Louis-Ferdinand Céline did not want to use his storyteller merely to retell the tale of his own experiences.

There are a number of inconsistencies, prominently posted by the narrator himself, that show one thing very clearly in *Rigodon*. He regards conventional storytelling as not so much beyond his capabilities as beneath him, unworthy of his talents.

Noting that he has need of memories, the narrator admits quite frankly, "and I can't remember everything... things and people...

12. At another point he remarks, "it don't matter you're waiting for me and instead of chronicling in order, I don't know no more where I'm at... oh yes I do!... we was talking about the coffee [drunk on the Red Cross train en route for Copenhagen]" (V, 485).
13. A hypothetical reader breaks in on the narrator's monolog to exclaim, "Come on Céline!... your readers have something of a right to see *you* too stop playing the clown! . . . your public wants something else!..." (V, 351).

I can't pick my way through them no more..." Some things, he is
ready to grant, he is sure to remember; "the others I'd have to sleep
on they'd come back to me... the proof, bit by bit... after a fashion..."
(V, 447). And yet, he is willing to concede, "I can't allow myself just
anything at all!... respect for the reader if you please! respect, yes,
indeed..." (V, 449). Caught between the danger of not remembering
enough and the temptation to say too much, he is not really contrite
when he observes, "I'm going to lose you!... ah, the exasperating habit
old men have of brightening themselves up with their youth, their
tiniest insignificant things, peeing cockeyed, whooping cough while
nursing, their dirty diapers..." (V, 441). Old age is not an excuse by
any means; it lends weight to an old man's pronouncements: "I mustn't
the state I'm in and at my age, leave nothing out for you... I owe you
an accounting, tough luck if I digress a bit!..." (V, 442).

As early as *Mort à crédit,* fever begins to color the recollections
noted sometimes in garish hues by Céline's fictional spokesmen, more
than one of whom confesses openly—insists on this, to be more accurate—that he is subject to severe mental stress. Quite beyond his
control, the latter leaves its mark on what he remembers and on the
way it is recalled, even when illness does not contribute to distorting
memories. By the time Céline had published *Nord,* it was no longer
possible for any attentive reader of his work to interpret the manifestation of fever at the beginning of a Célinian novel as an incidental
feature of the story. It was perfectly clear that narration and even the
impulse to narrate had become identified in Céline's fiction with the
projection of an hallucinated vision of the world.

In *Rigodon* fever takes a little longer than is usual in Céline's
novels to attack the narrator. But when he falls sick, it is with a familiar
fever-inducing infection, malaria. Referring to paludism, the storyteller
promises to take time later on to discuss its clinical aspects with us.
We really have no need for such a discussion, however. The effects of
malaria upon the way Célinian narrators re-create their past are well
known to their audience. Like the storyteller himself, we are prepared
to see him sink into delirium and to write under its influence.

Feeling an attack coming on, the narrator takes to his bed and waits, though not for long. Soon he sees someone sitting in the corner of his room. This "greenish" person is lit up like a glowworm, just as Mille-Pattes was. It is Vandremer, a doctor whom the storyteller knew once but cannot place—"just imagine, memory in my state of fever . . . I've the right not to be sure..." (V, 343). The narrator acknowledges this "fluorescent" Vandremer to be a "phantom," "anyway a kind of phantom," "a kind of Vandremer" in fact, who "fades away because the dogs are howling...," leaving the storyteller sweating and shivering at the same time (V, 344). His wife comes in to ask if he has been talking with someone. Told that it was Vandremer, she "don't labor the point... she thinks my mind's still wandering..." (V, 345).

When first one notices that the narrative is given impetus, in Célinian novels, by fever-fed hallucination, the permissible conclusion seems to be that the storyteller's physical condition gives special coloration to his story, in a sense excusing its tone by accounting for it. With *Rigodon*, readers finally have to acknowledge that narrative activity can be triggered in Céline's fictional universe by the stimulus memory receives from fever. Now the Célinian narrator takes us into a world that has ceased to be our own or even the one we would have seen had we traveled in his company, perhaps.

A touch of fever, the storyteller supposes, had put him to sleep. Waking up, "I didn't think I was seeing what I could see when I opened my eyes again, there, wide... our train had stopped and there was in front of us a mountain of scrap metal maybe a hundred yards away right in the middle of a field... and right on top, a locomotive perched... upside-down... and not a little one I tell you, a twelve-wheeler!... up in the air upside-down the twelve wheels!... I count them, I count them again..." (V, 430–31). At this point, "Not sure of my head, of my impressions, since I was seeing all queer," Céline's spokesman asked his wife and a companion, Felipe, if he was really seeing the locomotive lying up there, "it must have been an explosion, I'd say a volcanic one" (V, 431). This need to know whether he could trust his eyesight runs counter to his faith in what his eyes show: "Like Saint Thomas I only believe what I see!..."[14] He remains confident that

14. Later he will remind himself of Jesus' injunction: "Vide Thomas! vide latus!" (V, 441). Describing an incident taking place in a railroad tunnel ("the typhoon in the tunnel"), he concedes, "that must have happened to other people... Herz?... Taunus?... I've heard it claimed... but I'm not satisfied with 'it's said that'... if I ever finish this book I promise myself I'll go have a look,

he actually did see the abandoned boats with their propellers pointing
skyward; "as for that locomotive in the clouds?... I wouldn't swear to
it... phantasmagoria? possible! effect of fever..." (V, 441). It is interesting that he still is not convinced, even though Lili and Felipe both
saw the locomotive. The latter becomes his "*idée fixe*" (V, 432) for a
while, as—no more a drinking man than Louis-Ferdinand Céline—he
feels as though he were intoxicated: "I've told you too, fifteen... twenty
times... about that locomotive in the clouds I'm not very sure... fuck
being sure!" (V, 445).

The quite surprising conclusion to which these reflections bring
the storyteller may seem uncharacteristic of Célinian narrators, generally more inclined to fret about the strange sights they have witnessed than to pass over them. The truth of the matter is that fever
is not the only factor influencing the impression of reality set down at
twenty years' distance in Céline's *Rigodon*.

When this novel's narrator argues that, at his age and after
what he has seen, it would be only natural if he should turn out to be
senile, he mentions an incident to which he attaches special importance:
along the way, during his travels through Germany, someone threw a
brick at him, striking him in the head. Subsequently, the storyteller
notes, "I felt, myself, I'd say 'abstract'... the effect not so much of
fatigue, but surely of shock, of the blow from the brick... Felipe
had seen it... also of that loss of blood through the ear... blood still
all over my pants... I wasn't dreaming... dried, I must say" (V,
443). Now comes the unequivocal warning: "From that moment
on, I warn you, my chronicle is a bit chopped up, me here who lived
through what I'm telling you I can hardly make it out..." (V, 423).
He certainly needs the indulgence for which he appeals at this moment
because supposition takes over, now, from statement of fact: "I don't
know, I'm forced to imagine... I don't know no more..."

"Such reminiscences come out of me! full of them!" we read.
The narrator likens himself to an old toad "covering itself with warts
if you just touch it the slightest bit..." (V, 424). Because of the blow

---

see for myself, if they've flattened those hilltops... knocked down those tourist-
attraction ridges... sealed off those entrances... exits..." (V, 377). Mentioning
having traveled for a while in the company of lepers on their way to a colony in
Stettin, he remarks, "In fact we never did see them again, nor heard tell of
them... nor of that leper colony... nor of Stettin... I did ask here... there... so-called
travelers... towns and villages have changed their names, it seems... and the in-
habitants have left... would have to go there... to see... just think of that!" (V, 370).

received to the head—albeit some twenty years before—"I've the right
to a few memories, they come to me like a hair on soup..." (V, 453).
He is less apologetic than assertive when he remarks, "I can't tell you
things in order, here! the brick and my head...  . . . you'll excuse
me!... if you won't excuse me tough luck!" (V, 447). Now the word
*"ravitaillement"* ("you'll excuse me this word means a lot to me"),
diverts his narrative from its course so that it can let in a memory of
another war, of Verdun in October 1914. A similar interruption of
chronology accommodates recollections of the storyteller's stay across
the Channel in Rochester. Now he depicts weekend crowds of British
sailors and a Salvation Army band: "I don't want to give you no commercial for the magic of other times... other ports... let me catch
up with you! all well and good, my head, the blow from the brick,
blood from my ear and so on and so forth... but I can't take every
liberty!... respect for the reader if you please! respect, yes, sure...
all the same I must point out, I *am* taking the liberty, . . . it's absolutely essential for you to be there just a bit, for it not to be just
something out of a dream, those quays in Richmond [a slip for
Rochester], Chatham and Stroude [sic]... anyway you'll do what
you can... with the grace of God!..." (V, 449).

Now Céline's alter ego has an unimpeachable excuse: "you'll
say: he's doing it on purpose... no!... like with the brick... no!... it was
bound to happen, my head!... *prong!* in any case it's ringing!... like a
gong!..." (V, 459). The blow to the head naturally brings up mention
of the narrator's old head wound, dating from the First World War:
"God knows I'm used to it!... whistles... drums... spurts of steam" (V,
425). No objections can carry weight, at this stage: "Well now! if I
proliferate I lose sight of you... oh dear! watch out!... wandering in my
mind?... I warned you, sure enough!... my head!..." (V, 429). The storyteller grumbles about "percussion, hurricanes of mines," and declares
that "no ear can take it, nor the head neither, mine, you can imagine! I
don't want to talk to you about it no more!... nor of the brick" (V,
468). He confesses, "I didn't used to be naturally hare-brained but now
I admit I let things slide... fatigue; that's for sure, you know, and this
accident... I ain't going to speak of the brick... enough said!..." (V,
457). As before, he repeats himself at the very time he is assuring his
readers that he refuses to repeat himself. And in so doing he makes it
clear that he does not feel he needs the forgiveness he repeatedly asks,
for wandering from the point: "I can't stop myself... I got the right!
me too I'm spitting blood, there! dammit!... I got the right, since the
brick!..." (V, 438).

Vociferous about his own, the narrator of *Rigodon* appears to give little or no thought to his public's rights. In fact, the more we read of his story, the more sure we are that it imposes obligations on the reader without granting in return any privileges of note.

To begin with, from the outset Céline's spokesman approaches the task of storytelling in exactly the way he did throughout *D'un Château l'autre* and *Nord.* He addresses himself directly to an audience whose attentiveness he never questions and whose willingness to tolerate a disjointed account of past events is never of concern to him. His way of presenting facts and impressions exceeds the bounds of confidentiality. So, if there is any progress to be noted in the narrative technique applied in *Rigodon,* it is in this direction: the narrator apparently has stopped looking upon his reader as an uncooperative protagonist. He writes, now, with assurance of the reader's complicity, of the public's full cooperation. Moreover, instead of merely working on the tacit assumption that cooperation is guaranteed, he goes about his job in a manner that defies his audience to be uncooperative. In the process, the convention of narrative fiction is subjected to ironic treatment. One short paragraph runs, "Let me tell you about this waiting room, they had set it in order... four armchairs and four stools... that's all..." Evoking the waiting room, the storyteller asks to be allowed to do something he should be doing in any case, without need of permission. And requesting permission takes up almost as much space in his text (almost as much of the reader's time) as the succeeding descriptive details, quite anticlimactic after the paragraph's opening phrase.

Speaking of two forms of intelligence, the narrator of *Rigodon* separates the intelligence of the ant from "the other, inspired, genius, yours, mine" (V, 350). Being a chronicler, he explains, he has to choose to display something other than the merely amusing intelligence of the ant. "I could amuse you again, anyway try to, with my 'Nostradamus,' the yellow army in Brest, the black army at Montparnasse Station, the capitulation of Saint-Denis, but because I'll be seventy when this book comes out, these facts will have been gone over in your usual newspapers, their seamy side photographed by a thousand and one magazines..." (V, 349). The narrator's duty is clear therefore: to testify to what he has seen. And so too is the reader's: "can't you just see the cataclysm?... don't think I'm exaggerating... . . . I got the right to see people a bit fuzzy, I've reached that age, you'll rectify, and that's all! in short you help me..." (V, 456).

Irony touches the relationship Céline's storyteller establishes with his audience in *Rigodon*. "Here we are!... homage to the reader!... a bowl... we find ourselves once again at the very same spot... Harras has just left..." (V, 351). Yet, even though he asks his "honored reader" to forgive him (V, 401), he is less preoccupied with his failings as a teller of tales than with the demands he feels entitled to make on his public. The narrator of Céline's last novel draws his reader into the story more than ever before, denying him indifference or even detachment.

Recalling a bumpy ride in a railroad coach ("you're going to say, that's all he does is catch trains!..." [V, 428]), the storyteller interjects, "about the coach, you'll say that it's taken enough, that it's going to burst apart, open up, fall to bits, that it's ripe..." (V, 374). But this remark is too characteristic of the narrator for us to be misled. Through the reaction ascribed to the reader, Céline projects the very kind of hallucinated impressions upon which he lets his storyteller build his account of past experience: "just imagine if the coaches are having a good time of it, jigging about, the whole train swinging to and fro, the racket, chains and bits of windows, the whole lot in such a roar... ah, the chains snapping, unhooking, scraping along the embankment..." (V, 376). The novelist incites his readers to participate, whether they want to or not. He has his narrator solicit their speculation and interpretation of scenes, has him put into their mouths questions to which the text of *Rigodon*, significantly, often has no answers. And if anyone should object that, despite the narrator's urging to imagine this or that catastrophic situation, it is impossible to do so, the storyteller has an answer all ready: "you been real lucky if that never happened to you..." (V, 465).[15]

When Céline permits the storyteller of *Rigodon* to consult his readers, to appeal to their recollections of earlier stages of his chronicle (*Nord* included), to invite them to be witnesses to past events about which, after all, they know only what the narrator himself has told them, it is with one overriding purpose. He wishes to imprison them within the fictional universe through which his hapless alter ego wanders at the whim of forces to which he must submit, like it or not.

15. He grants that his companions and he were foolish to go to Berlin: "I admit, ridiculous... but, ain't this so, in the circumstances you might have behaved, yourself, even more unfortunately!... telling about it now is alright!... 'we're all pretty clever after the fact' yes by God!..." (V, 403).

In one sense, *Rigodon* subjects the novel, as a contract between author and audience, to hostile treatment. More than ever before in Céline's work it brings stresses and strains to bear both on narrative method and on fictional structure. In another sense, this novelist who holds no convention sacrosanct accepts the logic of his position: he acknowledges none of the conventional obligations to his public, yet writes as though his readers had agreed to surrender all their rights except that of placing themselves entirely in his hands. And so the narrator's self-conscious admission that he has digressed has the effect of stressing that a digression has interrupted narrative flow. "Enough memories," he cries, "straight to what's happening . . . this train was rolling along, pressing on, I was telling you, and . . ." (V, 374). This call to narrative order does not restrain errant memory for even a instant. Before his new paragraph has ended, the storyteller will have had occasion to reach back into the past—to the Passage Choiseul and, earlier still, to Courbevoie—and forward too, beyond the time span of *Rigodon*, to Copenhagen and Meudon, where *Rigodon* is being written.

The narrator has boundless faith in his public's tolerance. Also, he assumes the reader has enough mental resilience to keep up with temporal shifts that occur without warning in *Rigodon*'s re-creation of the past. At one point in their wandering through Germany, when he and his companions (Lili, Le Vigan, and Bébert the cat) are on a train in the company of lepers, the narrator explains that Allied planes always let that train through without bombing it, because its freight is fresh fish. He goes on to comment, "you'll see during the next war, the atomic one, they'll be sending baskets of strawberries, from Finisterre to Svarnopol, and by rocket... I'm joking but not all that much... I was forgetting to tell you about the snow... *now* there was some... . . . I was forgetting the seagulls too!... and yet they ain't left us... just imagine four cars of fish!..." (V, 365).

The presence and ungrudging participation of the reader are implied throughout *Rigodon*, even when they are not openly mentioned or directly solicited: "going forward, I see, there ain't many houses standing... more? less than in Berlin? the same I'd say, but warmer, more in flames... I must say these street of debris... green... pink... red grayer in a different way . . . than in their ordinary state" (V, 418).[16] Reader involvement helps heighten the hallucinating effect.

16. Cf. "I told you: not a habitable house left!... yes!... oh yes!... there! there!... no!... people upright at attention against the walls! there!... we can see them good now... a man!... we stop, we move up close, we touch... it's a soldier!... and another... a whole swarm of them!... backs to the wall, like that... at attention!... dead there, stiff... done in!... we've already seen that in Berlin... in short,

For it is noteworthy that Céline's use of a shifting time scheme in his novel is not meant to afford the narrator an opportunity, at the moment of setting down his memoirs, to correct the distortions and exaggerations of his original impression. Distance does not bring an attempt to reduce distortion but determination to record its effects with maximum fidelity. And in this connection, the blow to the head that the storyteller received in Hanover is of the utmost importance: "I've pointed out to you, since the brick, Hanover, I'd say that I get mixed up I find my bearings, the best I can, out of duty and automatism, in short pretty much like in the war... I mean like in the old war the way they used to have them real at once and not 'by hearsay'... . . . come!... come! let me get a grip on myself, this spasm of laughter you know since that bump on the temple, Hanover... the temple... the brick... I don't want to be absent-minded!... I don't want to laugh no more..." (V, 489).

"Suppose I lead you astray, what will you do?... no question of that!..." (V, 486). The storyteller's reassurance is firm, but hardly effective, when the reader surveys the patchwork of narrative detail, extraneous reminiscence, and hasty correction of errors that only leaves him wondering how many other details have been forgotten or deliberately left out: "I was forgetting to situate the place for you," the narrator confesses at one moment, "I must have lost some pages, I'd written everything down!..." (V, 384). Another time, he remarks, "meanwhile I'm forgetting you!... we was on that platform between dynamos, searchlights, and bric à brac all kinds, but only Lili, me and the kids left, Bébert in his bag... the others had disappeared I told you, La Vigue, Restif, etc.... you drop people, that's life, here... there... I was to lose a lot more still... I'll tell you as we go along... the ups and downs... funny more or less... it takes all sorts to make a world.... and what about a book!... you can think me pretty much of a dumb cluck..." (V, 470-71).

*Rigodon* illustrates forcefully the fundamental irony of Louis-Ferdinand Céline's approach to first-person narrative fiction. This novel epitomizes the kind of self-conscious novel he practiced. It shows how

---

mummified all at once!... . . . I was forgetting a detail for you, now that I can see good, all 'chameleon' camouflaged" (V, 418-19).

deliberate was his manipulation of narrative content, carefully controlled so as to appear quite haphazard and totally out of control. As with his earlier fiction, Céline's audience find that *Rigodon* involves them in a reading experience that offers rewards the very least of which is finding out what happened in the storyteller's past, or what he would like us to believe happened.

Reviewed in chronological order, Céline's novels can be seen to have an increasingly loose temporal structure. In *Nord* and *Rigodon* especially, the Célinian narrator shifts about in time, letting the present of narrative time intrude upon the past. Thus formlessness becomes, in its way, the shape of Céline's fiction, with narrative discursiveness its essential characteristic. Fictional form is so elastic that it can accommodate and assimilate anything and everything the novelist cares to include by way of his narrator's memories and thought associations. In this way, the governing principle according to which the story is rescued from the past is imposed by the mental condition of the storyteller far more than by the events narrated.

At times, then, *Rigodon* reads like extensive notes toward a novel that the storyteller plans to write. Its narrator tells us what he wants to talk about, warning himself in the process against his undeniable weaknesses as a teller of tales, faults he is quite unable to eradicate. This surface impression of ineffectuality conceals the originality of Céline's undertaking. Long before Alain Robbe-Grillet began experimenting with the "self-inventing novel," Louis-Ferdinand Céline had anticipated a line of investigation for fiction that had brought him, by the time of his death, to *Rigodon,* an apparently artless tale that marked his final, logical step in experimenting with the potentialities of novelistic form.

# CONCLUSION

Reading *Entretiens avec le Professeur Y (Interviews with Professor Y)*, published in 1955, confronts us with two very pressing problems. We need to establish what kind of a work this is and to determine how Louis-Ferdinand Céline came to write it.

Early on, the text itself offers a direct answer to the question of motivation that sounds quite plausible. Speaking of the publisher who has put him under contract since his return from Denmark, Céline confides, "Gaston said to me, 'Hurry up! get people to talk about you!...'" and adds, "I'm doing what I can" (III, 371). Now, by way of his habitual complaint that, in this day and age, no writer can make enough money since books can be borrowed and passed from hand to hand, Céline takes up a familiar theme briefly, representing all writers as victims of society. But this is only a prelude to his main topic: that he himself is really the only literary genius, "the only writer of the century! proof of this: no one never spoke about me!... all the others were jealous!... the only inventor of the century! Me! me!... the only man of genius, you could say!" (III, 382). *Entretiens avec le Professeur Y* ascribes to Gaston Gallimard the suggestion that Céline react to his unenviable situation: "I really ought to break the silence, that has done me so much harm! . . . to come out of my unobtrusiveness to have my genius recognized" (III, 352).

Whether Gallimard actually did advise Céline to write something calculated to attract attention and promote sales is not really the point, however. What matters is that bringing out *Entretiens* was a tactical move of real importance to Céline's career as a novelist. Now with the war over, he was back in France, having been granted amnesty in April 1951. He was legally exonerated, but his most recent two-part novel, *Féerie pour une autre fois,* had been less that a popular success and a decided failure with the critics. It was imperative that he define

his outlook as a writer of fiction clearly and positively. The stigma
still disfiguring the man must not be permitted to obscure the virtues
of the writer.

A strong undercurrent that makes itself felt in *Entretiens avec
le Professeur Y* is supplied by the author's firm conviction that the true
artist is not merely neglected or scorned by society but actually considered a menace, and is treated as such. Hence, not content with
ostracizing him, society aims to eliminate him altogether. This idea
surfaces in Céline's text the moment he begins talking of the Impressionist painters: "The public, for its part, has only ever thought to hang
them! the Impressionists! and if Emperor Napoleon hadn't stepped in,
they'd have been done for" (III, 360). This statement carries forward
another, describing the tragic alternative open to the artist: either
execution by hanging or simply not being taken seriously.

Céline reminds his readers at this stage that Robert Denoël, his
first publisher, was assassinated in December of 1945 and that, moreover, the risks run by a writer of quality are multiplied when he happens to be unfortunate enough to bear the name of Louis-Ferdinand
Céline: "how many articles," he notes, "have been passed on to me
in which assassins ate their hearts out for having missed me... by
a minute" (III, 362). When he thinks momentarily—just for a joke,
he stresses—of throwing his annoying interviewer over the parapet of
the Pont des Arts into the Seine ("this bit of fun! you can imagine! I
thought of it for a laugh!" [III, 405] ), the other man has the very same
idea, "and not for the fun of it!" He takes hold of Céline and tries in
earnest to toss him over the parapet.

By the time *Entretiens avec le Professeur Y* came to be written,
Céline had reached the firm conclusion that his role as a strikingly original artist had alienated the public. As he sees himself in this book, he
is rejected by a society that misjudges his genius because no one can
understand it. Society, he states contemptuously, is "sadistic, reaction-
ary, . . . it turns to the false, naturally . . . it loves only the false,"
exclaiming in admiration, "these innovators shit ideas!... what messages!... Just look at them!... they're liberating us! they transcend us!"
(III, 369).

When he set to work on *Entretiens,* it was quite apparent that
Céline had little or no hope or expectation of drawing to himself a
loyal, appreciative following in France, such as Jean-Paul Sartre and
Albert Camus had gained while he was in jail and exile in Scandinavia.
His show of contempt in *Entretiens* for all writers who have a message
to convey (to purvey, he implies) and who command youth's respect

for this reason must be read, partly, as an acknowledgment of the fact. Louis-Ferdinand Céline realized that during the fifties respect of this kind was reserved for others than he. *Entretiens avec le Professeur Y* will end with an admission of concern for these "memoirs in interview fashion." The author will recall, as he brings his book to a close, how much grief Harvey's ten-page memoir on the circulation of the blood caused him and the misfortune that four little words brought down on Galileo's head. He brings his text to a stop with the words, "it's not of so much importance" (III, 411).

As for the other basic question facing us when we open *Entretiens avec le Professeur Y,* a response begins to take shape as soon as we appreciate the following fact. Céline was fully aware that, if he was to win notice from the postwar public, it could only be as a creative writer whose unquestionable artistry kept him pure of the taint of suspect sociopolitical ideas. Still smarting from the failure of his most recent novel, he proceeded to unburden himself of the explanation so many readers had proved unable to deduce for themselves from *Féerie pour une autre fois.*

The circumstances under which *Entretiens avec le Professeur Y* came into existence alert us, naturally, to the self-interest at the origin of this text. Here Céline indulged in veiled attacks on individuals (journalists whom he found guilty of misrepresenting his work and fellow novelists whose success, so much wider than his own, he considered unmerited). He waged war too on those who presumed to arbitrate in matters of taste and quality—the French Academy and the Académie Goncourt notably. At the same time though he responded with a theoretical exposition to the incomprehension that had turned readers away from *Féerie pour une autre fois.* On balance, he gave less emphasis in the end to personalities, facts, or narrative content in fiction than to style—the manner in which he sought to come to terms with life through art.

*Entretiens avec le Professeur Y* occupies, in Céline's work, somewhat the same position as *Comment j'ai écrit certains de mes livres (How I wrote certain of my books)* in Raymond Roussel's. It furnishes the key to its author's creative endeavor. Both writers had firm faith in their own efforts and credited the originality of their creative technique with antagonizing the public, with the neglect that greeted their publications. While Roussel spoke in *Comment j'ai écrit* of his *"procédé,"* his creative process, Céline undertook in *Entretiens* to explain his *"petit truc,"* his "little trick." Roussel had interpreted the public's disinterest as confirming his superiority as an artist of indisputable genius. Céline evidently did the same—or wanted to give this impression, any way, when he claimed in *Entretiens avec le Professeur Y* to be the only genius of the twentieth century. Yet, as his text eloquently bears witness, Céline did not enjoy the placid self-assurance that had led Roussel to plan *Comment j'ai écrit certains de mes livres* as a posthumous work.

Like Raymond Roussel, Louis-Ferdinand Céline was fully aware that he was crying out in a wilderness of indifference and even hostility. His book betrays more irritation, anguish even, than Roussel's. Both writers reserved their confidence for a more remote future than Stendhal had done, with Céline looking for vindication perhaps centuries ahead. In other words, the special difficulty the author of *Entretiens avec le Professeur Y* had to face was his complete lack of faith in those to whom he was obliged to address himself most immediately—his contemporaries. He found the public of his day perfectly willing to admire and adulate writers whose goals inspired him to the deepest contempt. Hence, of necessity it seems, he adopted an adversary posture in *Entretiens,* taking grim pleasure in provoking his audience, instead of attempting to speak persuasively to them.

In the second of no less than seven versions of this very short text (covering seven hundred nine manuscript pages in all[1]), when Professor Y points out maliciously that Aristophanes was punished for writing, Céline ripostes, "Oh, with a few clouts with a stick! but excuse me! did *he* do himself proud! he's still pissing the world off" (III, 576). The same redaction of *Entretiens avec le Professeur Y* ends this way:

> Go prove your good faith! with people the way they are! You'll make yourself even more grotesque!
> I didn't try, I left!... I came home fast to write everything down... Just so there's written proof anyway! (III, 592)

1. The air of incoherence that Céline gave all his novels after *Mort à crédit* should be considered in light of his statement "It takes me two years to get a book done, because I start each sentence ten, twenty times over. . . . It's all measured down to the last millimeter, man!... The only thing is, it's killing me..." See Robert Poulet, *Entretiens familiers avec L.-F. Céline,* p. 5.

The conclusion of this version testifies to Céline's ineradicable mistrust of the people around him. Also it reveals what motivated him as a writer: the abiding belief that committing something to paper enables it to survive, misinterpretation and slander nothwithstanding.

*Entretiens avec le Professeur Y* calls for examination in connection with Céline's fiction for two reasons above all. It sets forth his convictions about style, as they relate to his handling of the novel form, and it presents these in the course of a fictional dialog involving Céline himself and an imaginary interviewer.

Ducourneau sees *Entretiens avec le Professeur Y* as occupying a unique place among Céline's writings: "Here the author puts himself on stage under his own name, he is one of the acknowledged protagonists of this poetic duo and he relates for us, with no dissimulation at all, events from his life" (III, 572). Checking this naive interpretation against the text, we soon find that from time to time Céline dons a mask, making him look rather like the narrator of one of his earlier novels. More precisely, he now sounds just like Ferdinand, for instance. He speaks the same language, affecting the colloquial style, *le parlé*, of which *Entretiens* boasts.

One cannot say for sure that Céline's intention was to show his real face and only his real face in *Entretiens avec le Professeur Y*. He seems, rather, to have been content to hide behind the brutal mask that, over the years, he had fashioned with care and in the end succeeded in persuading a large section of his public to take for his own visage.

In the second manuscript version of *Entretiens* Céline's fictitious interviewer speaks accusingly of "your dear perpeutal 'ego,'" and "your dear center-of-the-world navel," then asks, "are you surprised that people hate you?" (III, 579). In the same redaction Céline remarks pertinently, "I'd be ready to believe, so far as it seems to me, that the François Villon legend: crook, informer, pimp, tough guy... he himself created, out of nothing, to cover up his 'I'... to give his 'I' a ridiculous appearance... curious acrobatics!... 'Look how despicable I am!'... at the very same time he was stuffing them all!... right up the ass!... all triumphant in his 'I' lyricism!... the sly dog!" (III, 580). Nevertheless, at moments Céline gives revealing intimations of past disappointments, through his mockery of the Académie Goncourt, for example. All in all, Louis-Ferdinand Céline attempted to maintain a front of unsentimental disillusionment in *Entretiens avec le Professeur Y*, protecting himself with an irony that served as his chief weapon of defense against a society by which he felt misunderstood, mistreated, and maligned. In so doing, he seems to have been quite prepared to accept the consequences, to see readers refuse to take his ideas seriously and end up looking upon *Entretiens avec le Professeur Y* as at best amusing and at worst a meaningless hoax, unworthy of their attention.

The tone of the imaginary interviews and the way these are conducted are quite bewildering, unless examined against the background of Louis-Ferdinand Céline's dissatisfaction with journalists, his negative attitude toward them, and his conviction that they are not only untrustworthy but congenitally incapable of reporting truthfully or even comprehending what they are told.

On one occasion in 1959, interviewing him for a television program, Louis Pauwels offered Céline what looked like a splendid opportunity. "It is often said that you are not understood properly. Here is a chance to explain yourself better. If you had to define yourself in one sentence, what would you say?" Céline's response to this well-intentioned invitation tells much about his outlook. "Well, it's this, I work and the others do damn all. That's exactly what I think."[2] It does not matter whether this was a considered statement or a spontaneous, irascible outburst of pique, whether or not it exaggerated the speaker's opinion of himself and other writers. The two facts worth noting are these. Céline's remark was characteristic of his usual reaction, when given the chance to comment on his own work and so to lead the public to appreciate its scope and direction better. And, on the occasion in question, his suspicions turned out to be well founded: the organizers of the series for which the interview with Pauwels had been telerecorded banned the Céline segment.

Incidents like this one account for the complaint attributed to Gaston Gallimard at the beginning of *Entretiens avec le Professeur Y:* "You don't play the game!..." (III, 531). Here, we are given to understand, was the point of departure for the text in our hands. "I didn't want to hurt his feelings...," comments Céline, "I set about seeking, posthaste, some aptitude for 'playing the game'!..." (III, 352). The author of *Guignol's band* appears to have come early to the conclusion that he was suited neither to television nor radio. "The little I've looked

2. Cited in André Brissaud, "Voyage au bout de la tendresse," *L'Herne,* No 3, p. 229.

at myself over the years," *Entretiens* tells us, as once again its author assumes the disguise he wore in *Mort à crédit*, "I've always found myself more and more ugly... that was my father's opinion too... he found me hideous... he used to advise me to wear a beard..." Céline now toys with the idea of arranging to be interviewed by Jean Paulhan, but he has to abandon this project because the respected critic and close associate of Gaston Gallimard is about to leave on a cruise. Céline therefore finds himself in a predicament: "I'm labeled 'exhibitionist,' rapist of the French language, bum, and not even a homosexual one, not even a habitual criminal,[3] since 1932!... . . . and since 1932 I've aggravated my case even more, I've become, as well as rapist, traitor, genocide, yetti... the man you mustn't even talk about!..." (III, 362).

From about fifty possible substitutes, all unnamed, Céline finally selects someone to interview him in Paulhan's place. "I found one," he reports, "it was best to do this, totally hostile to me... underhand and mistrustful" (III, 354). This is Professor Y, a man so mistrustful indeed that he refuses outright to meet Céline in the latter's home, insisting on conducting the interviews in a public place. Significantly, the location he chooses is the Square des Arts-et-Métiers, named for Arts and Crafts, Arts and Mysteries.

In *Entretiens avec le Professeur Y* Céline metaphorically descends into the market place, though without showing any sign of expecting to gain many converts or of really swaying public opinion in favor of his writings. He approaches the interviews he is about to grant knowing full well, so it seems, that he cannot count at all on the good will other writers—better respected by society at large, but for whom *he* has no respect—could expect in similar circumstances. He displays wry awareness of being an embarrassing figure:

> "What if we talked about love?"
> "Oh! not so loud! not so loud!... people can hear us!..."
> "Who, people?"
> There wasn't a cat!... close by!... and anyway I wasn't talking so loud! (III, 377)

When, alternatively, Céline offers to sing him a popular song, Y at once threatens to leave. Instead of framing intelligent leading questions, the professor now falls silent. If Céline has cause to regret his

---

3. The allusion, in all likelihood, is to Jean Genet, whose work was gaining popularity during the fifties, in no small measure thanks to the influence of Jean-Paul Sartre.

choice, then, it is only because Y is ridiculously taciturn: "I could have had another churlish lout come if I'd known!... I hadn't no shortage of them!... one who would have grumbled at me a bit... someone hostile absolutely mute like this Y, that's lousy!" (III, 354). Professor Y is the quintessential uncomprehending journalist–critic with whom Céline had to battle all the time. His singular inability to sustain attention and his incapacity to follow an argument are aggravated by a distracting physical disability, the result of a prostate condition.

Céline tries to stimulate the professor to appropriate activity. "How do you expect me to 'play the game,' if you don't ask me a single question? Think of Gaston!" That influential name elicits an echoing mumble from Y who—like every other professor, Céline reports—has a manuscript under consideration by the house of Gallimard. Yet Y's state still seems to border on the cretinous. Céline goes on to make it only too clear that he looks upon this halfwit as representative of his profession. Accordingly, he adjusts his remarks to the man's mental limitations:

"You're going over the same thing, Mr Céline!"
"Oh, not enough! never enough! proof of this is that you ain't understood nothing!... you got to learn everything by heart!... don't try to be smart!... You're a lame-brain!... you ain't understood at all the main point of what I've told you!...  . . . just repeat!... and after me!... emotion is to be found, and with enormous difficulty, only in 'spoken language'... emotion can be captured only in 'spoken language'... and be reproduced through writing only with great effort at the cost of infinite patience, that a prick like you doesn't even suspect!..." (III, 361)

Throughout *Entretiens avec le Professeur Y* Céline deliberately provokes his interviewer, selected, we remember, for his hostility. The novelist agrees to talk to this man, so he says, only to please Gallimard. As their conversation goes on, he repeatedly asks the professor how many pages of notes he has accumulated so far, as though the whole endeavor of explaining the Célinian method were merely a mechanical exercise, to be weighed solely by the number of printed pages it would yield a penny-a-line journalist.

Considering Professor Y's limited intelligence and the kind of relationship Céline establishes with him, one cannot help wondering how serious the novelist really was about explaining his method in *Entretiens*. If he was truly in earnest, then why did he not elect to air his views on style in a real interview with a carefully selected critic (Gallimard's influence would have been most helpful, here) whose respectability and objectivity would have guaranteed unbiased attention from a thoughtful audience? After all, Paulhan would have filled the role of interviewer to perfection, and vacation cruises do not last forever. Characteristically, Louis-Ferdinand Céline preferred to go his own way, dangerous though it was to do so. In *Entretiens avec le Professeur Y* he took the kind of risk that apparently gave spice to his career as a professional writer. The end of the text expresses satisfaction at the thought of "this dirty creature, Professor Y, Colonel! the hate he focused on me!" (III, 410).

Hate placed in Céline's hands a yardstick for measuring gifts so superior, to his mind, that they had brought him nothing but incomprehension and antagonism. A sign of the hostility separating this talented writer from society is Professor Y's alias: Colonel Réséda—Céline's scorn for the military mind has been no secret since *Voyage au bout de la nuit*. Meanwhile, the author interjects in his second manuscript version of *Entretiens*, "Oh, I wasn't taken in... as far as hating me goes, he hated me more and and more!... I could see from his pockmarked mug! That rictus!... that hate bubbling up in him!... that venom!" (III, 577).

*Entretiens avec le Professeur Y* is the natural extension of certain passages in *Féerie pour une autre fois* where the hypothetical reader raises questions and voices objections to the way the narrator goes about telling his story, that is, the way the novelist communicates with his public. Louis-Ferdinand Céline treats the professor-colonel just as the storyteller in *Féerie I* and *II* treats his reader, explaining as simply as he sees fit, though not necessarily as fully as listeners might wish. "I'm trying to get you to understand that the inventor of a new style is only the inventor of a technique! of a little technique!... does that technique hold up? does it not? that's all! that's everything... it's clear!... *my* trick is the *emotive*! does 'rendering emotive' style have any value? does it work?... I say *yes!*" (III, 363). When Y-Réséda, who obviously has something other on his mind than listening carefully, finally goes off on the first of several visits to a nearby public urinal, the novelist comments, "I'm sure he'd not taken nothing in!..." (III, 381).

With all the odds decidedly against success, Céline sets out to describe for Y's benefit the "little trick" that has made him, by his own testimony, the outstanding writer of the twentieth century. As he does so, his text methodically plots the curve of his interviewer's befuddlement. "You understand what I'm explaining to you?" the writer asks, "all I'm explaining to you? the refinement of my invention? the artfulness of the work! why I am the genius of Literature? and the only one, eh?" And the colonel, urine running down his trousers and forming a puddle at his feet, cries, "Yes! yes! yes!" (III, 393). But he is still not fully convinced:

> "The great liberator of style? all the emotion of 'spoken language,' through writing? that's me! no one else! you understand me, Colonel?"
> "Eh? Eh?"
> What a dense creature!

The claim Céline makes about his own worth in *Entretiens avec le Professeur Y* is wildly exaggerated. It is so extravagant that anyone who takes it at face value must be scarcely more deserving of respect, on the intellectual plane, than the professor.[4] Céline makes assertions about his genius to demonstrate that, however inflated his self-congratulatory remarks, he can count on Y to be neither impressed nor truly responsive to them. So the author contends that his "little discovery"—writing "in 'emotive style'"—has put an end to one kind of fiction, just as Manet, with his *Le Déjeuner sur l'herbe*, made it impossible to paint thereafter pictures like Géricault's *Le Radeau de la Méduse*. Moreover, he argues with mock gravity, his method has rendered the cinema obsolete. Does the colonel challenge this nonsense? Not at all. He is too preoccupied with other matters even to pay attention: "He's fiddling with his fly again" (III, 382).

Reasons, even reasons exaggerated for effect, mean nothing to

---

4. The narrator of *Rigodon* reproduces a laudatory text about his work, written by a fictitious reviewer. When another journalist arrives to interview him, Céline's alter ego—confined to his bed by fever—cries, "Unknown person, learn who I am! this epoch is megalomaniac!... I'm the greatest writer in the world! do you agree?" The unidentified man yells his agreement, but the storyteller is not satisfied. "Next to me," he cries, "nothing exists! only charlatans and blunderers... grotesque shitographers, purulent cockroaches!" (V, 346). Soon after, he predicts, "They'll still be talking about me, about my horrible books, when French people won't exist no more..." (V, 350).

Réséda, who personifies the blind hate of which Céline felt himself the unfortunate victim. Asked about the difference between other more popular writers and himself, the novelist categorically states in *Entretiens*, "I've invented a little trick... and them? nothing at all!"[5] His reply sets the colonel astride one of his hobby horses, causing him to retort, "Well *I* can bring you to your senses about your foolish pretensions! you want to know what people think? what everyone thinks?... that you're a sclerous, driveling, embittered pretentious old man, done for!..." (III, 368). Giving voice to the acrimonious feelings that Céline's writings have attracted over the years, Réséda dubs him "cantankerous" and "a washout" (III, 370). This hostile informant offers to tell the author of *Mort à crédit* what everyone thinks of him: "The worst Tartuffe in French Literature! so there!" (III, 371).

Céline's purpose is now clear. Bringing a hostile witness to the stand and allowing him complete liberty to malign the accused, he shows how his own achievement as a writer has isolated him from a public so prejudiced they have become quite incapable of understanding his motives or his methods. "Well," says Réséda in the second manuscript of *Entretiens avec le Professeur Y*, "I'm going to tell you what I think of your 'emotive'! of your novels and of yourself! you are worse than all the others!" (III, 578). Réséda's condemnation perfectly balances Céline's self-praise.

One of this interviewer's most serious objections is that he finds Céline's first-person approach to fiction quite offensive. In the second redaction of *Entretiens* he states his opinion in no uncertain terms: "You are vain as a peacock" (III, 575). On this score, however, Céline feels himself above reproach, victimized by a fundamental misapprehension. This is why he delivers a statement that challenges so many of his readers to review their smugly confident evaluation of his early novels as autobiographical studies:

> "Oh! Colonel! oh! colonel!... *I* am modesty itself! my 'I' don't go too far at all! I present it only with care!... immense prudence... I always cover it all over with shit! . . . the law of the genre! no lyricism without 'I,' Colonel. Write that down, please, Colonel! the Law of Lyricism!
> "One hell of a law!"
> "You said it." (III, 374)

5. The only writers whose efforts to model written language on spoken language Céline was willing to acknowledge, in his correspondence, are Barbusse in *Le Feu*, Morand in *Ouvert la nuit*, and Ramuz "a bit."

In other words, as Céline puts it in the second version of his text, "*You,*
Professor Y, I'm going to set you straight once and for all!... the
opinions of men don't count!...  . . . It's the thing itself that counts:
the object! it succeeds or it doesn't!... fuck the rest!..." (III, 575). In
the published version, he expresses himself with more restraint: "to
capture the emotion of 'spoken language' through writing! that's not
nothing at all! it's tiny but it's something" (III, 357).

Louis-Ferdinand Céline was well aware that a writer like himself is seriously handicapped in present-day society. The mass of the
reading public, "70... 80 percent of a normal population," he declares in *Entretiens avec le Professeur Y,* have no time for "lyrical
authors and I am one" (III, 358). More than this, "Lyricism kills the
writer, through his nerves; through his arteries, and through the
hostility of everybody" (III, 359). So *Entretiens* shows Céline to have
been keenly conscious of the high price paid for his distinctive brand
of lyricism. He notes that "the 'I' don't spare the man! especially the
funnily lyrical" (III, 374).

Even though referring to it with a show of casualness as "a little
trick," Céline does not want his technique underestimated. Applying
his method has cost him altogether too much, we discover when we
turn to the second version of the *Entretiens* manuscript. Here stress is
given "le lyrique drôle," more than in the definitive text:

> "Pornography is a mania, a masturbation, a hate like slang, a
> process! lyricism is something different again!... I am lyrical, colonel,
> lyrical born!"
> "And an inventor!"
> "Exactly!"
> "And comic!"
> "That's my humble defect! they'd forgive me for being
> lyrical... maybe... they'd maybe forgive me for being an inventor...
> comic? all's lost!... that's the unforgivable thing, comic lyricism!"
> (III, 579)

When Céline has enlightened Y about the purpose of their
meeting, the professor's first positive reaction is to propose "a little

philosophical debate." This suggestion meets a chilly reception. "Ah, Professor Y, I'm willing to respect you and all... but I do declare: I'm hostile!... *I* ain't got no ideas! not a one! and I find nothing more vulgar, more common, more disgusting than ideas! . . . the impotent are bursting with ideas!... and the philosophers!... ideas, that's their industry!... they hustle the young with them! they pimp on the young!... the young are ready you know to swallow anything..." (III, 355). This is to say that Céline counts on being remembered not as a thinker but as "a little inventor." He insists, "*I* don't send no messages out into the world! no sir! *I* don't congest the Ether with my thoughts! no sir! I don't get drunk on words, nor on port, nor on flattery of the young!... I don't cogitate for the planet! . . . I know my tiny importance! but anything rather than *ideahs*!... I leave *ideahs* to Cheap Jacks! all *ideahs*! to pimps, to confusionists!..." (III, 356).

The professor laughs derisively at all this. He obviously is unaware of hearing at this point something fully consistent with Céline's approach to fiction. For such ideas as emerge in Célinian novels, even as early as *Voyage au bout de la nuit,* are not borrowed from a homogeneous pattern of thought or belief. They reflect a visceral reaction to living, the activity of what Céline calls, in *Entretiens,* his nerves. Indeed, as he presents his case in this text, being a lyrical writer such as he does not mean coming before the public in this guise or that, but rather with "nerves all raw!... yours!... not other people's nerves!... oh dear no! really yours!..." (III, 375).

Because he is fully alert to the danger implicit in his concept of the novel, Louis-Ferdinand Céline reacts sharply, in one manuscript version of his *Entretiens,* to the unfair accusation that he was no more than an egocentric writer. The published text takes up the same irate protest. Here Céline shows how he believes he has broken out of the narrow confines we have just heard him mark out for his work. "The reader who reads me! it seems to him, he'd swear to it, that someone is reading to him in his head!... in the privacy of his nerves! right in his nervous system! in his own head!" When his interviewer now admits grudgingly, "Well, that's something!...," Céline answers with an unwonted display of excitement, "You can say that again! that's something, Colonel! you can say that again! someone playing as he likes for him on the harp of his own nerves!" (III, 397).

Not long after *Entretiens avec le Professeur Y* appeared in print, Céline returned in a 1954 interview granted André Brissaud, who was preparing an edition of *Voyage au bout de la nuit,* to stress some of the underlying principles of his work already cited in imaginary conversation with Y. "I'm not a writer, you know, one of those who hustle the young, bursting with ideas, who synthesize, who have ideahs! I'm only a little inventor, a little inventor, that's right! and only of a little trick, just a little trick... . . . I've invented emotion in written language." In one way, Céline's persistence in emphasizing the same motive yet again speaks for itself, demonstrating how much importance he attached to being a stylistic innovator. In another way, too, it is just as significant, considered next to the professor–colonel's inability to follow Céline's explanation in *Entretiens*.

Y cannot keep up with Céline's effort to clarify his working method by use of the image of playing on the reader's nerves as on a harp. Hence the novelist tries out another analogy:

> "You plunge a stick into water..."
> "A stick into water?"
> "Yes, Colonel!..."
> "What does it look like, your stick?"
> "I don't know..."
> "It looks broken, your stick does! twisted!"
> "So what? so what?"
> "Break it yourself by God before plunging it into the water! a good joke! the whole secret of Impressionism!"
> "So what?"
> "So you'll correct the effect!"
> "What effect?"
> "Of refraction! it will look straight, your stick will!" (III, 398)

Y's failure to grasp what Céline is saying brings to mind the obtuseness displayed (or feigned) by another professor, Hindus,[6] to whom Céline had proposed the very same analogy in one of his 1947 letters: "On the subject of style and the stick—it seems to me I've not yet explained myself very clearly—It's the 'nerve deep,' the spontaneous melody, the music of the soul that I try to capture in spoken language

---

6. There can be no doubt that the unintelligent Professor Y owes much to the opinion Céline and his friends formed of Milton Hindus, after the appearance of his book *The Crippled Giant*, a veritable act of betrayal and self-advertisement, in their estimation.

and to introduce into writing[7] . . . To achieve this, I go, by means of a trick, into the very soul of spoken language, by burglarizing, so to speak, I steal its secret."[8]

As they appear in *Entretiens avec le Professeur Y*, Céline's comments on style set the dominant principle of transposition on a broader basis than before. They show transposition encompassing, now, not merely the process by which historical event is reborn as fictional incident, but also the manner in which incident is recorded, is transmitted through colloquial language. Thus the analogy of the stick that must be broken, if the effect of refraction is to be counteracted, relates closely to the novelist's remarks about Impressionism. The latter, *Entretiens* bids us notice, did not attempt to compete with photography. After all, Céline points out, "the photo ain't emotive... never!... it's frozen, it's frigid..." (III, 360). In the case of the Impressionist painters, he argues, the "little trick" was not communicating the vaunted "open air" quality for which Impressionism is widely admired, but " 'rendering' the open air." The Impressionists' version of the open air is therefore, in his estimation, the equivalent of the "spoken language" quality of his own writings.

The artist's aim must not be simply to reproduce with the greatest possible fidelity. This is why, in the middle of *Entretiens*, Céline takes time to reject the use of mechanical means like the dictaphone for recording whatever he has to say: "all that machinery," he declares, "kills life!" (III, 384). Céline apparently believed it impeded attainment of his ultimate goal: "*The emotion of spoken language through writing!*" (III, 357). The artist's aim must be to render, not simply to transcribe. If he is an artist with words, then he has to try to capture emotion, not so much through spoken language itself as through "memory of spoken language! and at the cost of infinite patience! of very tiny re-transcriptions!..." (III, 359). Evidently, this

---

7. Cf. the following statement in a 1948 letter to Ernst Bendz, dated "the 22": "Nature has endowed me with a certain sense of rhythm, with a pseudo-musical imagination." *L'Herne*, No 3, p. 120.

8. Letter to Hindus, dated October 17 (1947), in *L'Herne*, No 5, p. 99. In another letter to the same correspondent, dated "the 22nd" (of June 1947), Céline confided, "I have little interest in men in their opinions none at all even... . . . the thing itself... almost always the contrary of what they say that's where I find my music... in their being... but in spite of them and not from the angle they present to me I rape them... very sweetly of course but pitilessly..." *L'Herne*, No 5, p. 83.

is his reason for assuring Professor Y that a book written entirely in slang would be boring, "Because the reader is depraved! he wants slang always stronger still! where would you find it for him?" (III, 376).

The main themes of *Entretiens avec le Professeur Y* become unified when Céline proposes one last major image: "No dialectic! it was in the subway that this came to me! there's no dialectic in the subway!" (III, 362). At his prompting, Réséda finally asks a pertinent question: "How did you get the idea for your so-called new style?" The response: "Through the subway!... through the subway, Colonel!" (III, 380–81). Even if Réséda had not been compelled at this very moment to make yet another visit to the urinal, it is unlikely he would have found Céline's laconic remark very enlightening. And when the novelist develops his explanation more fully, it surely must leave his half-witted interviewer confused: "*I* capture all emotion!... all emotion in the surface! all at one time!... I decide!... I cram it all in the subway!... my subway!..." (III, 384).

The laconic has given way to the cryptic, because Céline now is talking of his genius, revealed to him, so he informs Réséda, in the Pigalle station of the North–South line of the Paris subway system:

> I lead all my people on the subway, . . . and I step on the pedal with them; I take everybody with me!... nilly-nilly!... with me!... the emotive subway, without all the inconveniences, the traffic tie-ups! in a dream!... never the briefest stops any place! no! to the end of the line! nonstop! into emotion!... by emotion! nothing but the end of the line: right into emotion... from beginning to end!"
> "What?... What?"
> "Thanks to my shaped rails! my shaped style!" (III, 389)

The colonel cries, "Yes!... yes!..." but does he understand what Céline is saying?

According to Louis-Ferdinand Céline, earnest fidelity to the reality principle, to mechanically recorded colloquial language, leads to something far worse than a disappointing dead end. It actually threatens the writer with disaster. Alluding to the danger, while developing his subway image, he informs Réséda that genius means "not running off the rails" (III, 397). This definition leads him to emphasize two important factors. First, he responds vigorously to one of the colonel's objections ("In place of those three dots you could after all put words, that's my opinion!"), indicating that, in his private subway, the three dots serve the same purpose as railroad ties. Then he points out, too, that the rails laid on those ties are of a particular kind, "Quite special rails that look perfectly straight and ain't!..." (III, 397). These are, in fact, "rendered emotive" rails that seem to be absolutely straight while not being so at all (III, 393). By bending the rails, Céline tries to make sure the subway train he sets on them will never run off the track. "I warp them in a certain way, so the passengers are in a dream... So they don't realize... the charm, the magic, Colonel! the violence too!... I admit it!... all the passengers loaded, shut in, locked up!... All in my emotive train!... No fuss or bother! no question of them getting out!... no! no!" (III, 389).

This image of the subway is meant to emphasize that Céline leaves "nothing on the Surface!... everything in my magic transport" (III, 390). In his analogy, the surface stands for cinematic realism and also for psychology, philosophy, and "photographic horror." He tries to make all this clear, but without success where Y is concerned. "He ain't listening to me" (III, 391). Eventually though the professor does seem to have heard something. This representative of a group whose members have not stopped short, sometimes, of accusing Céline of insanity is driven out of his mind by the explanations offered him. He jumps out of a taxi in which he and Céline are driving back to Gallimard's office and tries to throw himself into the fountain on the Place du Châtelet. The unsympathetic reaction of critics and journalists to the novelist's "dangerous" work is dramatized, as contact with the theories underlying it renders the colonel homicidal.

The effect conversing with Céline has on Réséda highlights the problem facing Céline in *Entretiens avec le Professur Y*. It shows how difficult he found the task of making the public comprehend the originality of his approach, when current taste and fashion directed their attention toward the novel of ideas, objectively presented.

A text ostensibly written to make its author's position clear,

*Entretiens avec le Professeur Y* reserves surprisingly little space for expository material. At any rate, it devotes an apparently disproportionate number of pages to material of a fictional nature: the interviewer's bladder complaint, notably, and his conduct once being unable to cope with the subway image has driven him off his head. Céline's point is well taken, of course, as he describes bystanders and policemen offering assistance while he is escorting his demented companion back to Gallimard's. Still, the development given the text of *Entretiens,* at the end, does blur the focus of his statement of esthetic principle.

*Entretiens avec le Professeur Y* is a strange, somewhat elusive work. In many respects, it is an entirely characteristic piece of Célinian writing. Like his novels, it weaves fact and fancy into a fabric of boldly original design, coloration, and texture. It does so in a way that leaves many a reader undecided whether the factual is intended to give fancy an air of seriousness or whether, on the contrary, Céline deliberately permitted the fanciful to render fact suspect. Only when we realize that the novelist was not content with formulating the theory of "le style émotif" do the professor-colonel's antics take on full meaning. In *Entretiens* Céline's intention was to offer practice more than precept. Sure that his argument would strike many readers as no more convincing than they seem to Y–Réséda, he sought less to defend a theory than to illustrate it, showing it in operation. To anyone who protests that this is not what the situation requires at all, Céline has but one answer in *Entretiens avec le Professeur Y:* "I'm doing what I can."

Referring to Abel Bonnard's mother, an old lady with an astonishing memory for the poetry of the past—Du Bellay, Charles d'Orléans, Louise Labé—Céline's alter ego in *D'un Château l'autre* remarks, "I came close with her to understanding certain waves" (IV, 413). The novelist's own version of life in general lets those willing to listen hear sound-waves of a very different kind. He never went back for a moment on his declaration in *Hommage à Zola* that the function of the modern writer is to bear witness to the decline of the world about him. Historically flawed though his later chronicle–novels certainly are, they nevertheless offer a faithful reflection of his apocalyptic vision of human life in the twentieth century. Interviewed by François Gillois in *L'Indépendant français* on November 12, 1948, Céline remarked, "In Sigmaringen I knew guys who thought only of the day when they'd have the purge paid for by a counter-purge... What misery... Will we never be done with it?... There ain't no reason for it to finish no more!... At every turnabout must assassination, hate, calumny be the only sanction of success?... What a grotesque period!"

As a novelist, Louis-Ferdinand Céline did not devote himself to trying to guarantee his public a faithful record of historical events in which he happened to have been implicated. Instead, he aimed at sharing his sense of the mystery and irony of human existence in a grotesque period. It is this, and not the impulse to deceive or distort, that deprives objective fact of the power to command and hold his respect and attention as a writer of fiction. Hence, for instance, the storyteller in the second volume of his *Féerie pour une autre fois* bids readers be attentive to his "respect for sumptuousness." In Céline's novels, sumptuousness does not merely pass before history, it often takes the latter's place.

Truth seems to be disregarded, as transposition is substituted everywhere for transcription. Readers are entirely free, of course, to condemn Louis-Ferdinand Céline's infidelity to historical truth. They cannot accuse him, though, of having betrayed history inadvertently, while yet striving to record it with utmost accuracy. His spokesman in *Rigodon* confides, "it's fucking impossible for me to even look as a photo!... to transcribe, to betray! yes! to reproduce, to photograph, to rot! then and there!... what's existed ain't watchable!... transpose then!... treat poetically if you can! but who mixes with that?... no one?..." ( V, 426). In other words, Céline was profoundly aware that his concept of fiction set him apart, that he was not understood by journalists and critics from whom the public were in the habit of looking for guidance.

His unrelenting opposition to contemporary novelists better regarded then he should have made it clear that Céline did not stand on the same ground as they and was entitled to have his work considered from a different perspective. Instead, the violence with which he condemned writers enjoying far wider popularity than he was interpreted purely negatively, as a sign of pettiness and frustration. It failed to clarify the nature of the demands Céline made on the content of his novels, so offensive to some, so scandalous as to draw adverse criticism.

In *Entretiens avec le Professeur Y* Céline made no attempt to defend himself on the grounds that his writing possessed historical value. Nor did he, like André Malraux in a postface to *Les Conquérants*, claim to have surpassed history by showing "a type of hero" peculiar to our time. Rather than make grand claims for his narrators—like Albert Camus, calling the central figure of his *L'Etranger* "the only Christ we deserve"[9]—Céline tried to make one fundamental fact clear. He wished to show how much importance he attached to coming to terms with the raw material of history on the basis of creative language.

Born into European society at a time of upheaval which he associated with the imminent collapse of Western culture, Louis-Ferdinand Céline built a career in literature upon his misfortunes as a human being. Perhaps his greatest misfortune, however, was to have been born in France.

For the French, the words, *style* and *styliste* take definition in language within a frame bounded by the lucidity of expression for which Descartes's writings set an example and a rhythmic elegance for which the works of Bossuet and Pascal provided the criteria. Céline's unacceptable presumption was to declare himself a stylist while at the same time scorning and rejecting everything that meant style to the French ear and mind. The claim he made for his own work, in his attack on traditional style and those defending and prolonging it, never appeared more questionable to those listening than when he aggressively asserted his superiority as a writer while conceding his indifference to respect as a thinker.

It is easy to see how high a price was extorted from this man whose estimate of his own qualities appeared so flagrantly at odds with his capacities. The injustice of the treatment meted out to Céline by his contemporaries cannot be denied. The inadmissibility of his idea of style, in their eyes anyway, is not the whole issue by any means. In fact, there is something else to be noticed, as soon as Céline's novels are examined for what they are, not for what those condemning them believe they ought to be. Céline's emphasis on style directly affected his treatment of the subject matter of his novels by relaxing narrative structure. The debate over the virtues and defects of his style may continue, but it will never obscure one essential feature of Célinian writing. Louis-Ferdinand Céline's experiments with fictional form reserve him a place among the twentieth century's important innovative novelists.

9. Albert Camus, "Avant-propos," in Germaine Brée & Carlos Lynes, Jr., eds., *L'Etranger* (New York): Appleton-Century-Crofts, 1955), p. viii.

# INDEX

232    INDEX

*THE INNER DREAM*

CÉLINE AS NOVELIST

was composed in 10-point Linotype Caledonia and leaded two points,
with display type in handset Deepdene, and printed on 55-lb. Glatco Offset
by Joe Mann Associates, Inc.;
Smythe-sewn and bound over boards in Columbia Bayside Vellum
by Maple-Vail Book Manufacturing Group, Inc.;
and published by

**SYRACUSE UNIVERSITY PRESS**
SYRACUSE, NEW YORK 13210